Catching Foxes

A Book For The Bride

By

Fenella Stevensen

authorHOUSE®

AuthorHouse™ UK
1663 Liberty Drive
Bloomington, IN 47403 USA
www.authorhouse.co.uk
Phone: 0800.197.4150

Published by AuthorHouse 03/24/2016

ISBN: 978-1-5246-2866-6 (sc)
ISBN: 978-1-5246-2867-3 (hc)
ISBN: 978-1-5246-2868-0 (e)

Contents

Catching Foxes

PART ONE

...a book for the Bride

Foreword

Lana Vawser has been speaking words of confirmation over the last twelve months, through prophetic words she has received from the Lord, that speak to many people, but have spoken directly to me, confirming all that He was already doing in my life, including the writing of this book, whereby the Lord was speaking that He was birthing writers for such a time as this, who will be going through labour pains to produce. I can say for sure, labour was long and extremely painful as you will read.

Just two days before sending the book for publication, this word I received directly from Lana through my email. It speaks completely of all that the Lord asked of me to write, and indeed of my own testimony which was happening as I was writing. With her kind permission, she has offered it as the Foreword for my book, for which I am so thankful.

New post on ♥Lana Vawser Feb 2 at 9:21 AM 2016

HIS FIRE FALLING ON YOUR CHARACTER IS A KEY FOR THE GREATEST OUTPOURING OF THE SPIRIT WE HAVE EVER SEEN!
By Lana Vawser

I had an encounter with the Lord today where I saw Jesus standing before me and I knew that He was before me to speak to me concerning the greatest outpouring of His Spirit across the earth.

As He stood before me, I felt such a tugging in His heart, the only way I can describe it, was a deep yearning, I was undone by the level of yearning I could feel pulsating from His heart. As He looked at me, I was suddenly surrounded by the sense that He was about to let me see into His heart for the body of Christ in this season, and what I heard come out of His mouth surprised me and undid me.

"PLEASE, PLEASE embrace the fire upon your character, PLEASE allow Me to deal with your character so that people can see ME CLEARLY"

All in one moment I felt the purest form of love that I have felt, a line being drawn in the sand for the people of God to say "YES" to Him no matter the cost, to say "YES" to His process despite the uncomfortableness, and yet even while feeling this yearning of love for the people of God to accept the invitation before them because it was going to lead to something greater than they could have ever imagined.

I then heard Him speak again:

"I am bringing My people back to Me as their first love, I am releasing My fire on character in this season in deep ways, for gifting will not keep them in the doors of favour I am opening for them. I am wanting to deal with the deep hidden things of the heart, I want to clean out things that are holding them back, I want to deal with things that are tormenting them, I want to deal with the things that could be potential areas that could cause the enemy to come in and pull them out of the place of favour I have for them, because they have not embraced My fire on their character. Many are perceiving the fire upon their character as they have done something wrong, and that is not true, that is the lie of the enemy. I am dealing DEEPLY with the heart and HEART MOTIVES right now because the greatest end time revival that is going to be released upon this earth is going to be marked with PURITY, LOVE and CHARACTER. A whole new level of purity, love, character and integrity will be seen across My Church as I move in power and in signs and wonders from the place of the divine dance with Me as their first love. Holiness is going to mark the end time outpouring in ways the world has never seen. Holiness that is free of a religious spirit, but holiness that is pure and flowing out of hearts that are just seeking to be with Me and love Me. I am restoring the MANIFESTED FRUIT OF HOLINESS through My people AS they embrace this fire. My people are holy, and My people are righteous in Me because of the Cross and My resurrection, that is the solid biblical truth, but the outworking of the fruit of holiness is going to be seen in a whole new ways as My people embrace the fire. This fire on character must be embraced now so My people are KEPT in the

revival and the doors of favour and opportunities I am releasing. I am purging and pruning hearts and heart motives SO THAT My people are strong. I am restoring a deeper honour of My heart in My people.

"Who then, dares to climb up into the presence of the Lord? And who has the right to enter into the holy place where He dwells? It will be those who are clean, and whose works and ways are pure; whose hearts are true and who are sealed in the truth. Those who never deceive, whose words are sure. Those who live like this will receive the Lord's blessing and the righteousness given by the Saviour-God. They are the very ones who will stand before God. For they seek the pleasure of Jacob's God by seeking His face." (Psalm 24:4-6) The Passion Translation[1]

"If you burn away the impurities from silver; a sterling vessel will emerge from the fire; and if you purge corruption from the kingdom, a king's reign will be established in righteousness." (Proverbs 25:4-5) The Passion Translation[2]

"Some of the greatest doors of favour, opportunity and responsibility are upon My people in this season, but to attempt to walk through those doors without embracing the fire upon character I am releasing is moving forward without wisdom. My fire upon character right now is not only going to see My people move forward in this season with longevity and sustainability but pure vessels that I will flow and shine through."

God is going after hearts! He is going after heart motives BECAUSE He loves us! I really feel the fear of God in this season, the awe of who He is and what He has called us to do. The doors He has placed before us, and

---

[1] Scripture quotations marked TPT are taken from *The Psalms: Poetry on Fire*, The Passion Translation®, copyright © 2012. Used by permission of 5 Fold Media, LLC, Syracuse, NY 13039, United States of America. All rights reserved.

[2] Scripture quotations marked TPT are taken from *Proverbs: Wisdom from Above*, The Passion Translation®, copyright © 2013. Used by permission of 5 Fold Media, LLC, Syracuse, NY 13039, United States of America. All rights reserved.

some of the greatest doors of opportunity and favour are before us in this season and we NEED to steward them well. Part of that 'stewarding' is allowing Him to examine and deal with our hearts. To bring heart motives to the surface if there are any there, that aren't pure, so He can bring realignment in love, He can bring healing and a purification. He is coming as a GOOD FATHER who is shaping, cleaning out and purifying the hearts of His people FOR OUR GOOD.

I feel a line being drawn in the sand in the body of Christ right now, it's all or nothing. He is calling us as His people to be pure vessels, to be holy. To be people of NO compromise. To be people of integrity. To be people attentive to His heart and drawing back to Him as our first love in ANY WAYS that we may have placed our focus or affection on anything else before Him. Oh how He embraces us in our repentance and our surrender. How He draws us close to His heart and wraps His arms around us and restores us.

In this great move of God that is beginning to build across the earth, there is a great SHAKING that is happening and GOING to happen in the midst of it. The shaking that will see a great alignment come into the body of Christ on a scale that we have not seen before. An alignment and shaking that will begin to see PURITY AND POWER manifesting. Purity and HIS power manifesting. Integrity and character are being married with love in this revival. Out of this place shall flow rivers of the prophetic in the purest form that the Church has ever seen.

It is an exciting time! The greatest seasons and opportunities for the body of Christ is upon us right now to see the Holy Spirit move in us and through us in a way we have NOT experienced before. As we 'get our houses in order' and embracing the fire He is releasing upon our character, is bringing us to a place of DEEP surrender and recognition for our need of Him that is going to explode the GREATEST MOVE OF GOD in power than we have EVER seen before. This intense pruning and purification is setting up the people of God that embrace it for STEADFAST PERSEVERANCE, STRENGTH AND PROMOTION.

Lana Vawser
Email: **lanavawser@gmail.com**
Website: facebook.com/pages/Lana-Vawser/212479638795197

Lana Vawser is married to Kevin, and they are living in Australia with their two sons. Lana and Kevin's heart is to see the Body of Christ develop deep intimacy with Jesus and actively hear His voice each day. They have a heart to see people free and walking in all that Jesus has purchased for them as they carry Christ into their world each day.

Lana preaches regularly and ministers prophetically, through both the pulpit and the Internet, calling people into a constant pursuit of His heart and hearing His voice for themselves and others.

His Fire Falling On Your Character is a Key For the Greatest Outpouring of the Spirit You Have Ever Seen, copyright © 2016. Used by permission of Lana Vawser. All rights reserved.

"Fenella, Blessings to you, and may your book lead people into deeper encounters with Jesus."
Lana Vawser.

Introduction

In this book I wish to share scripture verses using The Passion Translation (TPT: **1,2,3,4** as listed at the front of the book), together with (NIV: **5**) and (NKJV: **6**). Some of you may not be familiar with The Passion Translation so I would like to just share here how I first came to read it – and how it made an impact upon my life.

In 2013, I was about to embark on a journey to Uganda that would be the open door of God's promises to me since I was 5 years old. The full story can be read in the first two books of my life story under the titles "Rejoice" by Fenella Stevensen. My author name and the character name in the books are different, but they were to assure anonymity to persons in the books, as I told the story of my life as seen and experienced through my own eyes. I was told by the Lord that I would write these books thirty three years ago – and I laughed... "Who me - write a book?" At that time I didn't even enjoy reading books and hardly saw myself as a writer, when the best school grades for English were C+. However in 2012 the Lord told me now – now is the time to write.

"Now Lord, Now? Could you not have asked me to write before I fell from Grace, and as in the story of the Prodigal Son, walked in rebellion, pride and arrogance to a far distant land called sin and debauchery. You want me to write of all the bad things Lord or just the good bits?"

His reply to me was to write ALL, especially the bad bits, because it is in the bad things I have done His love and grace and mercy will be revealed.

I returned to the Lord when I came to my senses, as in the story of the Prodigal, not truly believing that the Father would have me back, at least not as a daughter, as I had turned my back on Him and walked away, maybe I could be back as a servant – a lowly position in the Kingdom, but even that I doubted at the time. In 2010, however just as the story in the Bible tells, of which I will refer to later in the book, the Father ran with open arms and covered my shame with His cloak – the cloak of Jesus' righteousness, and began to restore me as a daughter of the King!

All my dreams and visions since I was five were dead and buried, and to be honest, I was glad. In this new love I had found in my return to the Father, I wanted nothing more than to just sit at His feet and to worship. I knew that He knew me at the utmost worse, and still loved me! And I came to realize, like Paul writes in his letters, that I am wretched – the worst of sinners. It was in the next five years the Lord would take me on a journey of healing and restoration. Teaching me how to overcome the sin which had become a stronghold in my life... I wrote the books as He instructed me with still the third of the Trilogy in writing, and He sent me to Uganda.

It was whilst I was there on my first week as a Seminar speaker for five days in a remote village of Fort Portal, feeling weak, vulnerable and out of my depth, when a sister from the church back in Malta sent me an email containing a prophetic word by Pastor Brian Simmons in USA. As I read it – it burned within my heart, speaking to me that it was my destiny to which God had called me. That this time in Uganda was not by chance, but by His perfect planning and purpose for my life.

The word so pierced my heart, that as soon as I was online I added this Pastor to my Facebook, and more and more of His prophetic words – which he calls "I Hear His Whisper", began to minister to me, encouraging me in the things I was doing in the Lord. At the end of my three months I returned home, and searched the Pastors website called The Passion Translation. There I saw the books of the Bible he had translated... I felt so led by the Spirit that I ordered all six available at that time as a bulk order with special price. Song of Songs was one of those books. However I also had seen there was an audio of the Song of Songs, and I decided to purchase it and download it – so I could listen to the word whilst I awaited post from USA to deliver the books.

9

Before the audio had finished Chapter One – I was in tears. The words just pierced my heart...

[The Shulamite]

> ⁵Jerusalem maidens,
> In this twilight darkness
> I know I am so unworthy—so in need!

[The Shepherd-King]

> **Yet you are so lovely!**

Already here, my heart began to respond to the words... indeed I knew my own unworthiness and neediness as I stood in the Presence of the Lord and all His righteousness... I was dirty... but what I did not expect to hear was the Bridegroom's voice. My heart broke. It continued.

[The Shulamite]

> I feel as dark and dry as the desert tents
> Of the wandering nomads!

[The Shepherd-King]

> **Yet you are so lovely—**
> **Like the fine linen tapestry Hanging in the Holy Place!**

Oh.... That was it – I was lost in tears of the love of the Shepherd King, that despite my sinfulness, He not only called me lovely, but saw me Pure and Holy as the Curtains of the Holy Place. I had no idea at that moment how long the recording would run for - I had been washed in His love and just waves of His love washed over me – I heard nothing more only the echoing sound in my heart of my loveliness to Him.

I thought I had received His love and forgiveness – and yet as I heard myself saying that I was dark and in need – His love washed over me as I gently wept in His Presence. It was not tears of fear, or shame, or that of being told off – it was not tears of pain, but tears of Pure Healing Love washing over me.

The next day – I prepared myself to listen to the whole recording, I laid down on my soft red leather sofa (a symbol I see only now of His Mercy Seat sprinkled with Crimson)... and so it began again... and still in Chapter One... as He tells of my beauty as He sees me – I am once again, in tears of joy and love fulfilled. They were the words I had longed to hear in all my desperate years in search of a love, a husband... and then:

[The Shepherd-King]

¹¹We will enhance your beauty
Encircling you
With Our golden reins of love
You will be marked
With Our redeeming grace.

Oh that the Lord ... Father Son and Holy Spirit would encircle me enhancing what He already sees as beauty, and to mark me with Their Redeeming Love! Again I barely heard what else was spoken, as my heart rested in these amazing words of love, allowing the words and music just wash over me again and again of His love.

I realised – God is not angry with me. He is not as an angry Father who beats his child for the wrong things done, something too many children experience in this day by earthly fathers and mothers... No... despite my dark and sinful ways that I know are still lurking within me, He doesn't call me a snake in the grass or a wicked person, He doesn't condemn me saying, "Call yourself a Christian" followed by scornful laughter, he says:

[The Shepherd-King]

¹⁵Look at you, My dearest darling,
You are so lovely!
You are beauty itself to Me.
Your passionate eyes
Are like loyal, gentle doves.

I will go more into the word later, but for now it is to know that this translation brought me through an unseen barrier into His unending, all amazing, all powerful, all consuming love for me. Many people fear new translations of the Word of God. Of course we are to be careful that we will not be led astray in the end days as indeed the Word of God tells us will happen, as wolves in Sheep's clothing will deceive even the elect – if that is possible. I have learned to test by one thing. Does the Word translated take me closer to the Cross of Christ, does it take me closer to a place of repentance – the fruit of His Spirit within me, and does it draw me to be more like Him as the Word tells us that we should become transformed from Glory to Glory into the Image of Christ. Does it draw me to the Creator and not the created... does it cause me to bow my knee in humility and worship, or to stand tall and proud as the tares in the field of wheat before harvest.

Without doubt, this translation has brought me closer to the Lord, feeding me a hunger for more of Him and less of me. I do not fear hell and therefore cling to salvation, I am truly in love with the King of Kings and Lord of Lords, He is my husband, and my Beloved! In Him I am fulfilled in every way, His Love is all I need. I am indeed a prisoner of His Love, and it is I who has thrown away the key – I never want to leave this place of being bound together for the rest of my life with My Perfect Valentine! He has captured my heart and I am a willing heart surrendered to His Wrap-Around Love.

It is out of His Perfect Love, His Passionate love for you and for me – the Bride of Christ that He asked me to write this book. His Love draws us ever deeper, past the place of being a contented Christian waiting for the rapture to take us away, living life to the best of our ability in trying times. His love draws us into the very throne room of God, empowered by His Grace and Mercy to drink of His love, and as over-comers, destroy the works of the enemy... He is calling His Bride to be dressed ready, for the Bridegroom is on His way... let us not be wanting oil for our lamps, like the five foolish virgins, who missed the Bridegroom because they had to go and buy.... It is time for the Bride to Arise! To be dressed ready in her bridal gown of Purity and Holiness, wearing army boots! It is time to Catch Foxes!

Isaiah 60:1

Foxes of Compromise

Since my return to the Lord five years ago, He has been teaching me how to catch **Foxes**. It was not apparent at the time what was happening. In clearer terms, the Lord was shining a search light within my heart and showing me the areas of hidden sin and iniquity still needing to be dealt with... but always one step at a time. Had he shown me all at once the condition of my heart – maybe I would have given up – seeing the impossibility of restoring so much darkness... but God is Patient and God is Love. Jesus said He did not come to condemn the world but to set the captives free. He came to the sick to heal them, and the ones in captivity to break the chains of bondage... the question is – do we know we are sick? Do we know we are prisoners of the evil one? As Christians, many believe that when they come to salvation through confessing Jesus as Lord, that is it – finished – all the suffering of Christ in our place at Calvary complete at our simple confession of faith. We have as such minimized His suffering unto death to a single prayer of confession of faith, and seem to think we can now access all the benefits of heaven. In a way – it is absolutely true... but there is more to it than that. There is a cost to salvation, which sadly is seldom preached. There is a cost to accepting His gift of love and eternal life... and that cost is ALL. He is not interested in our Sundays only in church. For some – even arriving on time and giving the Lord two hours on a Sunday is more than they can manage. He who gave His life – unto death, and we struggle to give two hours? He is not interested in the good works we do in our communities, though indeed they are commendable... He is interested in our love for Him and willingness to take up our cross daily to follow Him. To as such die each day on the cross to self and follow Him in the paths He has prepared for us to go, and to lay down all our own plans, and be devoted to His plans.

He is interested in our hearts being totally and willingly surrendered to Him! This is true worship! He calls us to Worship him, and it is not in the songs we sing, but in the surrender of our lives according to His will and purpose. That is worship in Spirit and in Truth.

We know that people sometimes marry for money or for certain benefits found in that marriage – more than their devotion and love for the person offering the benefits. We may look upon it and judge others in our hearts for such coldness of heart, and yet – many of us as Christians have done the same, if not all of us – accepting the offer of eternal life with the God of Love, rather than eternity in hell, wanting healing, a life of prosperity etc – being in love with the benefits and not the giver of them. With time as we read in the Word and spend time in the Lords presence, seeking His face and getting to know Him, we fall in love with the Giver and it becomes a relationship of a divine love that develops and flourishes. However if we accept the gift and refuse to get to know the giver, then this becomes not a relationship, because life is lived out of laws and rules, which is a religion. We have been called, not to another religion but with a living intimate relationship with God Himself. The Church, is His Bride to be... we are betrothed to Him, engaged awaiting the coming of the Bridegroom for the great wedding feast. He is coming back for His Bride, who is dressed ready and waiting. He is coming back for His beloved whom He loves passionately, which we can read about in the book 'Song of Songs'... where He tells us that He is "undone" when He looks into our love and adoring eyes.

We have all grown up seeing correction as a shameful thing – often because it was done in a way where we were humiliated before others. Maybe correction meant a beating and so correction by God causes us to fear Him, but I hope you will come to trust Him through this book that God's ways are higher than man's ways. When we deserve a lecture God instead gives us a kiss! He wants for His Bride to walk in the fullness of Grace that was intended for us, in His Power and Authority, yet instead we are seen as a crippled Bride, either in a wheelchair or limping badly, often under attack and being defeated by the enemy... but the time has come for His Bride to

"Arise shine for your light has come! And the Glory of the Lord has risen upon you!" Isaiah 60:1 (NKJV: 6)

As I have already tried to explain before, God is not angry with us, but is longing to set us free. The truth will set us free, free from the lies of the devil.

After my return to the Lord in 2010, I had returned by attending a church for the first time in many years on February 14th – Valentine's Day, again you can read about how the Lord led me there in my autobiography 'Rejoice... The Bricks Have Fallen; I Will Rebuild' (Book 2), hence my own name for Jesus is my Perfect Valentine! I was totally bowled over by His love and acceptance of me again, and this time it was going to be different... or was it?

In either late July – August 2010, I was introduced to someone who would help the family to move house. This person was everything I was against... though not certain of his current involvement, in the recent past was a provider to the wider community of drugs, specifically, Marijuana. He was a friend of my niece – who together with her husband were also partakers of the drug. I strongly disagreed with drug taking. I had heard that he was staying next door at my nieces flat – and I had not been interested in meeting him, however, my sister invited him around one evening to discuss the possibility of him helping to move some of the furniture to the new flat if we hired a van. He said yes. That evening he sat politely at the table with us, agreed to share a glass of wine with me, and was very helpful and charming!

We met and before I realised it – I was hook line and sinker involved with him. I would go to church on Sunday, and find myself crying all the way through the service. I walked and talked with him, cried telling him that I was in a problem because I knew I was doing wrong to be with him, walking in compromise of my faith and relationship with Jesus. He seemed very understanding, but didn't want to end the relationship. I wanted to leave but I could not. Once again – the past had raised its head and I was once again walking in rebellion and sexual sin.

One night I had a dream. I was in the mouth of a lion, and its mouth was about to close shut. I heard a tender voice saying to me; "Get out before it's too late!" I knew it was the voice of the Lord. I was so upset, I wrote to a friend a long way away in Denmark, telling of my shame and distress, wondering if I will ever learn. Why is it that I do the things I don't want to do and don't do the things I want to do? Of course it will sound familiar to you as Paul also struggled with the same question.

My friend replied immediately, not what I expected. I expected to be rebuked. She told me first of all; **"God is not angry with you! He wants to teach you how to overcome."** When I read this my heart filled with tears of repentance and love for the Lord. Suddenly I knew what I had to do. From that place before Jesus, knowing He was not angry with me, He told me I had to close the door that was allowing the sins of the past to keep repeating.

I did not actually confess the sexual sin in the church house-group, but what I did do was to make a covenant with the Lord before witnesses. The Lord had shown me that I was open to the sexual sin because I had never laid my desires for a husband before the Lord. This desire was still alive and of the flesh – not of the Spirit, so before the group I spoke out that I was laying my fleshly desires for a partner / husband at the foot of the cross. I again publicly asked the Lord to forgive me for withholding this part of my life from Him, and I thanked Him that His Word tells me that He is my husband, and He is able to meet my every need as a single person. I confessed that He is more than enough for me. From this day forth I will not seek after a husband... unless the Lord clearly shows me that I am to marry, I will remain single and faithful to Him the rest of my days.

To be honest – the group thought I had gone a little too far, but I knew in my heart that what I had done was correct. I have not fallen in sexual sin since that day! I have been tempted, but I have not fallen! Repentance for my rebellion, my sexual sins, and withholding my desires of the flesh closed the door through which the enemy had always had access. I can remember such joy in my heart after this moment, and He was not angry with me. He had not called me a naughty girl. He had not punished me – my own guilt had punished me enough through the accuser - Satan, but the Lord had gently led me – instructed me how to become free from the chains that were binding me. When the Lord had shown me the Truth, the truth being that I had never surrendered this part of my life to Him, (and it was not a conscious act of withholding it, but something I had not even thought about.) It was the Truth that set me free!

Sexual sin – sexual immorality is a compromise, it is a **Fox**!

What do **Foxes** do? Well for the most part they steal! If there are chickens or eggs they will steal to eat. In the fields they will steal and ravage the harvest. They are a pest to farmers, and of course where I come from in UK, one of the famous sports is the **Fox** Hunt. There has been a move for many a year to stop it because of cruelty to the **Fox,** but it was first started when the rich landowners would get together with their dogs to hunt out the predator causing damage to their land. It became then a sport amongst the rich combining work with pleasure. I am not condoning the sport, but of course I understand the need to protect the land and the livelihood to provide food for the families, guarding against the **Fox** from stealing.

I have never been on such a hunt, but I have been hunting. I was fifteen/ sixteen years old, and dating a very handsome young man. I have never been an outdoor kind of girl – but I was willing to be one with the incentive of a handsome boyfriend. We went off early in the day, with packed lunch. Of course he looked so macho with his twelve-bore shotgun over his shoulder. We came into the forest, and there in the distance he spotted a **Fox**. We slowed down, moving a little closer, he realised that it was injured and was dying slowly in pain. He asked if I wanted to pull the trigger to put him out of his misery, an easy target because it was not moving. I agreed, placing the butt of the shotgun to my shoulder, aimed then shot! The force of the shot almost wrenched my shoulder... but it was dead! We went to see up close, and I remember crying. It was beautiful, and I had killed it. Of course it was dying already and I had put it out of its misery and pain, but never the less I cried. I lifted it – and carried it over my shoulder all the way home. In one way – proud of my catch... on the other hand sad – that this beautiful animal was dead.

Why do I tell you this story? Well often the **Foxes** in our lives we see as fun, likeable, even love, and see the chase as sport, done widely maybe with others who we seek acceptance and fellowship with... yes beautiful to our eyes that we don't want to actually say goodbye to them. In the Garden of Eden, when Satan tempted Eve, do you think he looked evil and scary? No – he disguises himself as an angel of light. It says that in the heaven he was of great beauty. **Foxes** in our lives often seem as harmless fun, but the truth is that they ravage and destroy, stealing the fruit of the Lord.

Catch The Troubling Foxes

The Song of Songs was penned 3,000 years ago by King Solomon and is the complete inspiration of the Holy Spirit. It is a book that many have misinterpreted believing it to be a form of marriage guidance for Christian marriages. It is written with such imagery that many have failed to understand it and therefore dismissed it from the reading schedule. I could be counted as one of those people, until my books arrived in the post that I was waiting for.

I had by now managed to listen to the audio all the way through – though still with tears as His words washed over me with love. It lasts for forty two minutes, and I lay on my red leather sofa every day, to soak in the beauty of every word spoken. I was totally amazed how Solomon had as such written my own love story with Jesus. Indeed – it is the story of how Jesus – the Shepherd King woos, romances His Brides to be. Of course women have no difficulty imagining themselves in such a place, but men who are also the Bride of Christ somehow find it difficult seeing themselves in the same way, none the less – this book is not just for women, it is for men and women who make up the Church.

In both the audio and the book, there was one place that captured me every time... it still does. Chapter Two, I find myself time and time again in this chapter. Of course I move on in my life and at times see myself having reached Chapters seven and eight, with great delight and dancing in my heart, but chapter two is where I am, and chapter two is I believe where many people need to be.

Chapter one the Shepherd King has won the heart of the Shulamite, which is a female version of the word – Solomon. Male and female are one in the name Shulamite... so captured by His love we are learning to trust Him, look for Him, long for His visits. She becomes intoxicated in his love, as one who drinks too much wine, and she wants more but it's too much, and can't take anymore – then she wants more. She is completely lovesick for her Beloved. Then in chapter two He tells her that now is the time to arise and to ascend the mountain with Him.

[The Shepherd-King]

> **Arise My love, My beautiful companion**
> **And run with Me to the higher place.**
> **For now is the time to arise**
> **And come away with Me!**
> **For you are My dove,**
> **Hidden in the split open Rock.**
> **It was I who took you**
> **And hid you up high**
>
> **In the secret stairway of the sky.**
> **Let Me see your radiant face**
> **And hear your sweet voice.**
> **How beautiful your eyes of worship,**
> **And I love the sound**
> **Of your voice in prayer.**
> **⁵You must catch the troubling foxes,**
> **Those sly little foxes**
> **Which hinder our relationship.**
> **For they raid**
> **Our budding vineyard of love**
> **To ruin what I've planted within you.**
> **Will you catch them**
> **And remove them for Me?**
> **We will do it together.**

He asks her to catch the **foxes** in their vineyard of love that are causing problems – ruining all He has planted within her... how does she respond to her Beloved?....

[The Shulamite]

I know my Lover is mine
And I have everything in You
For to life we delight ourselves in each other.
But, until the day springs to life
And the shifting shadows of fear disappear,
Turn around, my Lover, and ascend
To the holy mountains of separation
Without me.
Until the new day fully dawns,
Run on ahead like the graceful gazelle
And skip like the young stag
Over the mountains of separation.
Go on ahead to the mountain of spices—
I'll come away another time.

She says no!

She turns him down so beautifully, but says no, because there is fear, or maybe she doesn't like climbing mountains, maybe there are things she still has to do, maybe she is still enjoying the **foxes** and not ready to catch them... the fact is she says no! What happens is the Shepherd King turns around and pretends to leave her – yet all the while watching her, waiting for her to change her mind. When we begin Chapter three, she is on her bed of travail because she let Him go.

¹Night after night I'm tossing and turning
On my bed of travail.
Why did I let Him go from me?
How my heart now aches for Him
But He is nowhere to be found!

This period of travail can last up to a decade bringing about all kinds of angst, depression, trouble, sickness... how do I know? Because, I am the Shulamite.

If you have read my books Rejoice... then you will know how I turned my back on the Lord because of hurt and anger. He had asked me to take a back seat from ministry as He wanted to do something important in my life… what happened - He allowed me to see the anger and hurt in my life – He was showing me the **foxes**, but I said no. I can tell you for ten years I walked in rebellion as the prodigal. Until I came to my senses, and returned – to find Him waiting for me… not angry, no lecture, no bad name calling or the things we would expect to come, He received me back and wrapped the cloak of Jesus' Righteousness about me to cover my shame. It was only then I was ready to catch the **fox**!

During those ten years of separation, I was twice sick with work related stress, I was suicidal and deeply depressed, and became chronically sick with ME. It was such a chronic onset that the Dr feared that another six months I would be in a wheelchair for the rest of my life. I had to leave my job unable to work. I had been on a search almost worldwide looking for a husband. I was so desperate for love – to be loved I became no better than a prostitute… finding myself always being used and abused, the victim. In my head I tried to turn it around and use others, but deep in my heart I was always the one being hurt.

Although I left Him, the Lord never left me. I look back at those years realising how so many times I could have gone way too far, and realised that He was always with me- protecting me, but He could not overstep my own will. Jesus is not like that. The Father is not like that! The sickness, the depression and planned suicide was not about Jesus or the Father, it was not punishment as some would think… it is the result, the consequence of sin. Jesus never coerces anyone to be with Him. Love that is coerced will never be a love from the heart. Surrender that is forced through being threatened will only give birth to anger and bitterness and even hatred. It is not what the Father wants – not what Jesus came for… He came in search of those who long after Him, who willingly surrender to His loving care, lovingly will die to their own plans to be one in His plans. He is looking for those who will die to self and the things of this world – just to be in His presence, to be His companion and friend, to be His Bride… His Beloved.

One of the many things I learnt from Pastor Brian Simmons is about Homonyms. It is a word that when spoken can mean different things. For example the word Plain, when spoken could mean aeroplane, simple, a flat piece of land, a tool used for levelling wood, a piece of paper that is empty... and so it is in Hebrew. One word when spoken can mean different things.

Some of the things that totally transformed my understanding are:

The Hebrew word for kiss – used in the beginning of Chapter One, means the Divine breath of God that was breathed into Adam and gave him life..... So it is not just about asking for a kiss – but for the Lord to breathe His breath of life into the Bride to be.... But it is also a homonym, which could also mean "Armed for Battle". I have already stated that the Bride needs to put on her wedding dress of Purity and Holiness, but instead of fancy shoes – Army Boots! The Bride is the army of the Lord in these last days, who will overcome the powers of darkness which will increase in these last days. Aren't we already seeing this, the terror and evil more than ever before? This is not a time for the Bride to sit back and wait for the rapture, this is a time for the Bride to be clothed with the full armour of God, not resting but dressed and ready, alert and fighting.

Another of the homonyms explained just blew me away! Four times in the Book, the Bridegroom calls the Bride to be "my sister, my bride." Now we all know in this day and age it is not acceptable to marry your sister, it is incestuous... so this always seemed a strange thing to say. The Hebrew word used which translates as sister can also be translated as "Equal". Now it reads "my equal, my bride". If I am dead to self and Jesus in me is everything, then Jesus (in me) EQUALS Jesus. The Word of God tells us that when we take up our cross, putting the flesh, the "I" to death, so that Christ lives in me, then as Paul says it is not 'I' that lives but Christ that lives in me. The Word tells us that we should not be unequally yoked, and God would not compromise His own Word. Therefore as the Lord is preparing us, by revealing to us the things of the flesh that need to die within us, so that He might live... that we be transformed from Glory to Glory into the image of Christ.... When that happens – "Jesus in me equals Jesus", the perfect partner for the King of Kings and Lord of Lords!

I will share one more then I will suggest that you get the book, where all the explanations are also added. Talking of her beauty He tells her that her hair is like a flock of goats running down Mount Gilead. In honesty – I failed to see anything beautiful about a flock of goats... then the explanation came – not as a homonym, but that in the time of King

Solomon, the goats that were selected without blemish for sacrifice to God; they were kept separate in a pen on the top of Mount Gilead. When the pen gate was opened, they would skip and jump with gladness down the hill to be sacrificed. His Bride's beauty is in her joyful, willing sacrifice to die. Willingly, surrendered unto death, she is joyfully running to lay down her life as a pleasing sacrifice. Once again, He looks not to the outward beauty of this world, but to the inner beauty of the heart totally surrendered unto Him.

The Lord is looking for a Bride who wants to be His totally, not in part. He is not looking for a Bride who is still enjoying playing with the pleasures of this world. Clearly it says we cannot serve two masters. When we understand His passionate love for us, it will draw us to the place of surrender. It is not about doing things because the Pastor tells you to, or me or anyone else, it is about allowing the intimate touch of God to set your heart ablaze for Him alone, willing to forsake **all**, just for Him.

His love is waiting for each and every one willing to surrender to Him wholly... to have no other gods before Him, and willing to catch the **foxes** that are hindering your relationship with Him in your vineyard of love. Will you catch the **foxes**? When you say yes – you are not alone to do it – He is with you... "We will do it together!"

Will You Trust Me in the Pain?

What do **Foxes** look like? Basically **Foxes** are the compromises to God's word. So anything that is in our lives and is contrary to the Word of God – it is a compromise.

Some years ago, approximately 29 years, God had revealed such a **Fox** in my life though I didn't know it as such at the time. I will leave it for later to describe it – in context with God's Word, but I was sent away to receive counsel and help catching the **Fox**. In all, I was nine months in a place of deep healing, and towards the end of this very special time, I was asked what I wanted to be. I was not asked 'what is my call' but what I wanted to be... which seemed to be a strange question to me. However, I replied something that I had not thought or considered before. "I want to be an arrow sent out from God's bow to pierce the hearts of people with the love of God."

"That's interesting," she said, "It matches your name." I was confused. I knew it had nothing to do with my first name. It was not my first name she had intended – but my family name – the name of my father. Before I was married my family name was 'Broadhead.' I had hated this name all my life, because as a child and teenager it was always a source of ridicule and name calling, and I had decided at that point the sooner I got married and changed my name the better. So I enquired as to how my surname could have any link with what I wanted to be. I was surprised. Years later when I was writing the 'Rejoice' books I wanted to check out the facts of what she said so I 'googled' my surname. It opened up as she had told me. Broadhead, is the actual arrowhead. Its type was used specifically for two things only, war and hunting.

As the Bride – called to Battle, wearing the full armour of God, of course I, and everyone else is at war against the enemy we know as Satan. Paul, in the letter to the Ephesians, tells us that we fight not against flesh and blood but against principalities and powers, but what about hunting? It was as I heard from the Lord that I was to write this book, that I realized I am hunting **Foxes**! I am hunting them in my own life and helping others to recognize them, helping others to catch them and throw them out of the vineyard of love.

These last five years back with the Lord, He has drawn me ever closer to Him, healing me, delivering me, teaching me, and filling me with more and more of His amazing love. I am in India as I am writing this. My first time ever... let me start at the beginning...

I sold or gave away my possessions in Malta where I was living with my cat (as it is written in the 'Rejoice' books about the author.) The Lord was sending me to fulfill the call upon my life from the age of five – to Africa. I am based in Uganda with a call to all of Africa, however my visa runs out every three months and I need to leave the country. At this point let me quickly update details from the last two books

I began and completed writing the first two books in 2012. As I began, sometime in the month of April, an elder from the church had asked me how the book was going. I didn't think I had told anyone I was writing, so I said I had started, but it was going slow. He replied to me by being surprised I was actually writing a book, which made me very confused. If he didn't know about me writing, how then could he ask how it was going? He then said – you are not writing one book but three books. I laughed because the book was my life story – one life one book. He had received a vision the night before of me, at a table of a book signing reception, with three books. I laughed, but sure enough as I was writing it was too much for one, too much for two. There is one event however that I failed to mention in the first book....

In January 1987, I travelled still as a missionary to South Africa – my first ever trip to the continent of Africa, to work on a conference and then to travel with my friend. All in all, a three month time. During the conference I was working with the hospitality staff, taking care of the guest speakers travelling from all over the world. I was to ensure their comfort at the hotel and make sure transport from hotel to the conference was in place. One of the guest speakers was an evangelist called Elijah from South Africa together with his wife and young son of 5 yrs. I loved them greatly and spent time with their son when I could, teaching him butterfly and eskimo kisses, which is eye to eye blinking and tickling with each other's eyelashes, and rubbing noses. The evangelist had to leave early due to a death in the family, but before he left he gave me his contact details and asked me what my call was. When I told people I had a call to Africa they would laugh because it is normal to be called to a certain country of Africa not a continent. I said I thought he would laugh if I told him; he looked directly in my eyes and said, "Do not tell me what I will say!" Then after a long silence he said, "You are absolutely correct. The Lord has called you to cross every border and culture with the love of God." I was so surprised; he was the first to somehow understand the depths of my heart. Although I had his details and I did visit him at his home after the conference ended for a few hours as we were journeying further, I had no further contact with him since that time.

In December 2012, after the first book had been sent for publication, I made contact with someone I had met in Uganda in 1989. His name, Haggai, was a student on the school I was teaching for two weeks. He invited me to be his Christian Mama, and when I left he would write to me. No Internet or Mobiles in those days. However after I married in 1990, his letters stopped and we lost contact, until I found him on Facebook. We were both ecstatic at being connected again, and something welled up in my heart that I was to visit him and his wife and four children. I learned at this time that he had continued writing to me but I had never received his letters.

Back in the year 1985, the Lord had spoken to me the words of Isaiah 54, that basically she who had not born children and was rejected by her husband would have many children. I was excited that Haggai was one of the spiritual children promised. I planned to visit him for three months later that year from August to November.

With so much to look forward to, during the month of March of the same year 2012, I suddenly heard a small voice telling me to contact Elijah. I was surprised and confused. It was now twenty six years later, how would I find his telephone number? The Lord told me to search on internet, so I googled his name. I found it, but only a blue screen appeared under his name. "What now, Lord?" "Look closer" He replied. Feeling somewhat stupid I peered closer to the blue screen, and suddenly I saw some numbers in white behind the blue. I wrote them down in case they disappeared, then tried adding a pre-fix for South Africa and dialed the number. It rang!

"Can I speak to Elijah please?"

"This is Elijah speaking." I panicked... shall I put the phone down again, what shall I say?

"This will be a strange phone call. I met you twenty six years ago at the Go Festival in Durban, and I am wondering if you remember me?" I forgot to even tell him my name... oh I should just put the receiver down, how ridiculous that he would remember me after so long.... The silence seemed a long time then suddenly he said;

"And you taught my son how to do butterfly kisses!" I was taken aback with surprise....

"Yes, how can you remember that?"

"You were the first white person to ever show me the true love of Jesus. My son was then five and now he is thirty one with children of his own and still does butterfly kisses... and you had a call into all of Africa, to cross every border culturally and geographically with the love of God – where are you?"

Now I was shocked, how could he remember what he prophesied over me word for word twenty six years later?

"I am like Paul in the Bible. My life was shipwrecked and I am on the island of Malta. But the winter is over and it is time to board a ship to take me to my intended destination, and I will be visiting Uganda for three months later this year."

"To reach all of Africa, you need to live in Africa."

I tried to change the subject as I was still a little overwhelmed that he remembered me, so I queried after his own life, what he has been doing....

"I have evangelized in one hundred and forty countries of the world, I teach in Bible Colleges, I have written many books, I have spoken before kings and presidents including the Whitehouse in the USA and I am known as the 'Black Billy Graham'."

I was speechless. He had met thousands of people, important people in the kingdoms of the countries he had visited, and yet he still remembered me because I taught his son how to do a butterfly kiss. He ended the call by giving me his family mobile number that is never turned off so I can reach him where ever he is travelling in the world. I was overwhelmed. Overjoyed! Humbled! "Oh Lord, you asked me to call this man, to re-confirm the call you spoke and confirmed all those years ago. You are giving it back to me! The vision.... You had prophesied it was to be, and that which you promise will come to fulfillment. Let Your will be done!"

I had an amazing time in Uganda. On arrival Haggai met me with three others, whom I shook hands with. "No mum, you don't understand, these are my biological brothers, and these are also your sons!"

"How many children do I actually have?" I said in total astonishment.

"We are nine." Nine!!!!! From having no children suddenly I have nine! Of course I thought they were just being polite 'til I met their father, who was showing me a house they were building and showed me my bedroom and my inside bathroom with sit-down toilet. I asked him how it was possible he was building a house with me in mind. He told me that I am the mother of his children, and it was his duty to provide a place for me to stay. I was shocked, he had remarried after his first wife had died, yet I am their mother? I found also to my surprise that their mother was called by the same name as myself!

During the time I was there I also returned to the YWAM missionary base, where I had been invited to teach again, on Spiritual Warfare, after twenty four years. Indeed, the Lord was restoring all things to me that the locust had eaten, as spoken of in the Book of Joel.

After that amazing three months of ministry – teaching and preaching, I also had to learn how to be a mother. It was a strange thing to me. During the time back in Malta, I was led to return to Uganda the following January of 2013 to rent a house with one of the sons and his wife and grandchildren. I did not know details of how the Lord was leading me, but the same leader in the church who had a vision of three books, came on my return in March, saying I will be gone within one month. I laughed. But the Lord was speaking loud and clear that I was to give up my rented flat in Malta and sell all my things or give them away, to go and live in Africa. Before the end of April, I had gotten rid of everything, with only suitcases to travel with. Following instruction from the Lord to first go to Denmark, I did and was there for two months before the Lord told me now is the time to return to Malta then fly out to Uganda, so before leaving Denmark I obtained a six month multi-entry visa for Uganda, so I could go to Tanzania and return for a planned conference...taking me to Feb In January of 2015, prior to my trip to India, I visited Elijah and his family for the first time since I met them twenty eight years earlier. It was an amazing experience, doing butterfly kisses with his son now in his thirties... they had never forgotten me, and had often spoke wondering where I was in the world.

Following my return from visiting Elijah, I was expecting to go to Ethiopia but the Pastor who had invited me was suddenly out of reach. I had enquired of returning to South Africa from which I had just returned, but I was told too soon... I could see that the Lord was closing doors and so I knew He had something in store. I tried to contact a Pastor in Kenya who had also invited me – but again no reply. At that point I received a letter from India – "Mum seriously consider coming to India!" India?? Why India?? However as I looked into it – the doors seemed to open up to me.

As a young girl I had seen myself in dreams or visions standing before the Taj-Mahal. But years later I heard of someone being there on mission and rats were running on them at night in their beds. The thought of that closed the dreams from any further occurrence. I had also been some years later to Singapore and travelling alone through an area of Indian population on my way to have a blouse made in silk, I was being pressed on all sides on the metro and fear arose within me. I don't know why – Singapore is one of the safest places to be – penalties for even the slightest offence is very strict. I had built up in my heart a wall to protect me – from what I did not know. But one thing for sure – I would never go to India!

Last year in 2014, it was a year of **Fox** hunting for me. The hunt took place in Denmark, more of which I will explain later in the book, however one day I had been visiting some friends for the day, and they had dropped me off at the train station where I needed to wait for the train to arrive. Looking around I saw only one free seat, but it was next to a black man who was drinking vodka and appeared to have been drinking the whole day. I didn't want to sit next to him, so I walked a long way to find another vacant seat. When the train arrived, I sat in a compartment to myself, seated by the window. Just before the train left, another passenger had joined me on the adjacent seat to my left. "Hello, how are you?" I turned to the person speaking to see it was none other than the black man drinking vodka. I was very curt with him, not wanting to invite further conversation saying, "I am fine thank you." And immediately turning my head away to look out of the window hoping he would realize I did not want to talk. I did not ask how he was, I did not want contact.

"I am also fine, are you here on holiday?" Within me I could feel anger rising, I didn't ask how he was, I didn't care how he was... suddenly I heard a soft voice within me; "How come you love black people in their own land, but not here in Denmark?" This voice pierced my heart, knowing it was the voice of the Lord. Within my heart I said sorry to the Lord and turned to speak to the black man. As I turned, he had re-located, closer, to sit on the same seat as myself, pouring a bottle top of his vodka to offer to me in fellowship. I declined the offer of hospitality, and we chatted. He was not on the train very long before he should leave... but I had managed to tell him of my plan to live in Africa as a missionary. After he had left the train, quietly I asked the Lord what all of that had been about.

"Your father!" And with that comment He gave me instant knowledge of what He was talking about. As a fourteen year old, I can remember dad saying to me that he was not prejudiced, but I was NEVER to bring a black person into the house, or marry a black man. Then the Lord also brought to mind all the jokes my dad used to tell of the Jews. Immediately I knew that the Lord was speaking to me of a spirit of racism and anti-Semitism, handed down as a generational sin, and it was hiding within me that I had been blind to. I immediately knew what to do, repented of the sins of my father and my own, and receive the forgiveness. I knew from that point the Lord had dealt with it. It was finished.

We know that the Word tells us that the sins of the fathers can be passed down for up to four generations. I had not really understood how it works, but I had recently read a book by Ana Mendez Ferrell called the Hidden Iniquities. I knew it was an important book for me – but there was something in the technical details of explanation of the sins transferred that I had failed to grasp intellectually. Suddenly the Lord was explaining it to me. At conception, just as the physical DNA of the father and mother are transferred to the baby, so at birth I got my daddy's eyes and my mother's nose etc., so also were the sins spiritually transferred. Their sins as such then are like a seed, which grows as in pregnancy within the baby/child, giving birth then to its own sin. Often these sins go unnoticed in our lives and become more recognized as a characteristic, for example being bossy or stubborn just like mum or dad. However, I had never seen any sign of racism in my life, on the contrary I had always wanted a black baby, and I had always been attracted to black skin – especially African black. As for the Jews – I had never really thought much about them. Even as a Christian, I had not considered much about the Jews as God's chosen people. I didn't have any negative thoughts towards them, but actually I didn't have any thoughts at all! In the last two years, friends that I had in Malta were closely connected with Israel, and they would share, but I never found myself intently interested, they had their call, mine was Africa. That was it – it was a disinterest of the Jewish people... but slowly through these friends – the Lord was beginning to awaken something within me showing a distinct link with Uganda and Israel. I became intrigued to read a book by a Messianic Jew in the USA called Jonathan Cahn – and the book 'The Harbinger'... bringing alive to me Old Testament and the behavior of the Israelites in the desert linking to modern times... then He wrote 'The Mystery of the Shemitah'. It was fascinating again based on the Jewish foundations... linking with modern times. Slowly the Lord was breaking through a hidden wall, and then suddenly the Lord gave me revelation and understanding of the hidden sin – the compromise in my heart against the Jews – and brought me to repentance.

Back to the blacks, I still wondered who I was against, I could not see any dislike of any kind within my heart toward an African black... then the Lord showed me – not African black – but Indian and Pakistan black! Yes my dad had also been to Karachi and somewhere in India during the war. He did not like either place and hated the food, and then the Lord showed me again at the age of fourteen as I had to walk to my piano lesson each week, that going through a Pakistan area of the town – I always felt fear. In those days there was the very non politically correct talk of 'Bashing' the people of Pakistan... nothing that I got involved with consciously, but it was part of the era I was growing up. There was a TV program – a comedy of a black family living next door to a white racist family... can't remember the name of it but it was widely watched and laughed at. It seemed ok to laugh at the racism, so joking made the problem acceptable? Comedy is a mask for so many compromises... I love to laugh, but I am learning that I need to choose what I listen to. Laughter is a way of accepting the compromise into our hearts.

After I left Denmark and this revelation, I was in Uganda – and received an invitation to teach on a YWAM Discipleship Training School in Kampala. It was a new base recently started. I agreed. The leaders were Indian. I went to start the week, to find two Indian students also... Since my time of repentance, this was my first encounter with people from India... and I fell in love!

Not sure if you can see it as I see it... but I had dreams as a child of being in India, then through fear the dreams were stolen! **Foxes** steal! Once God had revealed to me the hidden iniquity from my father, on two levels, He started opening doors that had been closed. It was one of the students from the school in Kampala that had returned to India and wrote asking me to seriously consider coming to India.

Since October (2014) for three months, I suffered a back injury – something I have struggled with on and off for approximately 29 years. The pain started as I lifted my 2yr old granddaughter onto my knee. I tried to keep moving but it started to get worse. My daughter in law was massaging the leg for me – when she noticed something, and suggested I put a sock on to keep the foot warm. Apparently it was grey in colour, and she offered to call her husband at work – but I said – not to – what can he do? However within thirty minutes fear entered my heart as the pain travelled like ice and numbness to my foot. I screamed for help and again Salome came in and massaged my leg and foot – this time I called my other son Haggai in Kampala, because I didn't want to disturb my son Samson at work. Haggai agreed to travel immediately to come to my home, he contacted Samson who left work early and they arrived almost the same time. They put me in the car and took me to a doctor who sent me for x rays. The report said possible discus prolapsed. I was due to go to Kenya – and before traveling it seemed to be getting better, but the night I arrived in Kenya I was in such pain that I couldn't sit or lay down. I spent the whole night in tears and leaning against a wall. The next morning we went to the hospital where they gave me pethidine as a strong painkiller followed by strong painkillers to take in tablet form. It got me through the time of ministering, but when I returned back to Uganda – again the pain increased. I went through agonizing times of pain – and it broke my heart to see my daughter in law crying in prayer over me – at a loss of how to help me more. She told me how her husband had been crying in prayer – something she hadn't seen before as he too felt helpless in helping me out of the pain. We tried everything we knew how.

Pastors from the churches prayed for me, I was anointed with anointing oil, people I know all around the world were praying for me. At one point I went to check on the pain in the leg in case it was a blood clot as I had been afraid. Thankfully the result was all clear. On the way home from the hospital – the Lord began to speak to me of fear hidden in my heart... He wanted me to trust Him. As I was beginning to try and trust Him, I received word from the landlady that she was putting up the rent. I went to bed and the next two days I had high blood pressure – why, because of fear. Fear of lacking financial provision. I repented and asked for forgiveness, but still the pain continued. As it was now nearing Christmas, I had felt I was doing ok, so went on the boda taxi (motor bike) to the shop. I was fine until walking into the Mall, and then the pain was almost crippling me, with tears in my eyes, not knowing what to do. At the shop – they all know me so well – they insisted I was placed in a wheelchair and they pushed me around to shop. I wept at their care for me. Staff ran to me asking what was wrong, and I cried more. Needless to say I was in bed all over Christmas.

God had been speaking to me... I had received a hunger in my heart to read of Joseph, Jeremiah, Daniel, Job and I downloaded films of their lives too. I heard the small voice of the Lord – "Will you trust me in the pain?" Many were beginning to question that I was not healed – many people of faith had prayed believing for my healing... proclaiming that by His stripes I am healed... but healing did not come.

"Will you trust me in the pain?" I had learnt to trust Him to heal the pain, now He wanted me to trust Him in the pain. He showed me how the Bible names mentioned suffered greatly, pains of all kinds. God did not deliver them – they trusted Him through their pains. Finally on January 1st 2015, as I lay on my bed, I prayed: "God – I am in Uganda because it is Your call on my life – Your Call, Your Vision and Your Provision. If it is Your best plan for my life right now to be in this pain – I will trust You." I woke up on January 2nd 2015 completely pain free!

I rejoiced each day in my healing, marveled in the Lord, travelled to South Africa for twelve days – completely pain free and on my return – that is when I needed to decide where to go in three weeks' time when my visa ran out.

As I bought my ticket for India, and now had to go to the visa office in Kampala – travelling on the boda bike, my back pain began again. It was a dull pain, but I had to go back the next day again and this time seriously set the pain in motion. When they called to say my visa was ready for collection, I was flat on my back unable to go anywhere. Again screaming from the pain and impossible for anyone to help other than Salome giving me hot water massages. She had seen me pacing the floor unable to lay down, unable to sit – and described it as she had also experienced every time she was in labour, and believed that I was 'Spiritually in labour', about to birth something of the Lord. My sons arranged to get the passport and visa for me. There were several words coming to me, of significance but not at this part of the story... then I cried out to Samson that I can't live this life in Uganda – it's too hard. That evening I spoke with a brother in Malta – he told me to remain in the Spirit at all times, and do not allow the flesh to rise up. Oops – I had already failed on that one, again repentance. Then the Lord showed me something. Through a picture He gave me, He showed me that I had become offended by something someone had said – and that I was not to become emotionally involved with the situations He was sending me in to minister to. Oops failed that one too!! I repented and immediately spoke out forgiveness towards the people concerned. On the morning of my travel to India – I was still unable to sit even for five minutes – but I was certain that God's Grace would take over when I needed it. While I was resting on the bed for the car to arrive to take me to the airport, suddenly I saw my own teaching.... The sin that offends you in another person is just a reflection of the sin in your own heart. Wow! Suddenly I saw the Lord showing me another **Fox**. I was offended by a spirit of Pride and Arrogance in the other people.... Hello!!! Time to repent again for Pride and Arrogance, and before the car arrived I called the person I could reach to ask forgiveness. They forgave me. I sat in the car – and continued sitting for fifteen hours with wheelchair assistance 'til I arrived in India.

Divine Appointment

It was so exciting – for the first time in my life – I had stepped onto the continent of India – in the Southern Region called Kerala. Apparently the Disciple Thomas – doubting Thomas was the one to bring the Gospel to India – to Kerala. It is a place where there are more Christians than other areas, and also a very large Jewish community, where they found acceptance and safety in their exile.

My son from the DTS met me and with another YWAM brother – drove me to their base in Kochi. Happy and tired, I ate breakfast and was shown to my room. The following day I was planned to share in the afternoon with the students first an English class then to share my life testimony as preparation to teaching thereafter. The teaching thereafter had to go on hold – my back was again suffering greatly, and that evening I went to my bed and remained on bed rest – unable to even sit to eat... my food was being served to my room. Students would come and visit with me and I got to share with some of them.

As the pain was increasing, my son contacted my other new Indian son from the Kampala DTS. He had friends who were friends with a doctor who could help me. He cut short his mission trip to meet me and escort me to the town of his friends. At the train station, grace was with me enabling me to lay down on a bench to wait for the train, and on the train again I had the grace to be able to lay down the two hour journey. I saw nothing of the countryside but I was just thankful for the freedom to lie down.

Arrival at the station, a friend was waiting with the car that my son had rented especially to drive me around. First we went to the friend's home where I met his wife and two gorgeous daughters, and I was given Kerala specialties with my favourite milky coffee. From there they drove me up into the highest point of the town – now in the dark, **when a fox ran out into the headlights of the car,** then quickly disappeared. We were on our way to visit a clinic to see a Dr – a nun. She talked with me, gave me some pain killer, and a paper to get an x-ray. From there we returned to the home, and then we left to go to another friend's home where I was to stay. As we drove into the drive, Pastor T, his beautiful wife, and their son, stood to meet me at the porch. I felt so incredibly honoured and again, a Kerala delicacy and a cup of milky coffee to welcome me were served, before getting back into the car – to go to the X-Ray department for the X-Rays. Nothing was too much for anyone to do for me. Even back at the YWAM base I had been a little tearful because of the love, and care I received from my son and his wife, and all the staff, now I was here being treated the same. The X-ray didn't take long to do – no-one else there except me, then home.

As we were sitting in the living room chatting, Rani began to tell me of the word the Lord had given her, before she had met me. "This was going to be a special encounter with the Lord!" Later we went to the kitchen to eat – and an amazing meal was put before me – it was a banquet, a feast – as I tried every different amazing flavour that had been lovingly prepared for me. One in the morning we finished eating. It was time for bed. The next morning we were due to see the Dr, friend to Pastor T. He has two hospitals, one close to where I was staying, but we were to have an appointment at the other one about thirty minutes' drive away. We sat to wait, but as we were waiting the pain increased and in the end it was so bad – they had to unlock a door for me to go in and lie down. The doctor saw me there. With the room full of spectators, before seeing the x-rays, he diagnosed my pelvis was out of alignment and causing a nerve to be trapped, and making one leg shorter than the other. He then looked at the x-ray and it confirmed his diagnosis. He said that if I continue to remain without treatment this could cause me to be paralysed from the waist downwards. They chatted between themselves of the treatment required and the cost. I was told that this was the poor man's hospital but the treatment itself is exactly the same as the other one. I could move into this very room for seven days treatment, followed by seven days bed rest at home, eating no meat in that time. The cost was decided and agreed, but it was requested instead of me remaining there, could I return on Friday – they explained it was my birthday! It was agreed. On our journey home I learned that this Dr is the Dr to the rich and famous in India and the best Osteopath in the country. Thank you Jesus!

I awoke to my birthday and it was a restful day. I had hoped to go to the forest to see the elephants and tigers, but the Dr had said no traveling. That evening I was called from my bed to supposedly eat, and with the lights all out – just a candle glow in the lounge, and a family of musicians as guests, they sang happy birthday and led me to my cake. Wow it was beautiful! What a surprise and I was completely overwhelmed. I had tried many times already to say thank you to this wonderful family for their love and support of me, but I couldn't get the words out as tears welled up every time. Earlier in the day, for the first time ever in my life – three men escorted me to buy night dresses for the hospital and Indian towels. Again the pain was too much – I could do nothing but leave it to my escorts to choose.

The next day I went to the hospital. I had been told not to take laptop or phone because it may not be safe, so with the only two books I had with me – my Bible and Song of Songs (TPT), we departed. I knew however it was going to be a time to meet with the Living God – who knows, I might even return from the mountain as Moses with a veil to cover the Glory of the Lord's presence!

Pastor T and Rani had thought of everything, bed sheets, soft pillow, cup and plate, spoon and fork, blankets, bucket, and then as we were all just sitting – one of the nurses came to ask the men to leave. Rani remained, and with very broken English I was asked to undress, it was time for the treatment to begin... it is enough to say that the treatment was invasive and for me embarrassing. The next part was going to be significant. They prepared for me an oil bath, where oil was heated up on a small gas cooker then and poured onto me. As the oil was repeatedly heated and poured, the fragrance of it became sweeter and stronger. This treatment was going to be repeated daily. It was a painful time and tears could not be restrained from release. My friends had waited throughout to know I was ok, then they left – having been told someone would have to return to spend the night with me.

Finally on my own, I just lay on the bed and cried. **I felt like I was a huge burden**. I was unable to do anything and having virtual strangers to do everything for me. The very nation of people the Lord had shown me I had a racist spirit against – the Lord was now using them to shower me unconditionally with such love. I had tried to say thank you as they left me – but I could not – the tears just welled up from within me.

As I lay there in the silence of this simple bare-walled room with two beds, a wash basin and a toilet, wet from the tears coming from somewhere other than my eyes, I turned to the Lord in prayer. "Why Lord – why all these tears, and this overwhelming feeling of love I cannot contain?"

"For almost all your adult life you have had to cope. Most of the times single, but also when you were married often despite sickness you had to manage to shop, manage to make food, manage everything on your own. Within your heart there has been a locked door to a room of Independence where there are also hurts still from not being loved and cherished as you had always longed for. I have been slowly **working to open that door** – to reveal it in your life. These people now are the ones I have chosen to pour out my unconditional love to you, through a situation where you could not use your independency, to become totally dependent."

"But Lord these people know what I need before I even need it, it is so humbling."

"Because I know your every need before you know you need it... it is my love for you that is flowing through them to you."

"But Lord – I have been able to do all things in you who strengthens me!"

"No! That is just it – you haven't. Though the word is true 'I can do all things through Him who strengthens me', your emphasis has been on "I" and not on "Him". The scripture has been a mask of religious spirit, used to hide the independent spirit behind. The scripture has become a Christian cliché thrown out at every opportunity giving permission for "I" to perform in the flesh. How many times did you ask for help from others? You didn't because you didn't want **to be a burden** on others, so you just soldiered on alone using the scripture as a mask to hide behind. If people didn't offer, you didn't ask."

"Oh Lord I am so sorry. Forgive me. Forgive me for the religious spirit, and for the independency, I repent and give you full permission to empty that room from all my independency, and fill it Lord with a dependency on You, and Father where there are hidden hurts towards anyone in the past who didn't offer to help me when I needed it – I forgive them Lord, they did not know what they were doing as I did not know what I was doing, I forgive them Lord, release now any spirit of hurt or rejection, or unworthiness from my heart, and fill it with healing, and full understanding of my priceless worth in you. Deliver me Lord from yet another piece of the religious spirit you have already been at work on in my life."

And I wept not in pain, but from an overflowing of love washing over me. I saw people that had helped me in the past despite my saying I didn't need it – and thanked the Lord for them in my heart... and I saw that as I had been stripped physically that day – the Lord was stripping me spiritually – to bring His ultimate inner healing of love poured out into the areas of coldness that had been locked away in the room of independency.

Day one – stripped! That afternoon – the pain was quite intense, as I prayed "Lord I can do nothing without **You!**" Staff came to give me some heat treatment on the bed before they went home, Pastor T returned to spend the early evening with me and to be there when his friend the Dr did his rounds. Dr told me that the following day he would do the correction for me. That night Isaac and Richi came as my carers for the night and Thomas went home. I shared what already the Lord had been speaking to me... and despite the pain, my heart rejoiced as I said thank you to them with eyes filled with tears.

Day two was a repeat of the treatment from the day before, with hot flowing oil over my body and massage. Back in my room I felt the Lord lead me to Song of Songs. Chapter one....

[The Shulamite]

> ²Smother me with kisses—
> Your Spirit-kiss divine.
> So kind are Your caresses,
> I drink them in
> Like the sweetest wine!

³Your presence releases
A fragrance so pleasing—
Over and over poured out.
For Your lovely name is "**Flowing Oil**." (TPT:4)

Oh – that was it – His name – the very essence of Jesus was being poured out over and over and over and over as flowing oil, being massaged into every part of my external body – a physical picture of His redeeming work in my spiritual heart. Physically and spiritually I was absorbing the oil of love into my hurting body, into my wounded spirit. I was being restored from the inside out! My heart rejoiced, despite the pain, my heart rejoiced. I trusted Him implicitly in the pain! To smell the fragrance of Jesus- one needs to be close. I remember arriving at a church and greeting the Pastor with a kiss on his cheek. As I drew close to kiss, my nose was close to his ear and neck, and I smelled the most beautiful fragrance. It was so beautiful, I asked if I could draw close to smell it again. The fragrance I was experiencing in the treatment room was symbolic of the closeness of Jesus.

Healing is in His perfume, His lovely name.

At that moment my heart could not stay quiet as I lifted my voice in song to praise and worship Him, midst the pain, my heart was rejoicing.

That evening the doctor came with two nurses to assist... it was time for the correction! Feeling vulnerable and weak, and a little afraid – not knowing what would happen, he began with my neck and working his way down the spine to the pelvis. He corrected my leg and knee, 'til both legs were the same length... and so it was complete. That night and the following day I was in indescribable pain. Isaac and Richi arrived again to be with me in the night, but there was nothing they could do for me. I tossed and turned in pain, and discomfort, struggling to go to the bathroom at night.

Day three, and the treatment continued. I had had a bad night – a dream...

I was standing with my son in the lobby of a Hotel when my son realized he had dropped his wallet and it was in the road, which we could see from the entrance of the Hotel. A car had stopped and someone got out

41

to pick it up – to keep it – but I saw the man – and thinking I recognized him, called his name. He was startled and handed the wallet to me, and I realized when I saw him up close it wasn't who I thought it was, just someone who looked very similar. Later in the night of the dream the man appeared knocking on my hotel room door. "I need to kill you, I am sorry." He said as he stood with a knife in his hand pointed towards me. Bewildered I asked him why... he continued to explain; "If I ever stand in line of an identification parade, and you were asked to identify me, you would be able to because I look like a friend." Then I woke up. It was very clear and yet without any understanding to it.

The day that followed I was in a lot of pain and feeling nauseous, so when the Dr came he prescribed me some medicine to help. That evening, after the doctor had left, I was feeling the need to wash my hair. It had not now been washed for four days and my scalp was itching and sweating – I needed to wash it out. I placed a bucket on the toilet seat then carefully bending my head forward; I used the toilet shower and managed to wash my hair clean. I was so proud of my achievement, having been able to do it myself – when there was a knock at the door. It was the doctor returning with the medicine. She saw my hair was wet – and I was lovingly corrected as it was not supposed to have any cold treatment to my body in the seven days or beyond – only hot water!!!! I guess it was that independent spirit rising again within me, and I had to repent.

Day four I was resting after the morning treatment session, and I had a vision. I saw a book cover. Front and back was a picture – a close up shot of a bunch of delicious grapes, and then on the front there was a small box with the picture of a **Fox**. The title of the book was: Catching **Foxes** by Fenella Stevensen.

"Lord – do you want me to write another book; a book about catching the **Foxes** of compromise? Surely Lord I do not have enough to write about of my own experiences – maybe of four or five instances six at the most!"

"I want you to write about the teachings of Jesus in the Gospels."

"But Lord I am not a Bible teacher, I have not studied the word at Bible college, am I qualified to write such a book?"

"You are qualified; you are a qualified **Fox** hunter, and what you do not know I will teach you. You are to reveal the **Foxes** that need catching for the Bride to get herself ready for me. I am coming soon, and my Bride needs to be ready and waiting. Many have forgotten or taken for granted the words I taught. Many focus on Paul's teachings but when they don't agree with his word – they dismiss it saying it might be of his own opinion not of the Spirit looking for excuses to enjoy the fleshly desires of their own hearts – but I am the Word, I am the Way the Truth and the Life, and my Word is unchanging, the same yesterday today and forever. I am the Alpha and the Omega. My Bride will have the eyes of their hearts opened to see as you have seen. As I lead you through the Hunt, so you will lead others. The battle is about to happen on another level as my Bride begins to understand the power and authority they have in me when they catch the **Foxes** that are ruining all that I have planted in their vineyard of love. There is a harvest – greater than any seen before about to happen, it is time for the Bride to arise and shine for the glory of the Lord is risen upon her. The enemy knows now that you can recognize him, **as in the dream**, but remember I am with you, a shield about you, I am your fortress and the lifter of your head."

"Lord, I can do nothing without You."

"I know, and that is just the way I like it, I will open the way and lead you forth."

Suddenly I see, the arrowhead may be sharp, but unless the shaft of the arrow is in perfect alignment it will not hit the target. Four years ago I had a vision that as the Lord was restoring me, He was re-feathering the end of the arrow so it will fly perfectly through the air... now I see my back is a picture of the shaft of the arrow. It has been realigned but the pain from inflammation still in the nerves, is like the fine sanding work as the shaft is streamlined for flight. I am in the time of final preparation to be sent forth from God's Bow, it is a time for stillness and waiting in Him. An arrow does not place itself into the bow; it remains in the quiver until the archer chooses to send it forth. The arrow does not place itself in the quiver, the master who restores it will on completion see it fit as ready to be used. Now is a time for allowing His word to flow through me in obedience to that which He has set me aside to do. It is a time to be still and know that 'I AM' God... and it is for such a time as this – the time currently being celebrated as Purim – the feast remembering that Esther was born for such a time... indeed I may have had plans – but God's plan supersedes all things. I am on His operating table yet again, as a willing patient under the master physician's knife, and I have my complete and absolute trust in Him.

(After I was out of the hospital but still on bed rest, I sent a message to the friend I thought I recognised in my dream and told him the story, told him of the book I am writing. He replied immediately, thinking it rather strange – the morning he was to read my email, **a fox ran across the road in front of him**.)

De-Mask-us Road

Paul, a Jew of excellence, in that he was a well learned man in Judaism and a Pharisee, a Roman citizen and was zealous in what he believed to be true – especially in the persecution of the Christians. On the way to Damascus, Paul had his own personal encounter with the Living God. Causing him to be blind physically, that the Lord would awaken his spirit to receive new eyes. Eyes to see the true and living God, Jesus crucified and buried, resurrected and ascended to the right hand of the Father.

God de-masked Paul, and he comes to de-mask-us. The masks we have used to cover up our insecurities, our sins, have begun to slip that we cannot see.

You made me, You knew me before I was born
What makes me think You like me better disguised
I paint a face, another personality
One I can't see through, the mask keeps covering my eyes.

Help me to be just who I am, and help me to see that with You I can
open my heart, the deepest emotion - spill out every part
the least little notion You already know, so stop this performance,
I'm ready to show You the me, that You made me to be

Let's leave the stage, draw back the curtains, go home.
No need for masks, this is the end of the play.
I am this face, this personality,
I need to know that You like me better this way

Help me to be just who I am, and help me to see that with You I can
open my heart, the deepest emotion - spill out every part
the least little notion you already know, so stop this performance,
I'm ready to show you the me, that you made me to be

You made me, You knew me before I was born
What makes me think you like me better disguised
I am this face this personality,
I need to know that You like me better this way
I know I know that You LOVE me better this way.

All of us – not just me, have painted masks to hide behind… to be accepted in the places we wish to be accepted, by the people we seem to think are essential in our lives. I am not saying the masks are **foxes**, but I believe that the masks are a hiding place for the **foxes** to live and multiply.

We put up masks often, so people cannot see our insecurities, our flaws. Indeed we step out of the front doors of our homes and step onto the stage of life, being the person that we believe the public want us to be.

I was at a party once, helping to serve the guests with wine, when I was asked by the group I was serving how I knew the host. I told them of our connection as being baptised together and being missionaries at the same time, sharing wonderful memories of a time in South Africa. They were surprised, they did not know. Later my friend reprimanded me, telling me not to tell any of her guests of those days. I believe that was a mask; to deny what had been an important part of her life in order to be accepted by these people now important in her life. I share this to paint a picture, not to judge. I have painted many masks. I have for many years painted the face of a clown. I found that I could make people laugh, and so I became the clown when I was out, the person always laughing, ever joyful. The problem was that no-one knew when I was crying or in pain, because the mask they saw I was always happy. I would make fun of myself, that way others wouldn't need to. The truth was however that when someone did – it hurt me, but under the clowns mask no-one could see.

I was out once with friends and new friends I did not yet know. Somehow the many mistakes of my life became the topic of conversation, and under the mask of laughter, I was torn apart in front of others. Did it hurt me? Yes it did, but I kept the mask of comedy on and laughed my way through the pain. I have since taken off the mask. It was difficult, and I felt naked and vulnerable, but the Lord helped me to do it. Actually the greatest part of removing the mask was when the Lord asked me to write the Rejoice books. When He asked me to be open about my past; I suddenly was faced with "Obedience to God, verses Fear of man." God had accepted me despite all my sin through the blood of Jesus, even if no-one accepted me, my heavenly Father did. Actually writing those books was my De-mask-us road! When people know our vulnerable places of weakness, our mistakes, often they wish to hang them up for all to see, because it takes away the spotlight from their own hurts and weaknesses. There is no malice, because I have forgiven!

One of the greatest masks in the church is the religious mask! On Sundays or at the prayer meetings or worship meetings, in the coffee shop, where we tend to wear our spiritual mask, our holy mask. We speak spiritual talk and impress others with our memorized scripture verses that are thrown about as Christian cliché's. We love all. Forgive all. Smile to all. Hug all then go home and gossip or discuss the negatives of the ones we have just hugged. We speak of discernment from the Lord of someone else's sin, but instead of praying blessing over them we tear them apart in discussion, but next Sunday we will hug them and not say a word.

Many years ago I had been away as a missionary and was back again for a short time working with the youth. I received a call from a parent to say that her daughter had tried to commit suicide and was in the locked ward of the hospital for her own safety. Would I go and see her. I was not to mention to anyone else, it was only me she was willing to see. I went, and the first visit she refused to talk but, I went the next day. Eventually she opened up that she had failed at her business and tried to take her life. I asked her why I can't mention it at church so people can pray for her. "No! I can't be a Christian if I fail." Where did that come from? No-one in church, who were professional business people, doctors and nurses, ever had any problems. You ask how each other are, and all say fine! They never said they had a problem; never a failing business or struggle. She saw that these people had Jesus and so thought they lived the perfect life. Hers was not perfect so she must not have Jesus with her. She felt a fraud and a failure. My heart just broke; because of this false religious mask that probably no-one actually knew they were wearing had been used to drive this young woman to kill herself. I went to church the next Sunday and my spiritual father came to me and said – Hi how are you. I said that I was not good. He replied – praise the Lord and walked away. He had asked a question out of tradition, politeness but had not been interested enough to hear my reply. I called him back calling him a hypocrite. He was shocked and I told him what he had just done. He repented. How do I know? Because his wife and daughter who I was talking with three years ago had never heard the story, but they said he suddenly changed and would ask people how they were... and when they said fine, he would say – "and how are you really?" He made a point to never be a hypocrite again.

As the Bride of Christ we need to be honest and open to all, in humility. We need to let Jesus De-mask-us!

I am writing about it because I have done it. I was living in a religious place in the world, or so I thought, and decided I needed to know how to witness to religious people. I was led to a booklet written about the Religious Spirit. Excited to open the pages as soon as it arrived in the post, the first page pierced my heart. It read something like this... "You have probably purchased this book with someone else in mind, but it is not for them but for you!" I read on – and indeed I was seeing myself as in a mirror through the pages, some pages more clear than others, but I was shocked to actually see any part of me in this book.

For two years I had a word for someone that the Lord would not allow me to give. During that time, on different occasions something would happen and I would ask the Lord if I should share the word now, and each time the Lord said no – just love them. I did love them, didn't I? Other people the Lord showed me with anger and other obvious sins going on in their lives, and I asked if the Lord wanted me to confront them, He said no, just love them. I did love them, didn't I? God doesn't want us to love with our love – but with His love! Man's love is condemning and judgmental, yet His love is unconditional. What the Lord was speaking to me about, was that I had a religious Spirit, which will heap condemnation if I spoke the word. The word that comes from the heart of God, NEVER brings condemnation. Condemnation comes from Satan, not God, Satan will accuse, but God convicts us in our hearts, not through fear, but in the midst of His love for us. When the Lord convicts us in His love, we are brought to a place of surrender and the place of humility in repentance because of His love. True love in the Lord will love regardless of the sin. God first loved us, whilst we were in the midst of our sin. We love not the sin but we love the sinner as Jesus does. I had to learn to love regardless, and instead of speaking what the Lord had told me, to hold it in prayer with Him, to the blessing of them. Two years later – the Lord gave me permission to share the word. I asked Him, why now Lord? He told me that His word for this person comes from a heart of pure unconditional love, and he is to receive it in the same way, but because of the Religious Spirit that was in me, the word would have been twisted through the wrong spirit and if delivered in that way would have caused more hurt and resistance. Condemnation cannot bring forth the fruit of the Spirit, condemnation is not of God but a fruit of the flesh.

I was surprised therefore when the Lord just last week in the hospital spoke to me of the religious mask of using the scripture; "I can do all things in Him who strengthens me." I recall another time when the Lord delivered me from a spirit of witchcraft, and nine months after I had repented and delivered, He gave me revelation and understanding. I will give testimony to this later, but one thing I realise is that sometimes deliverance is done in parts. Just as it is impossible to remove a layer of onion in one piece, it gets broken into pieces to remove it; so it is often with deliverance and any form of healing and restoration. The masks we are talking about have been in place for a very long time and the walls of the mask are layered and thick. God is patient and He will patiently work a layer and piece at a time, bringing us revelation and understanding bit by bit. He could just rip the mask from us – He has all power to do it, but it is so attached to us it would tear our flesh too... He waits for us to remove a layer at a time. He does it with love, not condemnation... again He asks us to do it with Him. He waits for our permission. The permission we give to move in power and authority is our repentance. Recognizing the sin that the Lord is revealing and willingness to turn away from it, asking for forgiveness (which He has already forgiven) but He wants us to recognize and repent. This is the permission we give to the Holy Spirit to sweep clean the house.

The revelation God gave whilst in the hospital, was not as much a deliverance from a religious spirit – He had already done that, but it was the revelation of how the **fox** of Independence had been able to hide and go un-recognized. Once the mask had been removed, He was working all things together for the good of being able to reveal it to me. How did He do it? By placing me in a situation where I had to become completely dependent on others, and still am, as I am writing this book. In a place where I am still having others to strip me and bathe me, give me the medicines, feed me. The Lord has me in a place of complete dependency on others... teaching me total dependency on Him. It is humbling.

In 2013, I travelled to Uganda for the first time in twenty four years. I was asked to teach on Spiritual Warfare on a YWAM Discipleship School. I had felt unqualified then, because of my time away from the Lord in rebellion. When I prayed to the Lord about it, He told me that I had been living a lifestyle of Spiritual Warfare for the last three and a half years, I am qualified. I wasn't sure if I had heard correctly so I told my Pastor of the invitation to teach and I felt unqualified. He repeated the exact same words I had heard from the Lord! I was amazed! So I began to put together the training material, including teaching on the Religious Spirit and Spirit of Witchcraft.

The week of teaching began, and after ten minutes I was asked to stop. I felt unqualified and they were going to stop me, but a student was in pain and they asked me to pray. I prayed – not sure of the spirit, but sure that it was a spiritual attack, so I bound all spirits in Jesus name and also of sickness and infirmity and released the healing power of the Lord. He lay down on a mattress in the classroom, and after half an hour he was completely free from the pain.

I had taken longer on some points than planned so on Wednesday I was behind schedule. Wednesday night I had to pray to decide what to teach and what to leave out the next day. The Lord told me to speak on the Spirit of Witchcraft. That night I went to bed and in the middle of the night awoke to excruciating pains exactly as the student had described the first day. I now knew it was a spirit of witchcraft. I tried rebuking, binding, worshipping, praying in tongues, I cried out to the Lord, but help did not come. I was intent on teaching what the Lord had prepared, so I dragged myself to the training room that morning, no food – I felt so sick.

The same time I was under attack in the night, another student had also awoken with the same pains, and went to the bathroom. Out of the window it is always dark, but she saw blackness so dark and evil she was afraid and returned to her bed – put on worship to sleep to and the pain disappeared. Mine however was very strong. In the break time I sat down and students worshipped over me. Unable to stand I continued the teaching from the floor and when it was over I released them for an early lunch, but they remained with me and continued to worship over me. God then spoke to me to repent on behalf of my mother's and my own sin. Immediately the Lord showed me my mother's sin. I didn't understand my own sin but I was obedient and repented on behalf of my mother's sin and my own of Control and Manipulation. In other words – witchcraft! Immediately as I had prayed, all hell broke loose in my stomach like huge punches from side to side and a fever. They carried me to my room, and a car drove me to a private hospital. The doctor was convinced I had malaria and stomach ulcers, so sent me for tests. Blood was taken and an ultra-sound of my stomach. I returned to the doctor. He was confused. There was absolutely nothing wrong with me despite the pain, and in fact there was a lot of gas – which also there was no explanation for. He gave me painkillers but he could not treat me because there was nothing to treat. I returned home to the bed, and as I lay there, I had problems breathing. I heard the Lord speak telling me to exhale repeatedly. As I did so, suddenly I was free.

The next day I explained what had happened. I had been delivered of the spirit of witchcraft – Jezebel – control and manipulation. How did it get there? My mother!

As a child she was an only child, and never shared anything. Love from her mum and dad all for her, gifts and presents all for her. When she got married – husband's love all for her until my older sister was born. She was jealous of my dad's love for the baby! Her way to handle that was to give my sister to dad, and the next baby (me) would be ALL hers! No sharing!!! Control, manipulation and domination. And I grew up with that – and I escaped from it at the age of eighteen when I left home, though it wasn't apparent to me then what it was.

I was free, I understood in part, but despite not understanding all, I had prayed, I was obedient and I was free. Remember I mentioned the Fox hunt in Denmark 2014. I was staying at my friend's home, and had a dream. The dream was the Lord asking me to ask my sister's forgiveness. I asked the Lord what it was I had done wrong so I could ask for forgiveness. He began to tell me of something I said to her when I was six years old! What? I am now fifty eight years old and I need to repent of something at the age of six? I had apparently said once to my sister that if she did not stop what she was doing I would kill her. I was afraid of small moths, flies, yet she was afraid of me because I would kill her when I couldn't even kill a moth? Then the Lord said something that rang a bell. "It is not what you said – but the way you said it." Even as adults when we disagreed about something she would get angry with me saying "It's not what you say but the way you said it!" That was it – the light switch just went on and revelation came. As a child my sister was very discerning of the way I said I would kill her – and she was afraid of me. What she had discerned was not what I said, but the spirit of control and manipulation. The spirit of witchcraft – and she was afraid.

I explained how the Lord revealed to me the spirit transferred by my father, this was the big one transferred from my mother, and that was why it was my sin also. My mother's iniquities had given birth to my own sin of control but I had no idea I had it. Even my husband had recognized it – but He was so controlling I was the victim of his sins. Now I saw it with understanding. I wrote to my sister the next day – she didn't agree or understand, but she forgave me.

I was so amazed at this revelation and then the revelation that God used the black man drinking vodka took place some two weeks later! I was visiting a friend and telling them of my revelations. For some reason they were telling me how much I loved my husband. I didn't think it was love – probably more lust. No they argued back – I was so in love. I had had two marriage proposals at the same time – but I loved my husband so much and chose him. Funny, considering I had been so desperate for marriage, I didn't remember the other proposal. They told me the man from the church used to send me bouquets of roses, but I had no recollection. They had a book written by him on the shelf – he writes on Spiritual Warfare… there was a picture of him. I looked and still didn't recognize him. I opened my mouth and said something very strange. "He looks fat!" My friends replied, "He was not fat – like you we would say rounded." Now my reply was a revelation about to happen… "I would say that I am fat, and **I would never have married a fat man – I don't like fat men.**"

In the marriage I suffered for seven years, I was starved because my husband did not like fat women! God showed me that the same spirit of vanity that I saw in him, was also in me. In fact, as can be read in the second of the Rejoice books – I planned how I could kill myself because of the extreme control and manipulation, and vanity. God was showing me that the very **foxes** in my husband that tormented me, <u>were the same</u> **foxes** living in me <u>and had probably tormented my husband</u> but I hadn't realised it. "How did that happen," I asked? Sin attracts the same sin in others like a magnet. REVELATION! No wonder I didn't choose the 'fat man'...my sin was attracted to the man with the same sin – which he had also received from a very harsh controlling father. He was attracted to me despite being rounded, because the same sin of vanity and control and manipulation was attracted to me like a magnet!

Why do I call the sin **Foxes**? Because when we allow them to live within us, they destroy the work of the Lord within us. These sins / spirits are from the spirit of the flesh, not the spirit of the Holy Spirit.

How many of you have stubborn children? Oh little Jonny is so cute – and the parent will reply ah yes – but as stubborn as his father or mother! It is a characteristic we have accepted as being ok. What is stubborn? It is disobedient, rebellion. As the church of God – born again, with Jesus dwelling within us, what part of the fruits of the Spirit are stubborn, rebellion, disobedient? They are not – they are fruits of the flesh which we have supposed to have repented of and left behind with the old life. Instead we allow it as a characteristic and then pass it on to our children. Parents if you have controlling children, stubborn children, or other problems, then I will ask you, look to your parents and see if it is something they also have. If yes – then you have it too.

If you try to control your controlling children with the same spirit – the spirit will increase. The sins feed each other and it will escalate. The only way to break it – is first parents to repent of the controlling spirit on behalf of the parent etc. and your own! Jesus does not use any form of control or manipulation. If there is a black dog and a white dog to fight each other to the death, which one will win? The dog you feed! If we feed the spirit of the flesh, it will be the one who will grow stronger and overpower unto death the Holy Spirit.

Out of interest – control and manipulation is the basic sales techniques to manipulate and control people into buying a product – it is witchcraft! Churches have also used such methods to try and bring people into the church – or control the church members. Can you pick an avocado from a mango tree? No. Likewise the spirit of the flesh cannot produce fruit of the Holy Spirit.

Just returning to; it's not what you say but the way you say it...

Living in Malta, I was unable to learn the language, so listening to the Maltese talk in their own language was always a mystery to me. However, I often felt fear, because they would be shouting very loudly at one another, I thought a fight was about to happen and punches thrown. I once asked my friend and sister in the church if they were having an argument, but she laughed saying no – they were just passionate when they talk. One day the Lord revealed to me that there was a murderous spirit. Another incident was a friend also speaking on the telephone of what was thought to be someone-else's misdeeds. I couldn't listen more – it was like venomous poison being spewed out. When I talked to the person about it, I was told it was no such thing but that it was because of being Maltese, and they speak with passion. Another incident was another church member rising as a statement of authority and shouting in a venomous way his point of view in order to press it over us all. It was a coercive and murdering spirit that I was feeling, and no-one else seemed perturbed by it. I cried out to God and asked what I was seeing. He showed me the history of Malta. An island that was first owned by the Italians, but was sought after by many nations. When such nations came against the people they would muster to defend themselves, fighting and bloodshed occurred, but when they were defeated, and a new rule took over, they had no choice but to surrender to the new regime. They hated the victors, but with hidden anger and bitterness had to submit. Then another country would rise up to take over the country... more bloodshed, anger, hate and bitterness as a new victor took over the land and again with hatred and bitterness in their hearts, submitted wearing a mask of acceptance and allegiance. It became not just a sin of one person but that of the whole nation, that was then handed down through the generations, 'til the hidden anger, murdering, jealous and bitter spirit became a way of speaking. It is described as passionate, but it cuts and maims and there is nothing healing in the spirit of the way it is spoken.

They lived under control and domination, which has now become a part of their own inheritance, spiritual DNA handed down as a nation... not the words spoken, but in the way they are spoken

As Christians I believe we all need to recognise that we are born again – we do not belong to this world, I am not British, they are not Maltese, you are not from the land of your physical birth, of this tribe or that tribe, we have all become born again, we are citizens of the Kingdom of God, of the Tribe of Jesus, and the ways of this world should be let go of, and not defended when it is not in line with the word of God.

Jeremiah 29:11;
Song of Songs 2:6;
Isaiah 40:31

Down Memory Lane – Women of Independence

I am following a train of thought that has come to me... (whilst in my bed of rest following the hospital.)

Today I had a visitor, who is staff with YWAM in Uganda – but just before I was to teach there last year, there was a death in the family that he needed to return to India for, so we never met. He had heard of me and of the week I had shared on the DTS from the Base leader, and also from my two Indian sons, and decided that now was a good time to visit to meet me whilst on my bed rest and to see Isaac again. He arrived with his Pastor.

I managed to join them in the lounge sitting in the only chair I could manage... not sure for how long, and began to share of the experience of Chapter 5. As I was talking he told me of the very first experience meeting the European spirit of independence, when he was in Norway, and it was very aggressive. As an Indian man it is in their nature if they see someone in trouble – especially a woman, to offer to help. This particular trouble was that a car had a flat tyre and the wheel needed changing. He offered to help the lady, where he was sharply told no thank you and that she was capable of doing it herself.

As I am still lying in my bed in India, the lights are out, the ceiling fan is off because the power keeps cutting in and out, the sweat is pouring from every part of my body on this very hot humid night, and I think back to a meeting in Holland, where there was a guest speaker sharing about the strong female spirit. He had traced it back to the Second World War. It was a time when all the men had been called up for service and were away fighting against Hitler. With the men called into service, many important posts back home were suddenly left vacant and causing a fall in the businesses, so for the first time, they called for women to come and work and taught them to do the jobs the men were doing. The women liked it and were good at it.

After the war – many of the women were kept, on and men coming home from war found it hard then to get jobs. The women were now the breadwinners, and the male ego was crushed. He was intended to be the provider for the family, now his wife was doing that role... hence the saying "Who's wearing the trousers in this house?" In many of the European countries women became strong, independent and domineering as they progressed in being able to run the family, go out to work, and manage the finances.

I had been blind – I saw it more on the continent of Europe, than in Britain/ UK, but as I lay in my bed I remembered some things from home. Indeed when dad was away in the war, they were not yet married but they were sweethearts – mum was also called into one of the old factories that were suddenly making parachute material. She was one who went out to work, filling in the empty gaps, in the later years of the war.

Something I also remember about my mum was that she was very good at mathematics. She later had work in the local steel company, in the office. She was the only woman among the men – and all the men would go to my mum to check their work when there were discrepancies, because she would find the problem in a very short time than if they searched for themselves. Usually it was their adding that had gone wrong. My mum could be given a list verbally, of numbers up to six figures, and she could add them in her head – and was always right. There was often talk at home how wrong it was that my mum was the best at the job but because she was a woman got paid less than the men whose job she did for them were paid. I was one of very few children at school, whose mum and dad were both working. This was possible because when I was about two years old my mum's dad died, and for whatever reason at the time, it was agreed that mum and dad would move in to live with mum's mum – my nana. She was home and so she was there for us coming home from school – it meant that mum and dad were free to work – giving us extra income and the honor of having a car and travelling abroad to France for camping holidays. Of course for me in the early days I was not at school, but I would have fun with my nana. She made glue from flour and water so I could cut out pictures from magazines and make a collage. I loved my nana. She was a dress maker professionally, and I of course managed to get lots of dresses along with my sister that others didn't get. I used to do ballet from about the age of five years old, and my nana made all my costumes, beautiful ballet dresses, whatever I needed. She also taught me how to sew, I learned much from her. I loved all the food she made – she was excellent in the kitchen.

There was an incident I remember though of being afraid of her. My sister had done something wrong, maybe answered her back – I don't know – but I know that she was arguing with my sister, and the next thing she had my sister by the neck and pulled her to the kitchen tap and held her head under the tap to stop her hysterical shouting. I have a fear of water on my face from an early incident of almost drowning at the beach, and this frightened me – if she was ever to do this to me I would drown and die. It was better to stay in Nana's good books! (Fear controls!)

My nana knew how to do everything! There was nothing she couldn't do – well except build I guess. She spent hours in the garden, where she had both flowers and fruit bushes and vegetables. Dad had built a greenhouse adjoined to his shed. He was very proud of his tomatoes he grew there. The shed was a no entry zone to my Nana – dad insisted. He had in there a gas stove we used for camping, and he would use it to make his own preferred recipes of vegetable soup or potato hash, where Nana was not allowed to interfere as she used too much 'Bisto' as I recall, and dad preferred the natural flavours to be tasted. We just used to laugh about it at the time, but it was last night as I was thinking on these things I started to see the truth.

My dad was an excellent engineer, and was wanted all over the country to dismantle large machinery, transport them to new locations and then rebuild it again. It meant that he could be away working for longer periods of time. I suddenly saw the reality also behind this. I remembered when he came home – all decisions had already been made – by mum and of course Nana. Her house – she was paying the rent, in her name... so the man who was ordained by God as the head of the household had in fact been usurped by two dominating and manipulative women. I had recognized my mother's controlling spirit through the story of when my mother gave birth to my sister and gave her out of jealousy to dad saying the next one would be all hers! However what I had not seen was in fact the controlling spirit of my Nana.

Even as I am writing I am remembering a conversation where dad let it slip once that living with Nana was a nightmare, and he had no say over the family because she made all the decisions and her daughter followed. There were often rows between dad and Nana, though I don't remember what about. I am sure that the thing holding the family together was actually dad's great and equal love for both my sister and I.

What am I saying? I suddenly realise that there was a line of dominant women, strong women, and independent women in the generation from my mother's side. Though I don't know anything about my Nana's parents, I remember her saying that the First World War started when she was fourteen years old, and then the Second World War began to surface when my mum was 14 years old... I remember because when my sister was fourteen and then me – I wondered if there would be a third world war! It was later in the war when mum worked in the factory making parachute material. If the men of my Nana's life had left for war then also – it would go without saying that the women had to cope in the absence of their husbands and take control of the home and finances in their time away fighting. My Nana would have been part of that as a fourteen year old and upward – she would have learnt to take on responsibilities and to master them. Although my nana did have a brother who was older – he may well have also been signed up to fight, so women at home alone learning to cope with all things

I was actually a very timid and shy girl as a baby, demanding my mother for everything; because that was the way she had raised me – to be totally dependent on her. Of course that dependency was unhealthy. It was not about receiving love – but actually my dependency on my mother was about her using me for her own needs of love. She had pushed dad away once she had me... I was the one who was going to meet all her needs. **There is one thing a person who has a controlling spirit hates, and**

that is being controlled by someone else! Although I had not recognised what was happening in my life then, my choice at eighteen to visit a friend in Torquay ended up with me living there... I can see that when my friend had made that decision for me through deception to not return home, the story is in my first book, I found freedom. What I thought was freedom... but it was freedom to sin! It was after I left home I began to see my mother's manipulations to control. I don't believe any of it was intentional on her part – because she was deceived.

I am, as I said, in India as I am writing, and thinking of the words in Genesis, that a man and woman shall leave their father and mother and cleave together as husband and wife, two becoming one... here in India, I am seeing the young man in the house, still living with his parents at the age of twenty three; almost unheard of in western culture, where, we are looking to leave home usually as soon as possible. Many leave home when they go to study at university, feeding them with an independency and ability to cope without the parents. I am not saying it is wrong – but I can see that it is not in line with the Word in Genesis. When I was away for the first time on holiday without my mum and dad, I was deceived and from there my life found freedom to sin without the watchful eye of my parents as I look back now! It was not the first time I had sinned – in my book, I lost my virginity at the age of fourteen but my parents did not know. Now I didn't have to answer to anyone what time I arrived home at night or where I had been....

My dad, after both I and my sister had left home, and he had been finally made redundant and needed to spend endless hours at home, with Nana as mum was still working. He had gone to meet mum from work one day as a surprise. He saw all the workers leaving, waiting for mum. In the end he walked to her office. There was light on but the door was locked. He tried it a few times then returned to the car. As he sat, a few moments later, he saw mum come out of the locked door followed by a man. Dad's hand on the door trying to enter had alerted what had been going on behind closed doors. It was some time after that my dad called me to tell me he is leaving mum. He had known someone purely as friends for some years, but now he could not take the cold rejection and the constant control of my Nana. At the time I could not throw stones I was now living with a man who had left his wife and children for me. It was probably the first time I had realised how unhappy my dad was... possibly two weeks after he had called to tell me – I received another call from him. He was postponing the move out as mum was sick and had been diagnosed with a tumor on the brain... now was not the time to leave her regardless, now was the time to support her through it.

She did come through it, slowly returning to health but never returning to work. Nana died in 1983. Dad never did leave mum. He remained faithful to her despite her possible unfaithfulness to him. There were many stories that eventually came out. My mum had a problem with money... we have no idea what she used it for but she stole from the family business that we onetime had, placing dad in a position of having to keep closer control on what was happening. Remember – my mum was good with numbers – so it wasn't because she was bad with the accounting! In her later years we found that she had many store cards, and would buy dresses maxing out the cards and not paying them off. The wardrobe was packed with hidden dresses never worn. Dad was forced to sell the house to pay off the debts, and go into sheltered accommodation for the elderly. He managed to get a ground floor flat in the same residential park his own mum and dad had once lived in.

Both my parents are dead, and I **do not** write this to judge my mum in any way, because I see not the flesh, but I see the unseen spirit that was freely at work in my mother's life, also handed down through the generational line.

The spirit of Jezebel is a man hater. She usurps man's God given authority in the home, she is independent and also a temptress into sexual immorality. She is the Queen of heaven spoken of in the Bible and she controls many **foxes**. The truth is when you find one **fox** – there are usually more in hiding... and it is important to find how they have access into the vineyard of love – because unless that opening is closed and sealed – we will be forever chasing or we will give up and allow the **foxes** to completely destroy that which the Lord has planted.

I am seeing my independent spirit not just from the hurts of traumas of my own life, the transfer from my mum – but through the generational iniquities that have formed a western culture passed down and then given birth to my own. I am happy that women are valued after years of being suppressed and often considered worthless, especially in the westernized world. What I am seeing however is that independency in our hearts can also mean independency from God. He is knocking not just on my own door to a room of independency but to nations who without knowing, have areas of their lives locked away from Him because of our national / cultural inheritance, and as Christians, hiding behind the words "I can do all things in Him who strengthens me." The emphasis on 'I' and not "Him;" giving us license to cope, and cope well in many cases, but in our own flesh and not in the Spirit of the Lord. Our locked doors of independence are holding back the fullness of God's love to provide for us, holding back the fullness of God's Grace, and providing an entrance for the **foxes** to freely access and ruin the garden, our vineyard of love, stealing the fruit He has grown within us.

Is it easy to be rid of this? Well, I am finding that it has deep roots. I repent and as such nail it to the cross of Jesus, but I am continually realizing that it seems to resurrect itself. This place of bed rest – total bed rest, being totally dependent on others is the place where I am seeing opposition within me rise. Ten days out from the hospital and something rises up within me when the family tells me it is bath time. Bath time means first bathed in oil and laying in that way for half an hour, before walking assisted to the bathroom and the plastic chair and buckets of hot water waiting with soap to wash off the oil. I am totally unable to do it myself. I believe that the inflammation inside the nerves, and the blockages of blood flow through the legs bringing the pain, will be with me 'til in Jesus name the spiritual door has been broken down and – and the room swept clean. I am as I write – catching **foxes**!

Indeed as I was waiting to be treated today, I have been two days without a bath in extreme heat and sweating, and today I just wanted to wash. Change my nightdress. I asked and they said no – the maid will come at two in the afternoon. I waited and no maid came, so I asked again at about three, and I was told I will get treatment at four. They covered me with oils then rest for thirty minutes... but every time they keep me waiting much longer – sometimes uncomfortably, on a plastic sheet- hot and sticky with mosquitoes in the air waiting for open banquet. Today I realised what was coming up within me... impatience, having to wait for others to do things in their time. That's why I like to have my own car – I can come and go without having to either wait for others or wait for buses... I know I am not the only one, but what I can see is more than just independence raising its head – it is also attached with impatience, time management, not that I have anything to manage at this point in time. There is nothing wrong with having a car or time management – but what the Lord is showing me are the things that are driving within me... I have to wait for others, and it is not feeling good.... **SO if I don't like waiting for others, how am I at 'Waiting on God'?**

How many of us try helping the Lord in the flesh? Abraham and Sarah who were told they would have a child allowed flesh thoughts to interfere instead of waiting and trusting. That independent spirit said – it is impossible for Sarah in her old age – actually it was Sarah who suggested to her husband to sleep with her maid servant, which he did and Ishmael was born. (It was also Eve in the garden who was deceived and suggested to Adam to eat the fruit. Eve was deceived but Adam was in outright rebellion through disobedience.) Ishmael and his descendants would always 'til the end of time be at war with Isaac. Ishmael was born of the flesh – Isaac was a complete miracle of God – born of the Spirit!

Why does God want to chase the **foxes**... well He wants to do amazing things birthed in the Spirit, to bring glory unto Him, but if we are not careful through being independent and unwilling to wait, we will find ourselves birthing in the flesh – good works – maybe – but unless they are birthed in the Spirit – they will only bring forth fruit of the flesh – always at war against the Spirit! We are born again and called to walk in the Spirit, but these **foxes** are hindering the plans the Lord has for us:

> **"11 For I know the plans I have for you," declares the LORD,**
> **"plans to prosper you and not to harm you, plans to**
> **give you hope and a future." Jeremiah 29:11 (NIV: 5)**

I have to say that another revelation has come as I talked with my son Isaac. I was talking with him and from my mouth, in the present tense; I said **I have no-one.** His eyes filled with tears and told me not to say that – I have him and the family here. Those tears were as though I saw the heart of God, and I too filled with tears as I realised what I had said. I had meant that everyone has a husband and children and they belong together – they are a family, a unit. Husbands and wives can turn to each other to their children when they are older, for help and support. Even husbands and wives share pillow talk and can help and support each other even if it is just to be held tightly in love whilst tears of pain fall. As a single, do you know how much I miss just being held?

I am learning to let the Lord hold me – hug me:

Song of Songs 2: 6

"His left hand cradles my head
While His right hand holds me close. I'm at rest in this love!"(TPT:4)

We are all one family... on Earth as it is in Heaven. I have withheld myself in the past as a gift, in **fear of being a burden**... but we are family, and I belong to you in Christ, and you to me. We are blood relatives, for although we are scattered all over the globe, the one thing that binds us together is "The Blood of Jesus!" If people did not offer, I did not ask. It is **my sin** of self-centeredness in my thinking, never thinking that my weakness could be a blessing to others to allow their strengths to be used as a channel of God's love.

It reminds me of an incident thirty three years ago when I was first born again and a family invited me to their home for Sunday tea at five in the evening. I cried because I couldn't go. When asked why I was crying, I told them that I could not accept theirs and everyone's charity any more by being invited for free food. They were smart, and said – "Ok – come at five still – we will eat whilst you just talk with us, we are not bothered about feeding you, but we do enjoy your company!" It had not occurred to me that someone might actually like being with me! (**Insignificant!)** Some years later when I felt a failure, standing in the kitchen peeling potatoes at a YWAM base in the UK, I had been sent there to receive healing in the Lord. The base leader quietly walked up to me and whispered in my ear, "We do not endure you, we enjoy you!" And again I cried. **Only the Lord knew how worthless, insignificant and a burden that I felt because they needed to help me**. Oh that I should have learnt then the lessons I am learning today!!!!! Maybe I did but did not close the place of entry so they came back, or maybe the layers were thick and He was dealing with the first levels of it?

God is revealing the lies of the enemy that have been sown and I have believed for many years; that I was ugly, un-loveable, worthless, and a burden to others. Insignificant!

This is the word that describes how I have been seeing myself, and although I can see that the Lord has been healing me of this over the years, still I know that not wishing to be a burden is because the root of my belief is that I am insignificant! But the truth is – <u>I am so very significant because Jesus died on the cross for me</u>! Everything God has been revealing to me through His Word, and through the testimony of my life – even my names have meaning and purpose. He knew me before the world began, and knew exactly which mum and dad would give birth to me giving me my family name – a family name which I rejected, and yet this name was part of God's purpose for my life. In some ways even as I write now I see how I have rejected that which God gave me... wanting to get rid of the name as soon as possible because of always being made fun of... deciding marriage is the only option to change my name. Even my first partner before I was a Christian that I lived with, wanted to change my first name, telling me it was an old fashioned name, preferring to call me Eve. Again Fenella is not my real name – because of protecting people in the first two books of Rejoice. But my name that he hated is actually 'so who I am' in the Lord!

Do you see how **foxes** steal? Steal the promises of the Lord, through unbelief and lies, the purposes for our lives that will bring fulfillment and eternal joy with the Father, Son and Holy Spirit.

"... but those who hope (wait) in the Lord will renew their strength. They will soar on wings like eagles; they will run and not grow weary, they will walk and not be faint." Isaiah 40:31 (NIV: 5)

Another revelation through Pastor Brian Simmons is the word to wait... can also mean to be entwined. As we are waiting on the Lord we are being intricately entwined in Him. I am repenting for my unbelief, and asking the Lord now to release His truth in power to fill my heart, and to indeed renew my mind.

I believe this day - these **Foxes** have been caught

A Question of Possession

I have been speaking of spirits, deliverance and healing, and for some I believe you are questioning if a Christian can be demon possessed? A born-again Christian CANNOT be demon possessed!

I want to try and explain using a picture form.

I have grown up in the UK, during a time when it became a moneymaking business to buy an old house, run down and selling at a cheap price, then to do all the work within the house to renovate it and increase its sale value, then sell it on making a good profit, to then buy another house and start all over again. Usually these renovations would take place in a short space of time in order to maximize the profits. However not all families worked like this, but took from it lessons.

I remember being part of buying a property, and indeed looking at the current state, but seeing potential in the making. I created a drawing to join two rooms together to create a bathroom with a sunken bath – all the rage at that time... another room to be repainted and new designer curtains made and twelve small pieces of art ordered to make the dining room into a special place to entertain friends.... Changes made to the kitchen... the huge lounge with panoramic views from two walls being windows. Together with my partner we purchased the house seeing the potential of change after we had bought it – but the changes would be made one at a time, as and when the budget was in place for each piece of work. At first when we purchased the house, we moved into it just the way it was.

We took possession of the house when the papers had been signed and the money transferred from our bank to the seller's bank. We were given title deeds and the keys to the property. Now it was our total possession! In theory it belonged to the bank as we had taken out a mortgage – paying it each month, but we did not have to ask the bank permission to improve the property, we had the keys of ownership.

When I invited Jesus into my life to be Lord, it is when I transferred the deeds of my body into His ownership, possession. Jesus became the new owner of this body. I think of my body as a house with many different rooms and levels. When I gave Jesus the keys to my heart – I invited Him in through the front door and into the hallway, bringing Him into the lounge. As He first moved in, He decided to make two small rooms into one large room, with windows at both ends causing a great light into that room. He stripped the old wallpapers from the walls, plastered the cracks and holes hidden beneath, then He chose a new wall covering, light in colour to absorb the natural light of the sun, which would create a warmth and cosy place to rest, and entertain guests... some being angels. Next He worked on the kitchen, the heartbeat of the home where food would be gladly prepared for the family and for guests. This was His first plan as He took over the possession of this home. Immediate and obvious sin and pleasures were dealt with in the stripping of the old away, and replacing with the new to reflect the Son's love in my body. It was a time of great joy – and even the stripping away of the old was not painful but of great delight as I allowed Him to sweep clean these rooms. And it was in these rooms that He dwelt for many years...

The bathroom is always a place where we long to have luxury and a 'feel-good design' about us. In the days of my childhood, I remember an outside shed for the toilet, where I used to hate going in the night in case the bogey men would get me. In the winter when it was wet and even snow – going to the toilet was a time of discomfort. I remember moving to my nana's house, and she had a bathroom upstairs with toilet in a small room attached at the top of the stairs. Wow, it was fantastic, although use of the toilet became more difficult, because now it was indoors my dad seemed to enjoy taking the newspaper with him to sit and read for long periods of time. As I grew older I felt the same need to take my comic book with me to read... like father, like daughter. The bathroom had a bathtub and a wash basin in. We would wash every night/

morning at the wash basin but on a Sunday – it was bath day ready for the new week. As I got older I preferred more water in the bath, and longer time to soak in it, more bubbles, especially in the winter because the hot water and steam would heat up the bathroom which otherwise would be cold. As the bedrooms were without heating, the bathroom could be the warmest place because of running hot water in the basin to wash – so it also became the dressing room too – which would put a time pressure on the family all wanting to use it before school and work.

Because the bathroom is upstairs and in most cases out of view to the guests, it is one of the rooms to wait to be fixed, making do with what there is until budgets are in place for the new installations. Now-a-days, although baths are still enjoyed the shower or power shower has taken over due to a savings of water, and less time used, much more workable in a time of fitting many things into a day.... So the day arrives where we begin to plan the new bathroom. The place of washing/cleansing.

For many of us as Christians we believe that the 'washing clean' at the foot of the cross when we come to salvation is the only time required, when we are as such washed clean by the blood of Christ and all our sins are forgiven – the sins of the past present and the future. However I would say that at the time of purchase, there is a huge umbrella over the house – the umbrella of Grace. We are covered by the blood, but not as yet been set free.

For example. God's grace has been with me, and when I gave my life to Jesus in 1982 my life changed a lot... but God waited 30 years before He revealed to me the spirit of control and manipulation in my life since birth. It is as if it was one of those rooms on the waiting list to be transformed. God's timing is always perfect, and His work in our hearts of transformation is always done together with us. I needed to understand or at least have my heart in a place of readiness for His instruction before He could deal with the stronghold in my life. Indeed for it to take place I had to repent... as such I needed to go into the washroom at the foot of the cross, recognizing that which the Lord has told me, and repent, before the Lord had total permission to sweep the room clean. I needed a power shower! The whole house was in His possession, but He waited for the right time to ask permission to transform that room... when I repented, it gave Him the keys to the room to sweep it clean, strip off the old wall covering and repair the walls before recovering.... It took time – and part of that time was nine months after the deliverance, when He asked me to ask my sister for forgiveness for the something I said when I was 6 years old. During those 9 months he was slowly at work within that room to prepare me for the next step of transformation that would bring revelation to further works in the house. It was then He showed me the room of racism and anti-Semitism, handed down from my father, and the room of vanity – of which I don't know where it came from, although it would make sense from the time I learnt how to use make-up to paint beauty because I had ugly 'cod fish' eyes... all I know is that the Lord revealed it to me – the same spirit I judged my husband for having was in me! Having then had those rooms renovated, suddenly this year the Lord tells me of another room in a cold-darkness, that He's been waiting to enter – waiting for me to give permission – 'Room of Independence', which I later found was also a hiding place for 'hidden anger' which I had no idea about, and feelings of 'insignificance' still hiding there too.

Jesus has had total possession of my house, since 1982, but throughout the years there were areas of my life that God needed to renovate before His victory was established. For years I had suffered with sexual immorality because of a door I had not closed. I had not refused in defiance, but I was ignorant of the presence in my life, so how can I surrender what I don't know? That is why it is God's grace, because He knew that for me to deal with these areas of my life and overcome, I would need to go through a valley – a wilderness of revelation... then with understanding, I would make the right choices, and overcome. Each room was a renovation awaiting His perfect timing. His grace covered me by the blood of Calvary but I was not able to overcome the sin until I allowed Jesus into that part of my room to renovate. Where sin dwells it becomes a place of demonic influence... and only when we come with the specific sins to repentance does the authority of Christ become full to deliver us. He works with us. As He says in Song of Songs: "Will you catch the **foxes? We will do it together!**"

Just as we wash every day and sometimes more than once, in our luxury bathroom, we need to wash daily through repentance to keep us free from the constant attacks of Satan tempting us to fall in bondage one way or another to his ways of compromise.

Maybe we have just decorated a wonderful master bedroom, but we see something that looks so beautiful... oh it's only a picture, of ornate Chinese dragons or something else... again we need to be careful we do not allow images of the devil to find a foothold in our newly renovated room... we need to be discerning in all levels as to the things we allow in our home. We need to be discerning of what TV programs we allow on the TV, what videos we watch... what we allow ourselves to see on internet... Everything needs to be in union with the owner – Jesus and of His Spirit... we need to be careful every day to be free from pride and arrogance – which is the armour of hell – it is what Satan was cast out of heaven for... and he will try to bring us out of the center of God's will with the same if we give him access in anyway. I believe strongly that the Lord wants to empty our agendas, false expectations and non-biblical traditions, so that Christ alone will be Lord over His church, His Bride. His Bride surrendered in every part to His Perfect will, with oneness in spirit with our beloved Bridegroom – Jesus.

I have to tell a story of living with my sister and her husband. In a way we laughed at it later but at the time it was far from funny. We were in rented accommodation, and we had completely decorated it through and through, cleaning all the walls of black mold, and painting it fresh and clean before moving in. We were happy with the home. The bath was also a sunken bath – yes we were happy. One day my sister was on the toilet... as described in Africa – a long call as opposed to a short call! As my sister went to flush the toilet, the nature of the long call started to bubble up through the drain hole in the bath tub. Horrified at what she saw she bent down into the sunken bath to put the plug in the drain hole.... But she didn't realise that it needed an escape route and so the overflow hole – which was at face level as she was bent over, suddenly became a fountain of all she had just excreted. Covered on her face with her own excretions, she screamed loudly to bring our attention to the fact there was a serious problem.

Indeed the problem was in the drains under the house... fortunately a friend knew to take up the drain cover in the road, to find a blockage there – a cloth of sorts that had at some point been flushed away by previous tenants – causing a build up over a long time until such a time that completely blocked the system. We were fortunate, because the blockage was accessible, but had it been a problem under the house, the house would have had to be ripped up to find the problem and repair.

Sometimes when we have moved into our new home with Jesus, without understanding, we seem to be happy for a short time, then looking for new relationships to replace the old and painful, but sometimes we have not been seeking these things in the accordance with the Lord's will... because there seems to be a blockage in our foundations that needs to be torn apart and rectified before things will fall into place. Maybe the foundation is built on a wrong understanding of who God is. "Surely God knows how unhappy I have been, He will understand my need for this new relationship, and because I am not allowed to divorce – surely God will understand if we just live together...." and every time the relationship tries to come together there is opposition, bringing the opposite of a blessing,... "but surely that must be the devil, because surely God understands my need for this compromise in my life to His word. Surely God knows how much I love him and need this person in my life." Yes sometimes we pay a lot of money to put in a new power shower and bath, tile the room and have shiny taps and mirrors, heated towel rails to bring comfort in the winter months, yet the foundation is not in line with God's Word – and the only way to bring alignment of all things is to rip up the floor, rip out all the new installations to get to the root of the problem – where we need to have a renewal of understanding about the Holiness of God, and that in no way can He allow compromise with the devil, no matter how sad we may have been, He cannot compromise His own word... it is us who needs to see the compromise in our understanding and renew our mind according to the truth of God's word.

Another thing I experienced – also in a rented apartment, there was a picture owned by the landlord and it belonged to the flat. I have to say – the size was good because it filled a large empty space, but I just did not like the picture, it was dark and it was abstract in a way I could not see what it was – and I disliked it.... So I removed it from the lounge to hang my own pictures and mirrors, and I put it in the guest room later to be hung but for now the room was not in use and it could just stand against the wall behind the bed – out of sight!

When my friend said she was coming to stay for 2 weeks, I decided I needed to make the guest room comfortable and relaxing. I moved the bed to another direction, moving the furniture around 'til I was happy with the way it looked. The space over the bed head however was big and empty. The picture I had been hiding would fill the space really well.... So I turned it around and lifted it up to the wall. I worked out where to place the nails to hang it.... But in the hanging I seemed to have turned it without realizing.... and as I stood back and looked at the picture I realized before it had been upside down – because now the right way up I could see it was a boat on the water with a sun in the sky... and it was actually quite lovely. Upside down it was alien and ominous and oppressive, but now as I had turned it – I saw it as it was supposed to be seen and it was beautiful!

This is a picture of how I saw my name. I hated my God-Given name, because I was made fun of at school because of it. I hated the name so much that I made a vow that I would marry as soon as I could, just to change my name to the husband's name. What I didn't realise was that this vow had fed my desire that grew over the years to be desperate for love and to be married. Although for some years the longing for marriage was repressed, it was still there bubbling to the forefront, that every man I ever met was a potential husband.... I was like a black widow spider in my thoughts of wondering how to catch this one or that one. God had to do a lot of healing and restoration, and one of the questions I was always asking Him, was "Why?" Why did I have this desperation for marriage and to be loved? It was only these last two years that He started to reveal all to me. I had always believed I was insignificant, and ugly with eyes of a cod fish – my sister told me when I was young, and I believed her... I believed I was ugly and unlovable... I had always believed I was unwanted – but even that was untrue – my mother wanted me to fulfil her needs for love – even if it was for the wrong reasons, I was wanted... I blamed my father's family name for being made fun of... I was seeing the picture like the one in the apartment upside down and couldn't make out the picture as it was intended. The Lord revealed to me the meaning of my name – which strangely was in line with my heart's desire to be an arrow sent out of God's bow, with the love of God to pierce the hearts of people. My surname means 'arrowhead' used specifically for war and hunting. (Spiritual Warfare and Fox Hunting) As I became more in line with the Lord's desire for my life and began to realise that His word tells me that before the creation of the world – He already knew me by name. He knew the exact time I would be brought into this world and exactly who would be my parents, because I would inherit the name that would give purpose for my life in the Kingdom of God for such a time as this. I had always felt insignificant – but all this revelation brings the truth which means '**I am significant**'... nothing has been an accident, but with a purpose to form me into that arrow that would bring the love of God. My testimony when I share it with the people, they stand in awe of God's love and mercy. Suddenly it was like hanging the picture the right way up and seeing the beauty of it all. Why did I have to wait till I am 58-59 years old before the picture became clear and beautiful? He took possession of this house, my heart thirty three years ago, and only now do I see the picture that I inherited, but had failed to see it clearly for so very long... oh and how beautiful it is when revelation comes – like a light being turned on for the first time in a room always in the dark.... all I know, God's grace covers us and He loves us with warts and all. It doesn't mean that the warts will remain, but in His perfect timing He will restore all things to the fullness of His Image – Christ in us, the hope of Glory. We are a work in progress, and He is the master potter, the master builder, the master surgeon, the master healer, the master renovator and restorer. He loves us in all our sin, and His life in us and His purpose is to set the captives free... we are freed in theory the day we come to salvation, but the working out of that reality happens over a lifetime of surrender and humility allowing the Lord to de-mask us, and teach us how to catch the **foxes** of compromise and close the doors of entry into the garden – His garden of love where He has been growing the fruits of His Spirit in our hearts. He is looking to harvest a bumper crop.... And I am ready to allow him that bumper crop – for the first time, like the goats of Mount Gilead, running down with joy and delight to be a sacrifice of love – laying down my life that He may live in me.

I do not know how many rooms there are in my heart still waiting for His hand of love to restore and open up to His amazing love and light, but I trust Him, that He will reveal to me the **foxes** that have been hiding to ravage the fruits of His garden in me.... and together we will catch them. Thirty four years ago, He took possession of a derelict run-down house full of squatters, in need of restoration, repair, even a re-modeling, and He has been turning it into a Palace fit for the King of Kings to dwell within. It says that His cloak fills the temple... I am His temple, and He fills it! Squatters are being evacuated room by room as we enter together to restore it to its former intended glory... I am His possession, I am possessed by my King, the Lover of my Soul – my Perfect Valentine, and I am His to do His will. I am His beloved, and He is mine. He has and still loves me, not focusing on the work to be done, but seeing that which I will become.... This house is beyond any price a man can afford, this house is valued at only one price – the blood shed for me at Calvary. Jesus covered me with His grace and righteousness, taking my sin and shame to pay my penalty on the cross.... And I stand in awe of You Jesus. Holy God to whom all praise is due – I stand in awe of You, for You are truly beautiful beyond description!

Catching Foxes

PART TWO

...a book for the Bride

Matthew 5:3-11
Luke 6: 20-26

Let the Hunt Begin!
– The Beatitudes

This is where I will go through some of the teachings of Jesus – as such the words He actually spoke. He spoke to me that many of the 'Bride' have forsaken His words and teachings for the letters of Paul. He was not unhappy with people learning from the Letters of Paul – but that when people disagree with Paul's words, decide that it was Paul's own opinion and not of the Spirit, thus looking for loopholes to sin. I want to add at this point, that at any time we are looking for an excuse to do something – we are already walking in rebellion, and we will bring this up in a later chapter.

In the Beginning was the Word (Jesus), and the Word (Jesus) was with God, and the Word (Jesus) was God. He (Jesus) was with God in the Beginning... He (Jesus) was with God and He (Jesus) created the world, and then later the Word (Jesus) became flesh which the Apostle John tells us of at the beginning of his Gospel. He (Jesus) would probably have been the finger to write on the tablets of stone known as The Law and the Ten Commandments... and later when He walked the earth became the Fulfillment of the Law.

In one of the stories we will discuss later, when the Pharisees were trying to trip Him up on matters of the Law, before He answered He stooped to the ground and as such wrote something with His finger. It was the finger of God that wrote in the tablets of stone for Moses, and it was possible that as He stooped to write with his finger on the ground – it was an action of saying that He is the One who gave the Law to Moses. We will never know – but The Word and Jesus are the same!

The Word – Jesus, is always in accordance and agreement with the Father. What Jesus says as the Son of God, is what the Father says! There are no discrepancies, and there is no question of The Word changing with man's progression in this world and fleshly desires. His Word is the **same, yesterday, today and forever**. Again I will discuss more re the Law in the chapter 10

I do not profess to be a Bible teacher, but I believe this book is not supposed to speak to the mind of the learned, but rather the heart of those longing to know how to identify and catch the **foxes** in the simplest of ways. The best way I know is to give examples, and in many cases they are of my own testimonies. It does not mean that my examples are a complete list, but rather that they will stir your heart, to allow the Holy Spirit to speak to you of the **foxes** in your vineyard.

Let the Hunt Begin!

I will not discuss all of The Beatitudes, as His teachings later also cover them, but just make comment for now on a few.

Matthew 5:3

"What wealth is offered to you when you feel your spiritual poverty; for there is no charge to enter the realm of heaven's kingdom." (TPT: 1)

[3] "Blessed *are* the poor in spirit, for theirs is the kingdom of heaven." (NIV: 5)

I remember I first was taught in the church that being 'poor' does not talk about poverty in the physical worldly sense, but recognising that we are spiritually poor and need more of God.

A 'religious spirit' is where we consider that we know the Bible, can even quote it, probably been Christian believers for a long time and therefore believe we know all we need to know. It is also in some cases an un-teachable spirit, because we have learned all there is to know as the

Pharisees, and that is pride. If we are content with our spiritual walk, we are not poor! God has more, for those who will drink and drink of Him and still not be full enough of His love.

I am interested to see the notes by Brian Simmons (TPT: 1) that also speak regarding **Independence**:-

"5: 3 or, 'humble in spirit,' or, 'poor in spirit,' which means to be humble and <u>*totally dependent*</u> *upon God for everything. It is synonymous with "pious" or "saintly," not just in the sense of those who possess nothing. It could be translated "Delighted are those who have* <u>*surrendered completely*</u> *to God and trust only in him." See also Isaiah 41: 17, 57: 15, and 66: 2*

(Emphasis of underlining and emboldened added: '**Independence**' is opposite of '<u>totally dependent</u>!' I continue to deal with this truth, and can assure you, as I am writing, this is no easy **fox** to catch. I have found it is a family of 'cling-ons'.)

However living in Uganda I also see 'poor' in the physical sense where there is maybe not enough money for food on the table, school fees to send their children to school and no social services provided by the government to sustain the people in such conditions. The Christians I have met, and seen their living testimony of Gods faithfulness as they cling to Him in the Spirit and see Him provide their every need in the physical; their joy and testimony is amazing. They truly experience the reality of the kingdom-realm! When they give thanks to God for their life today, it's because they take nothing for granted in a world where people are dying in the thousands from sicknesses and infirmities. No money means no medical treatment, meaning death and painfully so too. When they are sick and cry out to God to be healed, it is never half hearted – if God is not with them, they will die.

He is the same God whether we are rich or poor, but I have looked at life from both sides, and it is easy to put your trust in the medical services, social services available in the West/ Europe, Insurance Policies and if there is no money to pay the bills, there will always be a hospital that will give emergency... and in many people's lives such services have replaced God. I am not saying that they are not a blessing from God, and I believe Christian believers in our history have fought for such services to be available to all, and Christian men and women have dedicated their lives in the Lord to serve in this way of helping others... but the problem is when we look to them instead of looking to God. Who needs God when we have everything provided for us through our government system? There is nothing wrong in praying to the Lord to bless and empower the medical staff with wisdom and knowledge as they treat us... we thank the Lord for this service of dedicated men and women who work to save and prolong lives in the physical realm... but I do believe we should be looking to the Lord first. Let us ask Him, what has caused such sickness, let Him relate to us personally of such things. In the Chapter on forgiveness there is a testimony which will give light to this.

As I have written, I have suffered many years from back problems. In the Christmas of 2013 whilst standing at the bathroom sink cleaning my teeth, I don't know what happened, but I bent to rinse my mouth, and the back went into spasm. It was not serious, but it was very painful, and the pain remained with me for some days. When it happened, I remember asking the Lord as to when this first happened and what the cause of its re-occurrence was. I did not get an immediate answer. A couple of days later a friend came unexpected to visit, and stayed over, so we were having breakfast the next day and I suddenly began to tell her of an incident – I had no idea why. I had been going through a time of discipline / being discipled, when I had just finished my DTS, and feeling inwardly very bad about myself. A fellow staff member had asked if I could teach him how to 'tap dance'. In order to make myself look good, I decided to teach a step that took years to learn and master, however this step required a certain position of complete straightness in the back and neck. I was looking down in an effort to show him how to do this step... and the back went into severe spasm. As I was telling the story I suddenly realised it was the answer to the question I had asked the Lord a few days earlier. I started to laugh and get excited. I realised that I was full of pride and arrogance wanting to lift me higher, making my friend to look bad... and it was something I had not considered back in 1985 when it happened. As we sat together to pray, I asked the Lord to forgive me for the pride and arrogance in my heart back then. My friend interrupted and added 'hidden anger'. I stopped praying and asked why she was saying hidden anger. She didn't know why only that she had the words hidden anger as I began to pray. As I looked back to the situation that had caused me to be in a place of discipline, I had indeed been angry with the people then in leadership, not understanding that they were in fact acting in the Lord's love for me. I returned to prayer and repented for hidden anger. After prayer we chatted about something different and suddenly I realised my back pain had completely gone! I believed the Lord had taken me back to the source of the problem, and through repentance healed me.

You will now be thinking that the healing was not permanent, because of the recent problems out of which I am writing this book. I too became quite disappointed, wondering what had happened; I thought I had dealt with my 'Goliath'. Then I read an amazing word shared by a pastor and author saying: Goliath had a brother! Goliath of course was the giant who David killed as a young boy with a hand held catapult and a small stone to his forehead. Goliath had relatives that looked just like him, and they would come for revenge. Sometimes we think we have killed the giant, and then someone just like him returns and we become despondent and may even lose faith. The truth is Goliath died! Our new battle is with his brother or other relatives.

Matthew 5:4

"What delight comes to you when you wait upon the Lord! For you will find what you long for." (TPT: 1) "⁴ Blessed *are* those who mourn, For they shall be comforted." (NIV: 5)

(An interesting note also here by Brian Simmons regarding the seemingly difference in translation:-

As translated from the Hebrew. (See also Psalm 27: 14.) The Greek is "mourn (grieve)." The Hebrew word for "wait" and for "mourn" is almost identical. As translated from the Aramaic word for comfort, nethbayoon, which means **"to see the face of what (or who) you long** for." The Greek is "They shall be comforted."(TPT: 1))

Again I am seeing the 'independent spirit' the Lord is speaking to me about, that does not wait upon the Lord to be comforted. He who waits upon the Lord shall renew their strength, yet when we fail to be totally dependent on the Lord, we are very quick to find our own solutions of comfort... for example: what the western world call retail therapy. Not something that I can be called guilty of, I personally hate shopping, though it has not always been the case. I know of a friend who was going through a time of depression – a time of mourning a relationship that had ended. Feeling totally overcome with depression she went out for a lunch break from work and came back with a brand new car! Of course many laughed, and so did she for a short while – but it was just a sticking plaster over the wound – a quick fix for the moment.

Of course not all do as my friend above, but I see too many, for example when a relationship fails, we are eager to as such not wait but get back in the saddle into another relationship, thinking another partner will be the answer to our problems, our loneliness, our emptiness, a saddle which I have myself sat in. But from my own experiences – believe me there were many, it just fed the loneliness and emptiness, and it wasn't until I truly came back '**face to face'** with the Lord that I found true healing and comfort, because He is all we long for – He is our everything if we will wait up on Him. What the Lord wants to offer us here is complete healing by finding all we need in Him and not in the things of this material and carnal world, relationships or cars or whatever we long after... true comfort comes from seeing the face – His face, that we long for. The question is: *Do we long for the face of Jesus?* Or are our hearts still longing first for other things or people!

Matthew 5:5

"What contentment floods you when gentleness lives in you! For you will inherit the earth." (TPT: 1) "⁵ Blessed *are* the meek, For they shall inherit the earth." (NIV: 5)

The fruit of the Spirit, gentleness! Meekness and majesty describes Jesus. Though He is the King of Kings, He came not in aggression to make people follow him. He treated all with love and gentleness, full of compassion and unconditional love. He came not to be served, but to serve. Pride, haughtiness, arrogance demand recognition and service of others, but Jesus who has all authority and power came to humbly serve, as we see in the foot-washing of his disciple's feet. The word meekness actually means to be surrendered, as Jesus surrendered Himself to the Father's will.

Matthew 5:6

"How enriched you are when you crave righteousness! For you will be surrounded with fruitfulness." (TPT: 1)

"**⁶** Blessed *are* those who hunger and thirst for righteousness, For they shall be filled." (NIV: 5)

Luke 6:21 "**Happy are you when you are consumed with hunger and desire, for that's when you will be completely satisfied!** (TPT: 2)

If you have plenty to eat and eat often, I find that at times I do not desire to eat more, I am still full from before, and I am not hungry, so unable to put more food into my mouth and stomach. Maybe what I have done is, between meals I have eaten rubbish foods, sweets, chocolate, crisps, fizzy sugar drinks, cakes etc... or maybe a savoury hot dog etc. So when it comes to the food served or time to prepare dinner, I am not able to eat or even consider cooking a healthy meal. I have filled up on the unhealthy fattening foods which eventually cause ill health in my body. It is true when we are so hungry; the best meal is the one you sit down to eat with a stomach crying out to be filled.

I know from my own life there was a time when my life was so filled with the things not of God, be it TV - watching meaningless soap dramas that are depressing and mundane and full of immorality, going out drinking, socialising, night clubbing, or hours spent on the internet or computer games. Time consumed at the gym perfecting the body beautiful, or other time consuming hobbies.

I am not saying that the gym or hobbies are bad, they are ways that can bring us into contact with others – a potential mission field on our doorsteps, but as with all things – it depends on what is fuelling the need for the gym... is it good health, is it with the vision to share the gospel of love, or is it focused on how beautiful you will look feeding such spirits as lust and vanity as it was in my life. In my marriage, I was starved – deprived foods because my husband did not like fat women. It may sound harsh – but it was a reality. I lost weight, but one counsellor when I talked with him started praising the Lord when I told him what was happening in my life. I was unsure why he should be praising God as I was distraught, he continued to tell me that the length of time of which I had been experiencing this, I was a walking miracle and should have been in a coffin – dead and buried! We have read devastating reports how the media has so focused on the perfect female body according to the beautiful models in the world, fashion and what the magazines focus on especially to teenage girls about beauty; and seen how young and older women get caught up in anorexia or bulimia, causing devastating weight loss, sickness to the body and premature death. Even Princess Diana told of her own battles with Bulimia, and another of the royal brides was not as such affected (that I know of) but received terrible press about her size and shape. Sadly it is also affecting young men... or the extremes of excessive weight training using steroids also causing problems to the body. In such cases it is an addiction... the same as drug abuse, alcohol addiction. In fact many are addicted to the TV, to certain foods be it burgers and such fast foods. It is also possible to be addicted to sex. So what are we hungering after to feed?

The gym for me meant only one thing... will I be sexy in tight jeans and a top – to get the man of my dreams! It fed the spirits of lust and sexual immorality, and also my worthiness only being in what I looked like – in other words – the flesh. I am not saying that it is the same for everyone as it was with me, I am just owning up to the motive within me to go to the gym... if you are going to the gym for keeping the body fit and healthy it is good... but believe me it can so easily take over and become so much more and an idol. My husband, who hated fatness of any proportion, would ride his cycle, do weight training and running. He spent more time looking in the mirror than I did. He used to do his weight training at home, it would be done every other day and running in the between days, Sunday was a day of rest from fitness. Because he was so fit and trained, he could buy a whole cake normally for six people and eat half of it in one go – with the excuse that he trains so it is ok... but for me who didn't train, when I ate one freshly picked tomato in the afternoon, I was denied dinner in the evening on one occasion. If I wanted to eat then I had to ride my bike or start running... and bunions on my feet prevented the running, and a long distance on my bike was excruciating. I used it only to go shopping, and travelling to and from work

My favourite time waster after my divorce, for a long time was Farmville through Facebook on the internet – it consumed me. I would wake in the mornings, even set my alarm especially to immediately turn on the computer to harvest crops and plant more – I could sit for hours, and I know I was not the only one!

These can all be considered as foxes that are ravaging the vineyard of His love... hindering our relationship with Him to blossom and bear fruit.

Luke 6:21

"Happy are you when you weep in complete brokenness, for that's when you will laugh with unrestrained joy!" (TPT: 2)

Complete brokenness happens when in the presence of the pure, holy love of God we recognise our own filthiness, our sin, and turn in repentance from doing that which God hates. From experience, every time I have been in this situation, a joy beyond explanation has flowed through my body. It is not rules or following the law as a doctrine that brings about this, it is nothing else than the unrestrained, all consuming, all amazing, unconditional love of God that touches the blind eyes of our hearts – to see clearly the truth, and bow in total surrender. Without this touch of God, living according to rules will only produce **self-righteousness and pride** – fruits of the flesh and spiritual blindness, the opposite of all that the Kingdom of God stands for.

It is in this place of brokenness that the power of the Lord sets us, the captives, free. Brokenness, which brings about repentence, is handing the baton of authority from sin, to Jesus, for Him to take control and clean out the house. Once we have given Him the permission, not just acknowledging our sin, but truly having a heart of great remorse for the things we have done... with a desire to change. When we receive such a revelation it is life changing. Often we say sorry or ask for forgiveness because we have been found out by others, and placed in a position of humiliation – which is not the same as humility. Humility is when our own heart bows down in surrender, and humiliation is when others try to humble us often by using a public arena to embarrass us to say sorry – but often the sin in the heart remains – it has only been lip service, with nothing changed within the heart.

I had not long been a Christian and thought I might be pregnant. Realising that if I was and was going to be baptised, all would see the fruit of my sinfulness so I went to confess to the Pastor and his wife, to tell him I was not sure it was a good idea to be baptised and why. I had as such submitted to his authority as the leader of the church in open honesty and humility. He led me to read Psalm 51 and left me in the room with the Bible. As I read this psalm of David, unrelenting tears began to flood forth, coming from deep within me. It was such a sense of remorse, and these words had mirrored the very depths of what I was feeling, I could not control anything at that point. The pastor then returned into the room with a freshly made cup of coffee, and saw my tear stained face. He asked me if I was sorry, and I knew beyond words that I was experiencing brokenness. The pastor then explained whether I was pregnant or not, he would be privileged to baptise me come that time if I so wanted. My heart rejoiced! As I love to say; 'my cup runneth over' with joy beyond measure.

Indeed the Lord will turn ashes into beauty, and mourning into dancing... It turned out I was not pregnant... had I remained quiet and waited I would not have needed to repent, but the Spirit within me was calling me to humility and a contrite heart. Had I waited without repentance, I would have been happy but repentance that brought forgiveness brought also something far greater than mere happiness, it released a joy. Happiness is something fleeting that happens because of circumstances so it comes and goes, but joy can be present even in the darkest moments of life, in trials and tests that are hard in every shape and form, happiness is nowhere, but joy is a river deep within that knows we are not alone, Jesus who can calm the storm is in our boat, sleeping or not, there is no fear when Jesus is with us and He is our joy and our strength!

Our remorse and contrite heart comes out of knowing the Lord. It comes from a relationship. I know from being 'in love' in the beginning with my husband, that if there was something I knew he disliked I would change from doing it as my love for him wanted to bless him, and when I knew how much he loved cycling and watching the 'Tour de France' on TV, I wanted to like it to bless him. In the beginning I thought it was like watching paint dry... but then I started to get to recognise the riders and their teams, and watch with greater interest so I could report to him when he came home from work in detail. He was so impressed that I could tell him all, that it also was a great sense of joy to me at that time. Making the one I loved happy was my joy too. If we truly love Jesus, then we will long in our hearts to change and turn from the things He hates, and to learn to love the things He loves. But it is out of a personal relationship – not out of rules and regulations.

Matthew 5:11-12

¹¹ **"Blessed are you when they revile and persecute you, and say all kinds of evil against you falsely for My sake."** (TPT: 1)

¹² Rejoice and be exceedingly glad, for great *is* your reward in heaven, for so they persecuted the prophets who were before you. (NKJV: 6)

Fear of man – idolatry! When we place man before God, then we walk to be accepted by our peers, work colleagues, maybe friends in high places etc. This is when we hide Jesus under the table so no-one will know that we love Him and chosen to be His disciples. The question then is – do we really love Him?

In my experience of being in love – I wanted to shout it from the mountaintop so all could know the joy I had in being in love and the one who I was in love with. Again, the question arises whether the full Gospel is being preached so people truly understand the cost of being a disciple... I have recently questioned my own level of commitment when I saw the twenty one Egyptian Christians lined up on the beach in Libya, to die for their faith in Christ. And then saw interviews of the wives and family, rejoicing and praising the Lord for the privilege of choosing their husbands to be martyred in Jesus name. It is an unquestionable joy that is unexplainable in the midst of such atrocities, but that the Lord himself was with them even unto death as they cried out his name with the Holy Spirit empowerment – their last breath captured on video.

When I returned to the Lord six years ago, I was clearly not posting worldwide on the internet of my return... being sensitive to all my friends both believer and non-believers... but Jesus took hold of my heart beyond my control or even desire to control. His love, was washing over me bringing healing and restoration where my sin and the world had brought death and destruction. In the light of what He was doing – I could not keep quiet, and did not want to. Yes – also to the distaste of some of my friends who also publicly posted their views, but that which the Lord was doing was far greater than any words spoken by people I loved and trusted. I yielded to the Lord on a new level, and my cup 'runneth-over' with joy.

When the Lord asked me to write my autobiography, my first thought was "All of it?" There were things I had done especially in the time I walked away from the Lord as a Prodigal, that I did not want all to know. But the Lord told me to write all of it and especially the bad stuff because it would be in the bad stuff His Grace and Mercy and Love would be recognised. I remember standing to share my testimony in a seminar as the main speaker, and saw the faces on some of the people. Suddenly I spoke out that they were free to judge me if they wanted to – I didn't care, because the only person who I care about, has forgiven me and cleansed me with His blood at Calvary. He has redeemed me and I am clothed in His righteousness and not my own. As I spoke that out, and told them from the bottom of my heart that I understand Paul when he said he was the wretched of all sinners... I know from my own experiences that there is nothing good in me except for Jesus!! And His acceptance of me is all I need. At that point I knew there was a spiritual shift take place and the fear of man had been broken in that room and the people began to see their own struggles hidden from all as being able to bring to the cross without fear and condemnation. But it could have gone the other way – I could have been rejected.

It is not without challenges, Jesus does not promise us a life with Him to be problem free, and to the contrary, He tells us we will face trials and tribulation, as we take up our cross daily to follow Him. Despite the fact that Christians in many ways have minimised the suffering of Christ to the 'sinners' prayer, we are called to live a life of denying self... crucifying the flesh that the Spirit of God should live in us. And there is the unspeakable joy of the Lord! He has promised to us through the words of Paul – that His grace is sufficient for us, and in our weaknesses His strength will be made perfect... and so, "I can do all things in Him who strengthens me"... in the true sense intended, when I face pain, suffering, rejection, and more because of His name, His strength will be all I need to complete that which He has called me to do. Those Egyptians and many more in our time and throughout the ages lived that to the very point of death, that Jesus strengthened them to the end...

Luke 6: 24-26

"But what sorrows await those of you who are rich in this life only. For you have already received all the comfort you'll ever get. 25 "What sorrows await those of you who are complete and content with yourselves. For hunger and emptiness will come to you. "What sorrows await those of you who laugh now, having received all your joy in this life only. For grief and wailing will come to you. 26 "What sorrows await those of you who are always honoured and lauded by others. For that's how your forefathers treated every other false prophet." (TPT: 2)

"Woe to you who are rich, for you have received your consolation. Woe to you who are full for you shall hunger. Woe to you who laugh now for you shall mourn and weep. Woe to you when all men speak well of you, for so did their fathers to the false prophets." (**NKJV: 6**)

Oh how we spend so much on lavishing out our homes and the kingdom of self, whilst the house of the Lord lies in ruins. The word loosely quoted is from the book of Haggai.

"... Because of My house that lays in ruin, while each of you is busy with his own house."

In the Old Testament they first had the Arc of the Covenant, and later the Temple was built in the City of David – Jerusalem, but we now live in the New Testament times where I personally believe that 'My house' is the temple within our heart that lays in ruins as we walk in idolatry, filling The Temple with all that is temporal and shall perish. Riches may bring comfort now but it is false comfort that will lead to sorrows.

I believe that the Lord has blessed many of His Bride with finances intended for the Kingdom Of God, but instead it has been used to bring comfort to the kingdom of self. It is time for the Bride to march forth to do Kingdom business we have been called to do – and it is time for the finances to be released to those willing to do the work in partnership. Are we willing I wonder to live less lavishly and use the monies to which we have been blessed, to see the work of God be fulfilled on this earth? Better to store up the treasures of heaven than to store it up here and reap eternity without comfort!

Fenella Stevensen

The Beatitudes, are the foundation of everything Jesus taught throughout the time of three years before His death and Resurrection. The teachings are not about the outward actions seen by others, but about the hidden – unseen motives of the heart that only God sees. I believe in the following chapters, as I do not confess to speak on every single thing Jesus taught, but the ones I feel led to write about, everything will come down to our heart attitude.

"Father, I thank you that you have given me Your Spirit to dwell within me and to teach me in your ways. Lord, as I bow before you and surrender my will to Your will, may You search my heart, and begin to reveal the **foxes** that have been comfortably living in my life. I invite you Lord to reveal to me the place of entry so when I catch the **foxes,** I can seal closed the area of my life preventing their re-entry. As Your word says... 'We will do it together.' Let the hunt begin Lord, I pray in Jesus name. Amen."

Matthew 5:17-20; 5:21 – 30;
Luke 16:7

The Law

Matthew 5:17-20.

"If you think I've come to set aside the Law of Moses or the writings of the prophets, you're mistaken. I have come to fulfill and bring to perfection all that has been written. 18 Indeed, I assure you, as long as heaven and earth endure, not even the smallest detail of the Law will be done away with until its purpose is complete. 19 So whoever violates even the least important of the commandments, and teaches others to do so, will be the least esteemed in the realm of heaven's kingdom. But whoever obeys them and teaches their truths to others will be greatly esteemed in the realm of heaven's kingdom. 20 For I tell you, unless your lives are more pure and full of integrity than the religious scholars and the "separated ones," you will never experience the realm of heaven's kingdom. (TPT: 1)

"Do not think that I came to destroy the Law or the Prophets. I did not come to destroy but to fulfil. [18] For assuredly, I say to you, till heaven and earth pass away, one jot or one tittle will by no means pass from the law till all is fulfilled. Whoever therefore breaks one of the least of these commandments, and teaches men so, shall be called least in the kingdom of heaven; but whoever does and teaches *them*, he shall be called great in the kingdom of heaven." For I say to you, that unless your righteousness exceeds *the righteousness* of the scribes and Pharisees, you will by no means enter the kingdom of heaven. (NKJV: 6)

Jesus came to fulfill the Law – not to abolish it... what does it mean?

We all know of the Ten Commandments, and many of us try to live our lives as best accordingly to them. I have never gone to prison because of murdering anyone, and yet I have in the eyes of the Lord murdered twice by having two abortions. But I have murdered much more than twice, according to the scripture below, which I will tell more about when we discuss Matthew 18. Jesus tells us that if we so much as have hatred in our hearts towards someone – it is the same as murder. To think it – to even visualize it – though never physically do it – we are already guilty!

Matthew 5: 21

"You're familiar with the commandment that the older generation was taught, 'Do not murder or you will be judged.' 22 But I'm telling you, if you hold anger in your heart toward a fellow believer, you are subject to judgment, and whoever demeans and insults a fellow believer is answerable to the congregation. And whoever calls down curses upon a fellow believer (calling someone a worthless fool) **is in danger of being sent to a fiery hell.** (TPT: 1)

I am not proud of my past, but you must know I am not judging anyone or casting stones, I know who I am and what I have been delivered from, and in truth, there is nothing good inside of me other than Jesus! I would like to say that when I came to the cross of Jesus for the forgiveness of sins, received salvation and to be born again, all my past iniquities no longer had power over my life. I would like to say that, but it would be a lie.

Sexual Immorality was an area of my life that I struggled with, and for a time in my new faith, since the time of my water baptism it was not something that raised its ugly head... but after being three years a Christian and then in training to be a missionary with YWAM, I fell in love with someone working as staff at the base. He had been on the DTS (Discipleship Training School) before me, and we both liked each other to the same extent. Towards the end of my school, preparing for an outreach phase to Tokyo, I went to visit friends of his at the weekend. On the way home, we stopped the car along the way for a kiss and cuddle – and as far as I could remember nothing more than that. When I later realised I was late for my menstruation, I began to panic and wondered if I had in fact gone much further than I had remembered. Without discussing it with the man concerned, I felt led by the Spirit to confess the possibility to my leader. I was told immediately to pack my bags and be ready to leave the base, meanwhile discuss it with no-one. The full story is in the first of the Rejoice books – I Will Fear No Evil. It is a story of true godly leadership at its best, all of whom I thank the Lord for! It happened that after I confessed and was to face eviction, I was Not pregnant!! But still I was told to leave. I thought it was un-forgiveness on their part, but it was not... God was about to place me on His operation table of healing, and it was to do with exactly the following scripture, similar to the one above on anger / murder, but this time to do with adultery. I had allowed my emotions for this man to run wild many times, and in my dreams and thoughts we had slept together as man and wife. I longed for the day it could become a reality.

Matthew 5: 27-30

"Your ancestors have been taught, 'Never commit adultery.' 28 However, I say to you, if you look with lust in your eyes at the body of a woman who is not your wife, you've already committed adultery in your heart. 29 If your right eye seduces you to fall into sin, then go blind in your right eye! For you're better off losing sight in one eye than to have your whole body thrown into hell. 30 And if your right hand entices you to sin, let it go limp and useless! For you're better off losing a part of your body than to have it all thrown into hell. (TPT: 1)

Jesus is telling us the severity of not dealing with such matters of the heart – it can lead to an eternity in hell.

Jesus is the Way, the Truth and the Life. That is what Jesus tells us in the Gospel of John. Who is He the way to? The Father! He says that no-one can come <u>to the Father</u> except through Jesus. Jesus is the doorway to the Father. So many of us receive salvation and either remain standing still, or turn back to play with the things of the past, thinking we are now safe in His mercy and grace. It is time to change our diet – what we feed on, because we can no longer feed on the pleasures of the past – we need to eat new food – heavenly food, manna from heaven in order to allow the Spirit of God to grow within us, and the flesh life of the past to shrink away. Like the Israelites, though they were led forth out of slavery from Egypt, still they were on the Way to the Promised Land. It wasn't the Promised Land as soon as they left Egypt! God had delivered them from slavery, but there was still a way to go – and not all entered the Promised Land. In my testimony, from receiving Christ (my deliverance out of slavery) I walked along the Way, living and serving the Lord, learning more of Him with every step. Like the time Moses sent in the Spies to see if they could take the land promised, God was calling me to look at the enemy – recognise the **foxes** and chase them out, but I said no. Saying no, was like the Israelites refusing to go in because of the giants of the land that they reported. What happened – they had to continue their wanderings in the desert until such a time as those who had been negative were dead. Joshua and Caleb were the only two of the original spies that entered the Promised Land because they had believed that God was greater than the giants. I spent almost fourteen years in the wilderness before I crossed over as such into that which I believe is my inheritance... and even then I was presented the **foxes** I refused earlier to catch, but this time I said yes! – In the Promised Land, Joshua still had to bring down the walls of Jericho, and so it is with us. It is a time of the Lord still setting the captive free, in His timing. As I trust Him and lean into Him more and more, He reveals more and more of the areas that still need to be released into His hands to heal. Salvation is only the door onto the narrow way that leads to the Father! We have to keep moving forward – drawing closer to God, as He draws closer to us. This is when the devil has to flee. Our lifestyle is one of spiritual warfare, where we claim back that which the enemy has stolen in our lives. I know that at this point, though there is still work to be done, I am in a place where I can say that which Joel prophesied, He is restoring to me that which the locust had eaten!!!

I believe that as we draw closer knowing the beautiful love of Jesus and the Father for us, as we delight in Him, He is the One to reveal to us the strongholds that have been keeping us captive. Indeed He came to set the captives free, but from my experience, it is not a one-time only event, but is continual in life as we trust Him more and more, surrendering all to Him, He reveals other locked rooms in our hearts (or areas of the garden still overgrown with thistles, thorn bushes and weeds.) I believe that as long as we have breath to breathe on this earth, then the Lord will use the time to transform us from Glory to Glory. The very saying from glory to glory suggests it is an ongoing process, not an act of completion at the point of salvation. The moment Jesus has been invited into our lives – we are in as such Glory... the Glory of Jesus has entered into our hearts – like a seed that grows... we grow like a child – as we become more and more like Jesus within us – increasing in Glory the more we allow Jesus to fill every part of our lives.

The Law was used as an outward measure of godly behavior, but sadly behind closed doors and what others didn't see was far from the truth. The Pharisees, who were zealous religious men in the times of Jesus, placed legalistic pressures upon the people whilst failing to live up to it in their own lives. Paul writes of the Law being the ministry of condemnation and death. In fact after the Law was first given, three thousand were put to death. After Pentecost – the birth of the Church, 3,000 received life by Grace!

God expected the Israelites to obey all. The penalty for failing was death. It was not marked on how many you got right, but rather if you failed one you failed them all! You could get all but one right, but fall for example in adultery, the penalty was stoning to death. There was no chance to argue that about getting nine of the ten correct, and plead mercy for getting the rest right? No! – to fail in just one is to fail them all.

Jesus says that He has not come to abolish the Law, but to fulfill it. How? By taking our place on the cross and paying our debt for the sins we have committed, that we may receive forgiveness and to walk in a relationship of thanksgiving and love for the One who paid the price, choosing to walk in obedience, empowered by the Holy Spirit under the new covenant of grace.

I remember speaking with a friend I had lost contact with for many years. He had been sick and needed a kidney transplant or he would have died. A friend of his, a woman, gave without question one of her kidneys so he would live. It happens all the time – we hear of it, but I'll never forget what he said. He **felt so beholden to her** for the gift she gave him of life, he felt he had to live his life taking care of her.

Are we **beholden to Jesus** for paying the price? I remember hearing once the way God does math.

20% Obedience + **80%** Disobedience = **100%** Disobedience!
99% Obedience + **1%** Disobedience = **100%** Disobedience!

One of my favourite verses in the Bible is from the Book of Samuel, where Samuel has spoken the word of the Lord to King Saul to kill all of the Amalakites, to spare none! Take no prisoners, kill all the livestock, and take nothing as spoils of the battle. Of course Saul disobeyed, sparing the King and pregnant Queen, and took the best of the cattle and sheep. Samuel returned asking Saul why he had disobeyed the Lord, and Saul said regarding the sheep and cattle that he spared the best to use them as an offering to the Lord as a sacrifice. The word then spoken was **"Obedience is better than sacrifice."** I will no doubt mention this later in the book!

Jesus paid the sacrifice; He is expecting obedience from those beholden to Him. Those who truly love Him will keep His commandments, and it won't even seem as a sacrifice, but a gift of love to the One who is worthy. Obedience is true worship. He said that not a single letter of the Law will be abolished until the day He returns, which means the Law still stands to teach us of the ways of the Lord. The difference is that when we get it wrong, the price has been paid, when we ask for forgiveness, we are forgiven and free to go **and sin no more**!

What does the Law do?

Without a personal relationship with Jesus – the Law becomes a dead religion. Following rules and regulations in our own strength, and this is where it becomes the ministry of condemnation... The Law has "self" on the throne and is all about if "I" achieves or not, whereas Grace has "Jesus" on the throne and it's about Jesus in us that enables us to live according to His will because of everything He achieved on the cross. When we fall, His Grace forgives us and teaches us how to get it right next time, whilst His love is never condemning us or punishing us, His love for us never fails!

As with the Pharisees, the Law creates **hypocrites**. People stand in judgment over others condemning them of their sins, their shortcomings, their weaknesses, their failings... so already there is a "them and us' divide. A hierarchy has been established, which indeed is what the Book of Revelation talks about as the teachings of the Nicolaitans. We will look at this a little later as we discuss Matthew 7. It creates **pride, arrogance and false humility**. It creates **legalism**. It creates **control and manipulation**.

It creates **independence** from God, not needing Him but relying on self. It creates **self-righteousness**. It creates **perfectionism**. It creates **rivalry and competition**. It creates **jealousy**. It creates **good works of the flesh** - a need to be seen doing good in order to be recognised. It creates a **fear of failure**, because it could mean public humiliation, it creates **low self-esteem and worthlessness** for those who are unable to live up to the required standards. It creates **rejection**. It creates **suicides through hopelessness**. Just some of the things it creates because it is all done in the flesh. What happens when you are told not to do something? Doesn't something inside of us want to do it – at least try it? It creates **rebellion** in us to stir up. I believe that in my heart of hearts if the Israelites had said Lord have mercy on us, it is impossible, maybe the Grace of God would have continued. After all, since they left Egypt they complained and murmured all the way (both being sin), yet God's Grace still went before them opening the Red Sea, turning bitter waters sweet, sending manna from heaven to feed them, but when they continued to be a rebellious stiff-necked people the Law needed to be introduced. Until this time, people heard and obeyed the word of God, though they were not perfect! They were not without sin. Abraham was in deception about Sarah – only telling half a truth to save his own life omitting to say she was his wife, and impatient by sleeping with Hagar instead of waiting for the promise with Sarah. Isaac committed the exact same lie twice in order to save his own life. Jacob was a liar and a cheat – cheating his brother out of his rightful inheritance as the firstborn... yet God did not hold their sins against them, because they were walking in a relationship with God, in His Grace!

I mentioned false humility earlier and not all understand what it is, so I want to illustrate it for you through my own testimony. I was in love and had received a proposal of marriage. I was working for YWAM as a missionary, and I had gone to see my leaders, for their blessing. They prayed for me, and I went away happy. The story in parts will be in this book but can be read in full in 'Rejoice... The Bricks Have Fallen; I Will Rebuild'. The marriage went wrong from day eleven and I finally applied for a divorce after seven years as what I described as a living hell. When I had a chance to return to Denmark and realised the fulfillment of forgiveness that the Lord had done within me, I also met with the leaders from years back. She asked me if I had never been angry with them. I thought it was strange because I had used the fact that they had prayed as an assurance it was of the Lord's will, but as we were talking I said;

"Actually I realise now, even if you hadn't prayed the blessing, I would still have married him, because I had already made up my mind and heart that it was what I wanted and was going to have it regardless." I realised I had gone to them in an 'outward attitude of humility', but inwardly my attitude was proud and unbending. What amazed me was that she told me then that in fact they had not prayed a blessing on the marriage because they knew it was not from the Lord – which is why she thought I may have been angry with them. It was news to me – I had been so caught up in pride, I actually hadn't even cared what they prayed – it was all just a religious act outwardly... a show of doing what was right but within my heart was rebellion. That is false humility!

The Law was intended to show people the Ways of God and their need for God in their lives. Even now it is a marker that points to God, but it can never transform people from flesh to Spirit, only Jesus can do that through being born again which is what he told Nicodemus.

I have already mentioned that it is possible that Jesus wrote on the ground, when a girl was found guilty of adultery and the Pharisees were standing with stones in their hands ready to stone her according to the Law of Moses, that it was possibly His finger that had written the Law on the tablets of stone, but another possibility is that he may have written the hidden sins of the Pharisees, then said "He who is without sin cast the first stone." Whatever He wrote we will never know this side of Glory and I think Glory will be too wonderful to think to ask when we get there – who knows? They who would have stoned her could not (because of their sin and intent in the Law), and He who could have stoned her (because He was without sin and full of Grace) would not! Jesus came against the hypocrisy of the religious spirit of appearing to be godly yet walking in sin. He came to give life – not to destroy it. He came to heal the sick in body and spirit, he came to make the spiritually blind to see the Kingdom of God and the spiritually deaf to hear the loving voice of God say; "Yet you are so lovely... my darling... my beloved...my dove... my equal... my bride... my flawless one." As can be read in the Song of Songs; Chapters 1-8. He covers our sin and shame with His righteousness – and sees us without blemish or stain, the perfect partner to the King of Kings. He loves us, woos us, romances us, cherishes us, wines and dines us on His love, nothing is too much for Him because of His surpassing love for us! True transformation and change cannot come by our own determination and efforts to live according to the Law. But actually by 'falling in love with, and being beholden to, and totally surrendered to Jesus'. When we learn of and experience daily more and more of His unrelenting love for us, His love alone will overcome the powers at work within us holding us in sin. It is His love that brings about a spirit of repentance, which is the transferring of Satan's authority in our life to Jesus authority. We hold the key to who has authority within. We choose! But in all honesty – when the fullness of Christ's all-consuming love for us is realised, who would choose other than Him?

After the Law was given by Moses, I have said three thousand were put to death, at Pentecost when the Holy Spirit, who Jesus promised to send after He had ascended to heaven had come; three thousand were born again and given new life!

Jesus came to fulfill the Law, healing the rotten heart of fallen man. We are all born sinners – rebellion handed down to us from Adam and Eve, and there can be no way to the Father because sin separates us. What has holiness got in common with sinfulness? Nothing. Father so longed to have fellowship with us, His beloved creation, that He made us to be higher than the angels to rule and reign with Him in eternity. Despite the sin, God so loved us that He was willing to give His own precious Son, who was with Him in the beginning, who was and is the Word, who became flesh and lived amongst us – to become the eternal sacrifice for the atonement of our sins. What greater sacrifice of love is there, that another lay down His life for you and me? The miracle in it all is that God knows we are incapable of a sinless life without His help. So when we believe on His name, receive the gift of love through repentance and receiving His forgiveness, He then empowers us by the indwelling presence of the Holy Spirit to live within us, to guide us, strengthen us, to teach us the ways of the Lord, and to transform us into the Image of God, from Glory to Glory. Now Jesus is the fulfillment because He has paid the price, and lives within us to help us live what we otherwise could not. It's called Grace!

All of the commandments that were part of the Law are still upheld, and the consequences of disobedience are still standing. What? Surely not – Jesus became a curse when He hung on the cross, that we might receive the blessings! Yes that is true – it is so very true, and as we walk in His Grace, in obedience to Him, it means we have turned our back on sin, and through the forgiveness we receive the fullness of God's Grace in blessings and power and authority to live out His will for our lives. God is the One who ordained that to walk in disobedience we will come under a curse, and the curses can be handed down from generation to generation. How do we then access the blessings that Jesus became the curse for?

I have already mentioned it earlier as the Lord was directing me of hidden iniquities / compromises / sin in my heart because of the generational inheritance from my mum and dad. Once I had received the spiritual DNA so to speak it then began reproducing in my own life – thus becoming my sin, and with sin comes the stronghold of the enemy. There is only one way to access the freedom in Christ, and it is to acknowledge the sin as being theirs and your own, speak out forgiveness towards the persons that have passed on their iniquities, and repent on behalf of theirs and your own sin. Then receiving the forgiveness which is already there for you and waiting for this time of recognition, commanding the spiritual strongholds to lose their grip and rebuke them out of your life and then giving the Holy Spirit permission to fill that place. When I repented for the independent spirit I asked the Lord to fill me with a spirit of total dependency upon God to fill that place. That is then the time the Lord begins to do His transforming work. I told you that from the time of repenting on behalf of the control and manipulation of my mother's and my own sin, there was a time period of nine months, before the Lord asked me to ask my sister for forgiveness for the spirit that had offended and scared her some fifty-two years earlier! I don't know if nine months is specific to the time from conception to birthing as in natural child birth, but I do believe that it is a time which the Holy Spirit is doing the transforming work following the repentance, to the time when the Lord can take us the next step. It takes me more than a day to spring clean the house, and it is this that the Holy Spirit is doing once we have given Him full permission. I will speak later of forgiveness, but having forgiven someone, it was eighteen months later that the Lord put me in the position to realise that from choosing to forgive and it being fully accomplished. I made the decision and gave permission, but then He does the healing work. It doesn't need to take that long, if we forgive immediately.

If we continue to live under the Covenant of the Law instead of the Covenant of Grace, and yet say we are born again, it is like living with one foot in one Kingdom of God and one foot in the World. I personally see this area as being the place of 'lukewarm; in Revelation 3 to the Church of Laedocea, which I will talk further about in Chapter 20.

The Law is about what 'I' can do. The Grace is about what 'Jesus' can do in and through me.

The Grace does not allow us to keep on sinning knowing Jesus has already forgiven us, that is cheap Grace – a false grace – not the one that is offered through the pain and suffering of the cross. If we continue to live under the covenant of the Law – then that is when we will see the fruits of the flesh in our lives. Our garden of love is destined to produce the fruits of the Holy Spirit and experience an outpouring of the Lords power and authority in new and greater levels to live the life we are called to fulfil. We are destined as the Bride of Christ, to rule and reign with Him for all eternity! It's time to shake off the cloak of death and condemnation, catch and expel those **foxes** from our hearts, and arise and shine for the Glory of the Lord is risen upon us! It is time to rise up as on eagle's wings, it is time to declare to a broken and hurting world that the Kingdom of God is here! We are here for such a time as this! We are the army that will rise in the midst of violence and evil, not fighting with the weapons of this world but shining like a lighthouse in the dark storms of life, and leading those yet to come to Christ into the safe haven of Gods unconditional, all amazing, all transforming, all consuming love, where death has lost its sting, and His perfect love has cast out all fear!

Matthew 6:12-14; 18:18;
18:22 – 35, 24:12
Luke 11:4; 17:3-4

Forgiveness

Jesus taught us how to pray – which I will look into in another chapter, but we are taught to say "Forgive us our trespasses AS we forgive them that trespass against us."

Un-forgiveness is one of the biggest compromises (**fox**) in the Church today. It is hidden deep in the hearts of many who have pushed it aside and placed a smiling mask to cover the darkness within which is actually growing deeper into bitterness. How do I know? I was one of them.

When I was divorced – no-one asked me or suggested to me that I should forgive my husband as far as I can remember. However, if they had, still I would have ignored them –because I felt I had every right to feel the way I did. Instead I went on a slippery road of rebellion, and didn't care. In 2010 when I returned to the Lord from a distant land of sin and debauchery, He began to speak to me.

The Lord asked me to forgive my husband.

"But he doesn't deserve it Lord!" I cried out – with pain, and anger and bitterness as all the memories of such pain flashed again through my head. In the stillest of voices and in pure love, He whispered to me, "Neither do you, Fenella."

At the time I saw myself only as the victim, and I suddenly saw in my mind's eye Jesus being tortured and crucified, without sin, innocent of all the charges, yet He was put to death... He was as such the victim, and as He hung on the cross midst the excruciating pain, with all watching Him suffer unto death, He prayed to His Father saying, "Father forgive them, they know not what they do."

How could He say that – they had been part of the ones crying out for Barabbas to be set free – a convicted murderer, of course they knew what they were doing – didn't they? Jesus chose to believe that they were walking in spiritual blindness, deceived and therefore could not see the truth... hence they did not know what they were doing. In Ephesians, Paul tells us that we fight not against flesh and blood but against powers and principalities... and Jesus knew that – He saw the people blinded and deceived by the prince of this world, Satan and his demons at work to cause the people not to see or understand, and He chose to forgive.

I had this awful feeling in my gut as I thought about forgiving him... it seemed that everything in my body was refusing as the constant movie in my head relayed all the pain and misery, the planned suicides, I didn't feel like forgiving him, but nothing that I suffered can compare to Jesus on the cross, who despite the injustice – loved us with the unconditional love to forgive us. I knew then it is not about feelings, but about obedience. It is a choice, and I remember crying in my room as I spoke out the words without feeling but meaning every word, "Father I forgive my husband!" Then I just wept and wept. From time to time since that day, I was reminded of something he had done to hurt me, and inside me I felt rising anger, then I remembered I had forgiven him, and would repeat to myself – "I have forgiven him – get behind me Satan!"

Ten months after my return to the Lord, I had been hurt by the man I had become involved with and also by my sister. It was Christmas Eve, and I had been invited to a midnight mass with a Catholic friend. I had had other plans for the evening but it was all cancelled and I was angry and full of self-pity, but happy to be invited on the last moment for dinner and then to hear my friend read at mass. The priest got up to deliver the word – but I heard nothing of it – instead I had Jesus speak directly His message to me.

"Fenella, how many times does it say to forgive in the Bible?"

"Seventy times seven Lord." (Matthew 18:22)

103

Fenella, how many times have I forgiven you?"

"Seventy times seven Lord."

"Fenella, how many times do I want you to forgive your sister and others?"

"Seventy times seven Lord."

"Fenella, the best present you can give to me this Christmas, is to forgive everyone unreservedly."

I chose to forgive!

In November 2011, I was invited to Denmark to sing at a friend's 60th birthday, and it was there I got to read a book which was taking me on a check list of all I had done over the last eighteen months with regards to forgiving my husband. To be honest I had stopped thinking about him – I don't know when, but now I was back in Denmark and about to see his mum and brother. For years I had longed to tell his mother what a horrible son she had. I was surprised to be in her sitting room to still see the paintings I had painted and given as gifts, still hanging on the wall... I had expected she would have thrown them out after I divorced her son. As she was in the kitchen making the coffee, I was looking on the shelves at all the photos. When she came in I asked who the two girls were, and I was surprised to hear they are the daughters of my ex-husband. Remembering how I had felt when I heard he had a baby and now seeing he had two beautiful girls, I paused - to stare at the photo expecting the sickly angry feeling to rise up within me... and I felt nothing. I was able to look at the girls and smile and say a blessing over them. Then as we were seated drinking coffee my mum in law asked me, "Fenella, why did you leave my son?" Oh how I had longed for years to tell her the answer – and now the chance, but as I opened my mouth to speak, I said, "Mum, he is still your son who you love and I have forgiven him, so it is enough to say that enough was enough!" As I heard the words as they left my mouth – a great joy welled up from within me, and I knew, that the Lord had been healing my heart for the last eighteen months since I chose to forgive... now I was free, free to love without pain of the past, and forgiveness was complete... or was it? What is more – I saw that He had taken me back to the place of defeat as I saw it, to realise now the victory. In some ways like Samson after he had fought with the lion, he returned to see the carcass only to find honey in it. There was the sweet taste of forgiveness fulfilled, with a joy overflowing of what the Lord had done in my heart!

In the church where I regularly attended, there was a lady that had done something I thought was totally wrong, and I was angry. I had asked the elders to pray with me that I would do the right thing; meanwhile I was harboring un-forgiveness. She had gone early to the house group one evening to tell the Pastor, who had been away on holiday. Whilst she was outside on the balcony the Pastor who did not ask me my version of the incident instead asked me to hug her and tell her I loved her. I told him no. He asked me to do it for him as he knew I loved him. I said no. I would not be a hypocrite and give lip service when my heart remained bitter within.

When I went home I decided to write the lady a letter of forgiveness. Of course it was important to let her know what I was forgiving her for and I went ahead and wrote a huge long letter that took hours to write, telling of every incident she had done wrong... I sent it to her by email and she replied with a very short reply – "Thank you – love you." Of course I was furious – I should take such a long time to explain all her wrong doings and the only reply was Thank you... she didn't even say sorry for her wrong doings and ask for forgiveness. Of course as you are reading this you will know that I had not forgiven, but rather sent her a letter of condemnation, with a mask of forgiveness and self-righteousness. The following Sunday in church, suddenly all was quiet – as we waited upon the Lord. The Lord spoke to me in His soft whisper, "Fenella, go and hug her and tell her you love her.' The Pastor had asked me to do it and I said no – but now the Lord Himself was asking me. I quietly stood and tiptoed across the room so as not to disturb anyone. I had to kneel because she was bent forward in prayer, and I whispered to her that I forgave her and love her, then gave her the hug, quietly stood and tip toed back to my chair. As I had just passed the Pastor, I heard him say – Hallelujah!

Often we find it harder to forgive fellow Christian believers, because we think they should know better than to do something wrong in the first place. (That is such a religious spirit that denies the grace of God over others.)

I suddenly realised, God doesn't care what someone has done to me. Yes of course He cares that I am hurting, He is with compassion and love, but the Lord has allowed it to happen for one reason only. Is Jesus big enough in my life for me to say 'Father forgive them they know not what they do?" I suddenly saw that it is not about what another person does to us, it is all about Jesus, and if we love Him, if we are His Bride, then we will be like Jesus and choose to forgive regardless of the action, we will choose obedience over sacrifice. I suddenly began to see, it is not my place to judge others or to dispense revenge, those are the works of the flesh, and if I am now born of the Spirit, then it is about the flesh dying. I always remember my Pastor saying, "If something someone does or says offends you, the flesh is not yet crucified, because dead flesh cannot feel anything and therefore cannot be offended", and it is true! Believe me the Lord keeps revealing un-crucified flesh... that I thought was dead, but then something happens and I feel hurt. It is a process. Who am I, that I should be forgiven so much and then not forgive another who has trespassed against me?

This brings me to **Matthew 18:23-25 – the Parable of the Unmerciful Servant**. We all know the story, but I was reacquainted with it when I was preparing to teach a seminar on Spiritual Warfare. In actual fact I had been asked to teach and I felt unqualified as I had been a prodigal for many years living in the lair of the evil one, who am I to think I can now teach spiritual warfare. As I prayed about it – the Lord told me that I am qualified to teach because I had been living a lifestyle of spiritual warfare for the last three and half years. I thought maybe I was hearing things so I told the Pastor of the invitation and how I felt unqualified. To my surprise he spoke word for word the same as I had heard from the Lord, so I started to look at what I had been doing the last three and half years. The Lord had been teaching me to forgive! It was then I realised this Parable with fresh eyes.

The Master had loaned a very large amount to a servant that he would not be able to repay it. When the master asked for the money the servant cried out and begged for mercy – which he received as the master had compassion upon him and cancelled his debt. But on his way home he met a fellow servant who owed him virtually nothing at all, but because he could not repay it, refusing mercy towards him, he had the servant thrown in jail. When the master heard about it – he called the servant back before him and called him a wicked man, because he had been forgiven so much and yet he could not forgive another for so little. This next part is important! The master then turned the wicked servant over to the jailors/torturers until he paid back every last piece of his original debt. There is only one person in this world who is a torturer and that is Satan and his demons. This story is telling us, that if we fail to forgive another, then Satan has a legal right to torture us! Let me say this again! When we fail to forgive others, Satan has a legal right to torture us! Hello!!! The Church is limping, from attacks of the enemy, and there are many who realise it is the enemy and go into fasting and praying, praying in tongues, casting out demons etc. and yet fail still to forgive others, keeping them imprisoned in their hearts of bitterness. Obedience is what keeps the enemy from our doors... there is no sin that can separate us from the love of God, and that means there is no sin that we also cannot forgive, because the one who has forgiven us lives within us.

Matthew 24:12 - 13

"12 There will be such an increase of sin and lawlessness that those whose hearts once burned with passion for God and others will grow cold. 13But keep your hope (endure) to the end and you will experience life and deliverance." (TPT: 1)

In these last days, we are seeing the lawlessness and sin increasing, both in the unbelieving, but also within the church. False prophets leading the sheep astray with wrong teachings, where immorality has become accepted by both leadership and congregations... however I look at the atrocities that are happening in the name of religion, and think if we are true worshippers of God, we must remain on our guard against the contagious nature of an embittered heart. We must not allow ourselves to be conformed to that of 'angry' and 'loveless' Christians. When injustice wounds us, we must respond with mercy.

Thirty years ago, living as a missionary, I was part of a drama team. The team leader was preaching and suddenly stopped saying he felt the Lord wanted us to pray for the sick. I had never prayed for the sick at that point of time. As the whole church put up their hands wanting prayer, I scanned the room to find someone who hopefully only had a headache, so incase the person was not healed I could give a Panadol instead. I saw a woman who was looking rather healthy so I went to pray for her. I asked her what the problem was.

For **twenty years** she had experienced numbness with pain in her right hand. Many times she had received prayer for healing but never healed. (Not just a headache then!) I closed my eyes and in the silence of my heart I cried out to God to help me. He gave me a picture. I saw her standing in the corner of a room being pressed back by a plank of wood. The end of the wood was on her right elbow pinning her to the wall and trapping a nerve causing numbness. On the plank of wood there was a word – UNFORGIVENESS.

I didn't like to use the word as I thought it sounded judgmental – so I politely asked her if there was anyone she didn't like. She told me there was no-one, she had many friends and she loved them all and they all loved her. I said lets pray again, and again the Lord gave me the same picture. I asked her if she was sure that there wasn't someone who she had a problem with. This time she asked her ten year old daughter if she could think of someone. She couldn't either, as her mummy loved everyone and everyone loved her. I was feeling a definite failure at this point of time, and suggested I prayed one more time and if it didn't work I would have to pray a blessing instead. She agreed.

I saw the same picture for the third time only this time there was a difference. The word un-forgiveness was now burning with red flames. I decided to describe the picture I had received all three times. When I finished – she burst into tears. I asked her if there was someone she had not forgiven. TWENTY YEARS AGO, her landlady had done something to her that she said she would NEVER forgive her for. I didn't ask what it was. I suddenly had a thought, and asked her if she was born again, and she said yes. I asked her if she had Jesus living within her, she said yes. I asked her if I could ask Jesus within her, if He would forgive the landlady for whatever she did all those years ago. The woman thought about it for a moment then said yes. I began to pray and asked Jesus to forgive the landlady. This woman went home still sick, however in the middle of the week something extraordinary happened, which she told to me the following Sunday. On her way home from work Wednesday of the following week, she passed a flower shop and felt to buy a bunch of flowers. That in itself is not unusual, because we were in The Netherlands at the time. They always have fresh flowers in their homes. As she arrived at her home, instead of going to her own door, she knocked at the landlady's door. The landlady opened and saw her there and was afraid, but without any words spoken, the lady handed the bunch of flowers to the landlady. She was holding them in her bad hand. The moment she gave them, the woman's hand was healed instantly! She had suffered the pain for the twenty years because of un-forgiveness. The act of giving the flowers was her act of forgiveness at which Jesus healed immediately. She was delivered from the torturers. It is interesting to know people had prayed for twenty years prayers of healing, but no-one had asked the Lord the cause of the sickness… a lesson here also in prayer.

How many of the Bride are suffering years of ill health? Maybe there is someone hiding in the closet that is un-forgiven… I am not saying that every sickness is because of un-forgiveness, but what I am saying, is to search our hearts to see if there may be un-forgiveness lurking in the dark arena of our heart.

As I was preparing more teaching material I came across some information that explained to me what I had been suffering in the marriage but also since. I realised that my husband was suffering from it all those years and who knows maybe still suffering. With recognition in my heart, I began to weep and pray for him. I suddenly felt a love for him – not as a wife to a husband, I didn't suddenly want to be his wife again, but I realised I loved him with a love I can only describe as being the love of God for him. For sure now I had truly forgiven if I could now also love him with the love of God.

Last year, the Lord showed me my own sin as I have written about earlier, of a controlling and manipulative spirit, spirit of vanity and more. I said in prayer to the Lord.

"Lord, couldn't you have shown me my own sin in the marriage before now – it would have been so much easier to forgive my husband if I had realised my own sins?"

"Fenella, it is not supposed to be easy to forgive, and it is not supposed to be without pain. Do you think that what I went through on the cross was easy and without pain? No Fenella, if it is easy and without pain, it is not forgiveness."

Forgiveness is part of the cross that when we accept Jesus into our lives we have accepted to take up our own cross. Forgiveness is the way of the cross, and un-forgiveness needs to be repented of. Un-forgiveness is all about me, me, me. My pain, my suffering, my rights, but the truth is when we become followers of Christ, his Bride to be, we don't have any rights because we have surrendered our flesh life to the cross so that He will live in us. It's now all about Jesus. Is Jesus big enough in you yet to say "Father forgive them they know not what they do?"

I strongly believe also that we are called in humility to ask others to forgive us for the things we have said and done to others. When the Lord brought such revelation to me about my own hidden sins, hidden to me but not to my husband, I realised that my sins had offended him as his had offended me. Both of us were unable to see our own planks of wood in our eye. I wrote to my husband asking him to forgive me. I'd had no idea of my own sin and had always felt that I was the victim only, but realized that he too must have felt a victim and me the perpetrator. I do not recall getting a reply from the letter, but I know that he had read it as it lets me know when the letter has been seen. It doesn't matter if he has forgiven me or not. I truly believe it is about me choosing to forgive and about humbling myself to ask for forgiveness, that the Lord is interested in. The Lord is purely interested in **my** heart. He is equally interested in my husband's heart – but it is between my husband and the Lord – it is not my business. God wants me to take care of my own mess, so one day my mess will indeed become a message!

Matthew 5:23-24

[23] "Therefore, if you are offering your gift at the altar and there remember that your brother has something against you, [24] leave your gift there in front of the altar. First go and be reconciled to your brother; then come and offer your gift." (NIV: 5)

After I had first been saved and then living as a missionary, I had returned to my home church for a period of nine months, as the Lord had directed me back to build up my support for further missions. During that time I was happy to receive a guest that I had met in South Africa, as he was travelling to Scandinavia also with YWAM. He came to church with my friend and me, and felt completely free to dance before the Lord as David danced – as we were singing that chorus in worship. What he didn't know was that there were people within the church who did not agree with such outward expressions of joy in the Holy Sanctuary. It was OK in the church hall downstairs, but not in the Sanctuary. I was at work the next day and the guest had travelled on to visit others whilst in the UK. I received a call from the Pastor in the afternoon. He had, during the morning, received phone calls from people wishing to remain anonymous accusing me of being the leader to encourage such unwelcomed behaviour in the sanctuary, wanting the Pastor to put a stop to such irreverence.

My heart was heavy when I heard of the incident, and asked the Pastor what his reply was to the anonymous people. He had told them that it was not his job to tell the Holy Spirit what He may or may not do in the church. For that I was blessed and thanked him. I went home to pray about it. The Lord put the above scripture in my heart. The following Sunday I was about to take communion as it was being served, and the Lord reminded me of this scripture, causing me to quietly weep. He did not want me to partake in the Holy Communion because the problem had not been dealt with. After the service and after declining from taking the bread and wine when offered to me, I went to talk to the Pastor of how the Lord had spoken to me.... But how can I put right when the people who have complained about me want to remain anonymous? He agreed with me that it cannot be right to remain anonymous in the house of God, and so he revealed two names to me – a married couple. I thanked Him and went home to pray. On the Sunday evening I called the couple asking if I may come Wednesday evening for coffee with them to discuss the issues that I had done to offend them. They were a little embarrassed but agreed. That day, the time before going to visit them, I fasted my evening meal and instead took time to worship the Lord in my room, and I still remember weeping with tears, as I asked the Lord to help me.

We sat to discuss how I could be considered as an instigator. I was very surprised that they had watched apparently on Sunday evenings all the youth from the Sunday school would sit beside me or behind me, and unbeknown to myself as I was raising my hands to worship the Lord – so were they. I didn't know because I always closed my eyes to worship.

111

Whilst the couple recognised that I may well be led by the Spirit, the others were just copying, and for that they were offended. I asked them how they knew they were just copying me, or if they too were being led by the Spirit and were for the first time obeying, using my boldness in freedom to lean upon. They couldn't answer that. I asked them why they considered dancing in the Holy Sanctuary to be offensive. The specific occasion after which they complained about, I was not dancing, yet I was accused because my friend danced. Again they believed there should be reverence in the presence of God, but I reminded them of David who indeed was accused by his wife for such a shameful behaviour, and she died. Is not every place according to the Word of God, Holy Ground where ever we set our feet? Isn't God present everywhere because He is within us? Is it not the joy of the Lord within us that causes us to look foolish without care of what others think? Therefore if the Lord has called us to dance for joy in praise and thanksgiving, to allow the Spirit within us to be released in sheer abandonment, do they have a scripture or direct word that would tell us that it is wrong to do so? They had not. I suggested that just as I was willing to give them perfect freedom to worship the Lord without smile or movement of body according to how they felt they should worship the Lord, I asked if they could not be willing also to give others in the church the freedom to worship the Lord how the Spirit was leading them. They agreed and asked my forgiveness for judging me, and others. We agreed that the following Sunday we would sit together in the church as a picture of love and forgiveness, and that we will each allow the other to worship in freedom as a sign of our love for the Lord and for one another. The Pastor looked and looked again in astonishment that Sunday morning to see us together, and after the meeting he gave me the other names also anonymous, and we were able to settle matters over the phone. I was also free then to partake in Holy Communion again.

The church at that time entered into a time of 'a move of the Spirit' especially among the teenagers of the church. If we know we have offended someone – rightly or wrongly accused, it is our duty to put it right. God has called us to love one another in perfect unity.

Luke15:11-32; 15:1-10; 7:47
Matthew 5:5; 13:44-46;
John 8:1-11; 10:14-16; 14:9
Song of Songs 1:11;
1John 4:18

The Prodigal Son

This story is indeed so well known – that to be honest I would skip reading it believing I knew it – no need to waste time... how wrong I was! This parable was indeed to become my own life story in so many ways.

When I was first saved and working in a Christian Boys Boarding School, a friend of a friend was visiting and taught us a drama based on this parable, which we made and performed for the boys' one Sunday service. I always saw it as an evangelistic story of the younger son finding salvation. It is true that "he came to his senses" and indeed found forgiveness and reunited with his father.... But the part of being re-united had failed to have meaning to me.

The truth of this story is that the son already belonged to the Father, and was living with his father, in his father's house. This is a picture of already being saved, when we come to Jesus, this is when we are born-again into the family of God, and we are now His children, sons and daughters. We may not physically be in the Father's home of heaven yet, but spiritually we are! This is the story of one who is saved that has received salvation through Christ and is born again, which rebels and turns away. In truth the story tells us that the Father had two sons, not one son and one sinner.

I have to realise that the fullness of that truth had always escaped me in as much as the story represented the rebellious son... but first let us look at the fact the Father had two sons. Anyone who has children, will understand this... no matter how naughty a child is, a parent is always protective of that child... you can tell your child off or say something bad – but don't think anyone else is allowed to do the same. There is a protective love in most cases that is the natural love of a parent to their child. They are the flesh of their flesh – their own offspring and a bond between such is stronger than anything else. Because the children are naughty you do not divorce yourself from being their parent... a parent's love truly covers a multitude of sins. Often we look at the negatives of a person, but here Jesus tells nothing of the failings of the children only that he has two sons.

As you know, I was very bitter and angry with God, because He had not given me a good marriage, and I turned my back on God in search of a husband better than the one He gave me – or so I thought He gave me at the time. What the younger son does in this story is the worst thing anyone could do. With selfish ambition, arrogance and pride, he virtually told his father that he wished he (the father) was dead, so he could have his share of the inheritance now.

It is interesting to note at this point of the story that the love of the Father is so great that he does not resist his son's request, or argue, or send him to his room for his evil thoughts or beat him. I am sure that the father at this point of time is all-knowing that what the son is requesting will only bring him pain and trouble, which the son is blinded to – he is deceived by the rebellion and greed in his heart. The son thinks the grass is greener on the other side so to speak and the wealth of his inheritance will serve him well.

Having received what was his, he left the home to live a life in a distant land. We know that it is distant, probably not in miles, but spiritually distant from God. He left to live a life of sin and debauchery with the money he received from his father, and squandered it away. A life that was full of drinking, and women. Yes – I can identify, not with the women but with men; – I walked away from God in anger and bitterness believing I could find someone better for me than God had already – that is also pride and arrogance, that I (the created) should know better than God (the creator)! Satan himself was created and the most beautiful of all the angels, but selfish ambition, pride and arrogance made him think he could be equal to God, wanting to be worshipped rather than to worship, rebelled taking others with him, to a place that became as distant as can be – outside the Kingdom of God... Never to return home! I squandered my life in a life distant from the ways of God.

Indeed there came the time when I came to my senses, which brought me home to my Father again, but I have to tell you, in my time away I was convinced that I would NEVER be allowed back home again – like Satan, vanquished to spend eternity in hell, believing I had committed the unpardonable sin. After all – I had been in my Father's house, I had been forgiven, and I turned away. I remember my first day back at a church in Malta, and the presence of God loving me, embracing me in His arms of Grace and I wept. I remember talking to the Pastor that week, and telling him of my sordid past expecting him to say – 'sorry you are not welcome here'. But instead I just heard of the Father's love for me that had been longing for my return, just like in the parable the father had seen his son whilst he was still a long way off, and his heart filled with compassion, and ran to his son, throwing his arms about him and kissing him. The narrative shows us that the father was always watching and waiting for the son's return, that in his heart he had forgiven him, and that he too was in great pain during the time his son was lost to him. I realised that there was indeed a party in heaven when I returned, just like the father in the story had the fatted cow slaughtered for a great feast to celebrate his son's return.

Culturally it was not normal for the father to run, it would have been normal for the father to maintain his dignity and wait for the remorseful son to come and beg for forgiveness. But such is the love of the father, filled with great compassion, and went against all cultural laws, powered by his great love and joy for his son, to meet him; and instead of waiting for the son to repent, just hugged him and kissed him. According to the Greek text used which translates as kiss, it is actually a verb written in the tense of a continuing action, and therefore it was not just one kiss but that he kept on kissing him. It had never entered the fathers heart that the boy was no longer his son when he left the home... the heart of the father was always focused on his beloved, looking for him hoping that one day he would return home again. Never a question arose in the fathers heart that the son could not be a son, the son will always be a son loved of the father no matter what! It is exactly what I experienced, an overflow of grace and love, forgiveness even before I had asked for it. The father already knew for his son to be home, that his heart had already changed, seeing the error of his ways and willing to walk home in humility. His journey had indeed changed the son from pride and arrogance to humility and meekness. The father did not chastise him. Why? The consequences of the son's sin had already ravaged his heart. He was no longer dressed in fine clothes but in filthy rags, he had not been able to feed himself having considered eating the food of the pigs he was tending. He was barefoot – without sandals or his sandals were tattered and torn. The shoes are also representing the Gospel of Peace, so he was a young man tormented because of the lack of peace, but to be without shoes was also a sign of a servant or slave, not a son... These were the consequences of his sin, not just his outlook but inwardly his heart and soul ravaged, in complete and utter ruin.

This is what DID NOT happen... the father stood at the door of the home so the son could see him knowing that terror would rise in his heart with every step closer as to the reaction awaiting him. With fear and trembling, the son was rehearsing his lines of repentance, but was expecting the beating stick for his rebellion and total lack of respect for his father and his brother. As the son approached in the ever increasing nearness, the father stood and said with such distaste and self-righteousness; "So you have come back have you? I thought when you left I told you never to return that you are no son of mine, but here you are, wearing the smell of rotting garbage, even worse, of pigs. Look at the state of you, your clothes are an absolute disgrace and I am mortally ashamed of you. Servants! Bring me the beating stick and let me teach this boy once and for all who is boss in this house, so that in future he will treat me with the respect I deserve. Get on your knees boy and grovel, beg for forgiveness, because when I have finished beating you, you will wish you had never been born you selfish, good for nothing, disgraceful boy." As the son fell in fear before the man he called father, the cane lashed at his back ten or fifteen times, maybe more because the boy lost count as the stick tore through what remaining rags were left covering him, and ripping through the flesh, causing blood to flow freely from his emaciated body. The rage of the father towards his son for squandering his hard earned wealth, withheld nothing in strength, that the son would never ever think well of himself the rest of his miserable life... and the scars on his back would be forever the reminder of his wretchedness. When the father had spent his last energy with the rod of discipline, he said to his son; "Go and get yourself cleaned up, and don't show yourself again until you are worthy to be seen. You can sleep with the cattle in the barn for you are unfit even to be called a servant... you are lower than a dog... I will teach you never to treat me and your brother with such irreverence again."

That is not what Jesus tells us happens in the story, **but instead**:-

The father was overjoyed to have his son home, that he ran to greet his son whilst he was still a way off and before the son could speak his rehearsed prayer for forgiveness, the father threw his arms around him and kissed him again and again, regardless of the son's filth and smell. The father had not even considered the thought of him being a servant in the house, because this is his son. Flesh of his flesh, always was and always will be! Calling the servants to bring everything, the father restores to him his sonship by placing not just 'a robe', but 'the best robe' upon him representing the Robe of Righteousness, to cover his shame – his tattered and torn rags called clothes. A ring was placed on his finger establishing before the servants and all, that he was indeed a son not a servant able to transact business on behalf of the father... and sandals were placed on his feet a sign of dignity and peace restored. Oh such love, such unconditional love. The son deserved at the least a lecture but the father welcomed him with a kiss!

I too experienced all of this, the best robe – the robe of righteousness – the blood of Jesus! A ring was also placed about me as in the **Song of Songs 1:11** when the Bridegroom says the Father, Son and Holy Spirit form a ring about me... encircling me, not just my finger but the whole of me... with their golden reins of love! When I deserved a clenched fist, something I had experience often before I was a Christian from my live-together partner, Jesus opens his hands instead to show me His nail scarred palms.

He received me back not as a maidservant – but his daughter, and there is not a word in the parable of the father chastising, but of great joy! Having been born again for the first time in 1982, in 2010, I understood, for the first time in my life this parable. I am his daughter... I became his daughter in 1982 when I received salvation, and His love for me as a daughter never changed because I was rebellious. Nothing can separate me from the love of my Father, no amount of sin could stop the Father's heart of love longing for me, waiting for me, watching for me, running toward me when He spotted me on the horizon of my return... He already knew the prayer of my heart I would have been practicing on the way. He knew already the great remorse within me, the shame, the guilt, my low self-worth... I expected a lecture, I deserved a life of servitude, but He instead

117

celebrated his daughter's return and hugged me and kissed me over and over... His daughter was home! I wept and wept for joy, uncontrolled joy and a spirit led repentance for all my known sin. I had come home – and wanted nothing more now but to sit at His feet. I had lost all desires to serve as such, no grand ideas of being a missionary or any title within the church or even in the world. I knew nothing I could do could impress Him to love me more – He loved me! With all of His heart He gave His son Jesus to die for me that I could come home... He cannot love me or you more than He already has and does. Despite knowing the worst of all I could be, He loved me as He had always loved me, He is my Father and I am His daughter... and now I wanted never to be separated ever again.

There are many in the world who as Christians believe that **Proverbs 13:24** when it says **"He who spares the rod hates his son, but he who loves him is careful to discipline him."** (NIV: 5) is instruction from God to use a cane or stick to beat them so they should learn from their wicked ways. Indeed it links back to **2 Samuel 7:14 -15 which says; "... I will be his father, and he will be my son. When he does wrong I will punish him with the rod of men, with floggings inflicted by men. But my love will never be taken away from him."** (NIV: 5) (I believe this to be prophetic because of what Jesus later endured, who took upon Himself the wrongs/ sins of the world. For this He was inflicted by men, with the rod of men.) **Proverbs 23:13** says; **"Do not withhold discipline from a child, if you punish him with the rod he will not die. Punish him with the rod and save his soul from death."** (NIV: 5)

In the Book of Exodus, the Staff of Moses was extended to bring forth the plagues that God sent over Pharaoh and Egypt, as God's decree of punishment because he did not let the Israelites leave Egypt. It was a sign of Gods authority and judgement, however, Moses never used this rod or staff to beat a person. God brought about plagues of misfortune over Pharaoh and Egypt... but he was not beaten. **Isaiah 11:14** speaking of the Branch of Jesse – which is in fact Jesus says; **"He will strike the earth with the rod of His mouth"** (NIV:5) Here it clearly describes that what comes from His mouth is a rod that will strike... it is the words spoken to disciple / discipline, not a physical beating.

We can discipline a child without beating. We can still hold out the "Rod of Discipline/Authority" by saying for example; "If you refuse to obey me, there will be no TV for a week, or you are grounded for a full week including any club activities planned or the removal of iPads / iPods and digital games for a week..." In this day and age it works! I did it with my grandchild for lying to me. Others apologised but he did not. I removed the TV and placed it in my room. Everyone suffered for his refusal to apologise... just as all of the Egyptians suffered because of the Pharaoh's disobedience. It was maybe six weeks later without a TV when the matter was discussed and explained in a time of prayer and reading the word before bedtime with the children. The children understood that disobedience reaps consequences, and they have learned it without the use of 'the beating stick'.

Moses was a shepherd before he was called to lead the people of Israel out of Egypt, and the staff was his tool to keep the sheep in line if they went astray. If they were straying from the path he would tap the sheep back onto the path supposed. Later a shepherds staff would have a crook on it – in the times of Jesus, so they could tap the sheep to keep them in line, however if they were way off they would stretch forth the staff and place the crook around the neck of the sheep to yank it back into the correct ways. If there had been violence with the staff the sheep would have been injured and of no value.

John 10: 14-15 "¹⁴I alone am the Good Shepherd and I know those whose hearts are Mine,

for they recognize Me and know Me, ¹⁵just as My Father knows My heart and I know My Father's heart. I am ready to give My life for the sheep. ¹⁶"And I have other sheep that I will gather which are not of this Jewish flock. And I, their Shepherd, must lead them too, and they will follow Me and listen to My voice. And I will join them all into one flock with one Shepherd." (TPT: 3)

Jesus is the Good Shepherd (Psalm 23) – and indeed He will find ways of placing the crook of his staff around the neck of the sheep to yank us at times back inline... or tap us to instruct us of His ways – but again, He is not violent with us, and the New Testament is a New Covenant. He brings comfort, correction and direction!

In Africa it is horrendous to see children at school caned first as a display of their punishment if they break the rules... they put fear into their hearts to control them. Parents carry with them a beating stick to beat their child if it is naughty, even to church. Other forms of torture are used in the name of discipline; for example of being made to kneel on a stony ground with hands uplifted for long periods of time until the one in authority says it is over. The stones could cut and cause bleeding, and the blood rushing from the hands over a long period of time of being raised.... I witnessed it and when I realised what was happening, put an end to it immediately.

The word discipline comes from the word to disciple, and to teach new disciplines. For example someone who is a gymnast would be trained in different disciplines, maybe the bar, or floor discipline, the high bar, the horse or the rings. It has nothing to do with punishment but everything to do with being taught – being discipled in different elements required to achieve in those specific areas of expertise. The twelve disciples were never beaten to rid them of their wicked fallen sinful nature, they were taught by example. Even Judas who was to betray the Lord Jesus was not dealt with unkindly by Jesus, it was his own guilt and shame that caused him to kill himself. The problem we have really is that we have no time for our children to teach them, because it takes time, especially to change old habits, so to use fear through beating, tends to shorten the process, however it also lessens the trust. Many abuse the authority, and children die through brutal acts of control. I can see no New Testament teaching of Jesus that authorises us to beat one another with a stick or rod!

A 'man of God' once said that he had been 'beaten' by God as punishment as a young man. I said it is not possible. Why? Because Jesus teaches us through this very parable of the Prodigal Son about the heart of the Father. The beatings or floggings as mentioned in **Matthew 27: 26; Mark 15:15-20; John 19:1-3,** are those which we deserved, but Jesus took for us. They stripped his outer clothing from him and they sentenced him to thirty nine lashings. It was considered that forty would kill a man and they wanted Him still to die enduring even more pain on the cross in a long and suffering way. It has been said they used the cat-o-nine tails, which had nine long tails to whip the flesh at one time, but at the ends of this instrument of torture was tied flint / stone with a sharpened edge, so as they were flung at the back of Jesus the flint would pierce the flesh and rip it from the body. Those were the stripes that he took for each and every one of us, so that we would not endure the wrath of God in punishment. After that, He was robed and mocked as the king of the Jews, and the staff they had placed in his hand was then used to beat him again and again on his head where the crown of thorns had been placed causing the thorns like nails to pierce his head. Jesus paid the price! He took my beatings from the beating stick of men! He was flogged in place of me! That is how I know that any punishment I received was not from God. The Word of God is absolute truth... Jesus took all the pain and the beating we deserved once and for all, then as he died on the cross He prayed to the Father for our forgiveness, and Jesus tells us in the parable that the son who returned deserving at the very least a lecture, received arms of love about him and kisses.

If we are punished then it is not by God our Father. It is not His nature, and it is not the message of the New Testament which Jesus came to share. What happened in the Old Testament – Jesus fulfilled once and for all. He taught that in the old days an eye for an eye – revenge – but He then says "but I say..." and He then proceeds to tell us to love and pray blessing for those who persecute us. To beat us is contrary to the words Jesus teaches.

Even the story of the woman found in sin and according to the Law of Moses, was to be stoned to death for her sins; Jesus says **"Let's have the man who has never had a sinful desire throw the first stone at her."** John 8:7 (TPT: 3). Jesus was and is the only one without sin, but He came to save not to condemn. He came to bring life and not death.

"¹⁰Finally, Jesus was left alone with the woman still standing there in front of Him. So He stood back up and said to her, "Dear woman, where are your accusers? Is there no one here to condemn you?" ¹¹Looking around she replied, "I see no one, Lord." Jesus said, "Then I certainly don't condemn you either. Go, and from now on, be free from a life of sin." John 8:10-11 (TPT: 3)

Without a single beating or stone thrown at this woman who deserved to be disciplined... she was shown compassionate love. How can we then say that God has punished us? If we are punished then it is by the carnal spirit of maybe our earthly fathers or mothers, teachers etc who do not understand God, by the consequences of our sin, and/or our own guilt and shame fuelled by the Accuser of the Brethren – Satan. If Satan can cause us to believe wrongly about God, then he has already limited the power and authority we have to do the Father's business on His behalf! Only a son and daughter can do that, and if we are afraid of our Father, fearing the punishments we will receive for our waywardness, then forgiveness will never be something we fully receive, repentance will not happen and thus the power of Christ fully unleashed upon the enemy of Satan and his demons will be severely weakened. I therefore suggest to you that the beating stick is an instrument of torture used and promoted by the devil to prevent us from drawing close to God, because in drawing close to God – the devil has to flee!

1 John 4:18 'Perfect love casts out all fear.' (NIV: 5) Fear is not a fruit of the Spirit of God, and therefore it is impossible for God who is Love, to use the spirit of the flesh (Satan) to control and disciple his children. Fear will cause us to compromise, when we fear at missing any of the pleasures this world has on offer to us. We are so afraid of what others will say if we say no because the Lord has called us to lay down our lives for Him. Fear of man imprisons us to follow the crowd... but it is not the way of the cross. Fear of an 'angry' God will hold us back from being with this person especially when we have done wrong, therefore denying us the fullness we have in our sonship through Christ Jesus. 'The Father' gives us a free will to love and obey Him... and yes we are to have a reverent fear for Him because He has all authority and power in heaven and on earth, but it is not something which we are to be scared of, but rather to worship and adore Him because there is no-one like Him! He is awesome and majestic and though he has the power to destroy, His heart is compassionate and full of perfect love for His children, longing for no-one to perish but that all be saved.

Song of Songs 1:8, Jesus says to me and you calling us His 'radiant one" – that if we ever lose sight of Him.... then He tells her how to find Him again. Many in the church – including also me at one time would have rebuked one for losing sight – and I would probably have called someone dark and deceived, devious, rebellious, sinful, but certainly not radiant one. Our God is not one to be feared in anyway – His love is compassionate, forgiving and His memory is very bad – because it says He remembers our sins no more when we ask forgiveness... He sees us robed in Christ's righteousness, radiant and pure.

If you are reading this as one who has been away from the Lord, maybe in secret and not as I had been in a public way, the same is for you, and the same love and forgiveness is yours to receive if you will, as such, turn around, and you will see the Father in the distance running to you! I say – blessed brother or sister, come home, there is a feast being prepared for you in celebration not condemnation! We love you!

Jesus tells us that of another story where if a wicked father will give good things to his son, how much more will our loving Father give to us. The prodigal son believed, though deceived, that the wealth of his inheritance would give him a better life. He asked for his share. The Father gave to him what he asked... He did not withhold anything. The son was asking in what I would describe as fleshly desires. The Father had every right to refuse the son, for the father was still alive and therefore the inheritance not legally due to be shared until after his death, but He knew that refusing it would not bring his son's cold heart to a place of warmth. The son was intent on a new life – a life to build what he thought would bring happiness, and he thought money could buy these things. The father did not consider the wealth of his possessions above the heart condition of his son... he was willing to give all, that his son's heart would one day return to find love beyond anything that this world can offer.

The greatest love is one that sets another free. What we often do, we try to control others as a form of protection, and maybe whilst still small children we need to do such to teach our children right from wrong, but there comes a time when children mature and they need to make their own decisions. A parent's love hopes that their grown child will make the right choices, but they cannot be sure, and there is a time when the child leaves the nest to make their own life. Every child at some point needs to make his and her own mistakes, and to learn from them. Often however we find ourselves not learning but making the same mistakes... like me. I kept making the wrong decisions many times until that precious day when a friend told me God is not angry with me but about to teach me how to overcome.

Of course the story does not end there, because we are told of the older brother who was working in the fields – as he did every day. He was angry and jealous when he heard of the noise and merriment in the father's home. When he heard that the father had had the fattened cow slaughtered and prepared for feasting, he was jealous. After all, he had been the dutiful son, remained home all the while working for his father diligently, and never once had his father even slaughtered a goat for him to share with his friends! Yet his brother who had left with half of the fathers wealth, squandered it on a life of sin, and then returns – and father gives him the fatted cow to celebrate. Where is the fairness in that?

I thought I could only be the prodigal son, but through the first three years since my return the Lord showed me this same jealousy of the older brother. I was jealous of Christian families that had been together with children now for many years, and the children were grown and they were still in ministry and had been living the blessings of God all this time, and I was jealous of them. Why did you bless them God and not me? In some ways it is different I know – but the jealous spirit is the same. I would wear a mask on the outside, but when a pastor stood and shared it was his wedding anniversary and how he loved his wife more now than ever before – I felt sick in my stomach wanting to vomit. I smiled and clapped like all the rest – but in my heart I was asking the question, why them and not me Lord? Why has no one cherished me in marriage and loved me and is more in love with me than ever before? Why? I had felt that the pastor was rubbing salt into my open wound – unintentionally of course.

God was showing me a **fox**! I didn't know it as a **fox** then, but that it was a fruit of the flesh and not of the Spirit, and I needed to repent. I indeed went home that day, and asked God to forgive me, for comparing my life to others, forgive me for thinking that God loved them more than he loved me. (Insignificance again). I had not considered it after that, but for one year later when the Pastor stood and gave thanks for his wonderful wife now of so many years, how wonderful she has been to him both as a wife and a mother of now beautiful teenage daughters. I was rejoicing with the church, when I suddenly realised – I was truly rejoicing and not feeling as before with the seriously sick feeling in my stomach. I don't know exactly when the Lord had completed the healing, but once again, I look back and see that after I had repented for my sin, recognising it and asking the Lord to forgive me, He was the one to bring about the healing.

In the next chapter I will refer back to the older brother, but I realise that both sons had been in a distant land. After all, had he not been the dutiful son who despite all, had remained on the farm working, not off somewhere distant having fun and laughter and enjoying the pleasures of this world. Perhaps it would be better to have done the same, at least he would have had the fatted cow when he returned too? Father told the older of the sons that all that He has belongs to him and asked him to rejoice that his brother had been lost but now he is found. But jealousy is hard, it cannot rejoice in another's victory, it will always be focused on 'my' loss. Jealousy is a distant land in the heart.

Let us just focus on what the father said to him... all that is mine is yours! The son was free at any time to take a goat or even a fatted cow to party with his friends, but he had not realised this truth. All that I have is yours... if it is yours (mine) it is mine to choose what to do with it. I can choose to invest in it to produce more or I can choose to use it... I can choose because it is mine. I am looking at this with fresh eyes, because I had not seen it before. In fact let us not forget that the father in the beginning, divided the estate between both his sons... if he had already been given it – then he could choose for himself what to do with it... perhaps it comes back to jealousy because maybe the fatted cow was part of the older sons inheritance? Was he jealous that the father had given away what was his?

Our Father in heaven is telling us that all He has is mine/ours. As His daughter, what is His is now mine... and my inheritance is now not after death! However in many ways I have lived my life in a way of being an orphan. I have not understood that what is His is mine. I have lived a life saying I do not belong to anyone, and yet I not only belong to the Father – but He belongs to me! As the future Bride of Christ – I belong to Jesus and He belongs to me... All that is His is mine! When I think back to my own earthly father... whether as a small child when I would run to sit on his lap and he would share his dinner with me even though I had already eaten, or anything that he had bought for the home if he thought I would benefit or would like it he always gave it away - to me or my sister... he never considered anything to be his alone – his heart would have given us the last penny in his pocket if we needed it. The truth is – I never asked. The older son in the parable had never asked... because if he had asked he would have received. (Again seeing the spirit of insignificance... afraid of asking in case he said no, so rather than feel rejection, because an insignificant spirit would take no as rejection manifesting a wounded spirit of poor me – nobody loves me... better not to ask.)

Now I have to come to the question, will God give something that we ask for even if it will hurt us? The truth is – in this story he did. It was not His perfect will for His son, but He could not deny the son his request. He must have known from the heart attitude in which the son asked for his inheritance that nothing would come good of it… except for the lesson of life learnt. The truth of the matter is, he was willing to give the son what he asked for, believing that he would learn the fullness of his love for him, and return to it. Though my marriage was not the Father's will for me, He did not stand in the way, because He knew that through it I would learn the fullness of His love and return. The Father will not control us to love Him… it is not that kind of love He desires. He desires the fullness of our heart to recognise the fullness of His love and run towards it, in meekness and humility. In that love He can then shower us with all good gifts… gifts to bless us and not to destroy us… but we need to trust Him and to know Him. A child knows, at least the majority know, the parents will never cause them harm. I am speaking in the natural. I know there are many children throughout the world that are not protected, used and abused by their parents – but it is not the natural of a parents love.

Jesus shares two more parables, before he tells of the Prodigal.

Luke 15:1-10

We are told of a shepherd that has 100 sheep that he cares for. When counting the sheep he realises that one is lost, missing from the fold. Does he say oh dear not to worry I still have ninety-nine, and forgets about the one missing? Of course not – we all know the story so well, that the shepherd left the ninety-nine to go and look for the one, that he might restore it to the flock. Perhaps that sounds amiss, after all is it not possible that whilst he is away searching for the lost that another will stray from the flock? If it would be the case – then for sure we know that the shepherd would then leave the flock to look for the other. The shepherd is not wanting for a single one of his sheep to go astray and be lost forever. The story then says that the Shepherd carried the lost sheep on his shoulder back home, and tells all his friends of how his sheep was lost but he found it again with great rejoicing. The last words Jesus says of this parable is that in the same way in heaven there will be great rejoicing in heaven over one sinner that repents than over the ninety-nine righteous persons that do not need to repent! The truth is that within the church of God there is a mask of self-righteousness, just as the older brother has – a religious spirit, that deludes many of us to be complacent and satisfied with the Christianity we have, and yet, whilst we have subtly allowed the compromises of this world to enter into our home and church life, we are still feeling there is nothing to repent of.

Next he tells of a lost coin. At first I didn't understand this – thinking it was just a piece of money, but I remember being explained many years ago that in fact the coin was part of a set, often found on a chain that was used around the waist as a kind of belt. One missing meant it would have a space where the coin should be, and the woman would find it ugly, much like now to wear a shirt with a button missing, or a necklace that has lost a stone, it would look untidy and ugly. Indeed any woman would search high and low in an effort to find the lost coin so it could be restored to the set. She would have told her friends that it was missing, and she is wracking her brain to try and remember the last place she had it – to see if it was lost there, and return to look in that place. It is typical of a woman, after searching all day to call her friends and rejoice when she has found it. I recall a friend of mine calling me to tell me she had lost her favourite ring, asking if she had left it in the bathroom at my home when she was visiting. I looked immediately and had to tell her no – it was not there. She had been distraught the whole day trying to think where it could be, and terribly sad at the thought of having lost it because of great sentimental value. We both prayed and asked for the Lord to reveal its whereabouts. The following day, she called me very excitedly, to tell me that she had left it at her place of work in the wash room, having removed it to wash her hands, and the cleaner had found it and placed it safely in the office. I can still remember the great joy in her voice – truly rejoicing having found the ring and having it back on her finger. Jesus finishes this parable with the same remark saying that there is great rejoicing before the angels when a single sinner repents.

I am beginning to think they must be drunk on laughter and rejoicing with all the repentance the Lord is bringing about in my life, as he reveals to me **fox** after **fox**! How does that make me feel? I have to say ecstatic! I feel ecstatic because instead of the picture we have all had of an old man with a long white beard with a beating stick waiting for us to receive the punishment for our sin, there is a picture of dancing and rejoicing, great laughter and happiness, indeed when we deserve a lecture God gives us a kiss! Do you want to make the Lord happy? The Word tells us how; when we humble ourselves in repentance and acknowledge our wicked ways and turn away from them. Not just one time at the cross of salvation, but on a daily basis as He reveals it to us. Indeed this is a lifestyle of worship!

Is it possible to be righteous without a need to repent? Well strange as it may sound – in the times of Jesus there were the Pharisees who indeed saw themselves as righteous and holy and beyond reproach, knowing the Law, as leaders in the synagogues... and times have not changed. Jesus' word is the same yesterday, today and forever. The same people are with us today in the church, not suggesting just leaders but within the congregations– believing that they have nothing to repent for. Is it not true that there is only one person who is good and that is God alone, according to the words of Jesus in the story of the rich young ruler, which I will come back to later? To think that we have nothing to repent of is to say that we are perfect, and therefore not in need of God's grace.

A friend once told me that he had always been a good person, never really doing anything wrong, thinking it would be better to have been like me and sinned in a big way - then he would understand more of God's forgiveness and love, but as mentioned in the Chapter on the Law, God's math is not as ours. If we have not committed murder, but have lusted in our thoughts about someone, we are guilty of adultery for which the penalty was death. Murder would appear to be a huge sin, in comparison to naughty thoughts about another person or even being angry with someone.... but both are deserving death. There is no big sin and little sin – there is no big death for big sins and little death for little sins. It is the same penalty for all. If I am dead I am not able to try and get it right next time – there is no next time. Our thinking that we have nothing to repent of is a deception of the devil. It is a lie – as I have said – Jesus says, no-one is good but God. I think how this way of thinking is so in line with what we know of the big brother in the story, considering that the sins of his little brother were great, and he had always been the good son!

What was it that one of the beatitudes said; "Blessed are the poor in spirit for theirs is the kingdom of heaven." These are the ones who recognise their wretchedness and in need of Jesus on a daily basis, hungering and thirsting for more of Him, not complacent and fully satisfied with the Christian life they have already. I am not saying that the Lord reveals a **fox** every day, but I am conscious every day that I am checking my heart for pride and arrogance less I find myself in a distant land again. One thing I can be sure of – having fallen from grace as some would say – but in fact it is not true – because God's grace never deserted me, it was me that deserted the Lord, but His grace remained, and the more I look back the more I see the incredible presence and grace of God that held me from falling too far! But pride and arrogance took me away, and I never want to stray again… so I allow the Lord to search my heart everyday – to show to me any bad thoughts or compromise I may have hidden. Does that make me 'holier than thou?' No, it makes me as Paul came to realise – there is nothing good inside of me except for Jesus!

I want to come back to the Father in the story of the Prodigal son. I have to say that a book called "The Return of the Prodigal Son" brought great revelation to my heart in this parable. I was always focused on the younger son… whom I can identify with, but then the Lord showed me I was also the older brother – filled with jealousy and resentment and insignificance. The book suddenly speaks of the writer being told by a work colleague, that it was time for him to stop being the rebellious child (the rebellious prodigal and the jealous son) to now become the father! To be the one who is offering grace and mercy to others instead of constantly in need of it as the rebellious children. We are called to be like the Father. The word tells us that we are being transformed in the image of Christ, and Jesus Himself says that whoever has seen Him (Jesus) has seen the Father. **John 14:9**. To be like Jesus is to be like the Father! Jesus is everything the Father is. Just as two in marriage become one, it is the divine mystery of the three in One God. Father, Son and Holy Spirit as One God.

We are called to reveal the Father-heart of God to a world of orphans, waiting to be adopted into the inheritance that has been already theirs since the beginning of time. How will the lost and hurting world understand the love of God if we cannot portray the Father's heart full of compassion and love? Was it not the Father, who so loved the world, even in its sin, that He gave His only begotten Son, that whosoever believes in Him (Jesus), shall not perish but have everlasting life! When God asked Abraham to offer his son Isaac to the Lord, after he and his wife Sarah had been unable to have children, and then the miracle happens and Sarah gives birth to Isaac. Abraham is given a promise that his children will be as the stars in the sky too numerous to count, so how could that possibly happen if his only son with Sarah is going to be sacrificed... and yet, Abraham trusted God that he was willing to tie Isaac to the wood that was to be the burnt offering. God seeing Abraham's obedience and trust in Him alone, He stops Abraham from killing his son, and instead provides a goat for the offering. It was, back then a picture of what would happen, when God would send his only begotten Son, to give up his Divine Nature as the Word, and become flesh, to become the eternal sacrifice for all of mankind's sin.

Recently I was sick. I had been experiencing prior to this, things that I would share with my son, but they were not received. He would hear but did not listen, considering that which I had to share was not relevant to him and his family. Then when I became sick and taken as an emergency to the hospital, needing someone to remain with me in case I choked to death, he preferred to go to a church meeting to pray for me. I was very hurt in my heart, because I knew that prayers from the empty bed by my side, prayed in secret would have been heard by our Father, there was no need to make them public. He was going because he enjoyed all the singing and dancing... I told him that he did not need a mother. He had managed all his life since his biological mother had died when he was young, that he didn't need one now he was a grown man... and I spoke out that I was 'divorcing myself' from the role. Oh how much I was learning! It was his wife, my sweet daughter-in-law, who came to me one day and said to me; "Mum, you didn't choose to be his mother, and he did not choose to be your son, the truth is God ordained it for a purpose, and it is not your right to terminate that which the Lord has put in place." The truth is as she has spoken it! I needed to learn a parent's heart from God's point of view. Once we become his child, no matter what, we are His child! The father in the story did not say – ok I am not your father anymore if you leave this house... if you do not do what I say, if you do wrong. I was to learn something through my son more of the Father's love for me, and more of what my love as a mother should be!

I know a Pastor who was not in agreement with the person his daughter had decided she wanted to marry. The one she loved wasn't from a family of riches, in fact, from a poor part of the country, and living as a missionary, having nothing to his name in land or home or material wealth. He was a recent convert from a different religion, but totally in love with the Lord, willing to lose everything for Jesus.

Matthew 13:44-46

Jesus tells us of the man who found treasure hidden in a field; he went away and sold everything he owned so as to buy the field with the hidden treasure. Or the merchant looking for fine pearls, and when he found one of great worth, he went away and sold everything he owned so as to purchase it.

This young man, had as such found the hidden treasure, the pearl of great worth – Jesus. Though it would cost him everything because to give his life to Jesus would be against his family beliefs and therefore would be cast out from the family and lose all his inheritance of land and buildings that would otherwise be his.

The Pastor was not happy, preferring his daughter to marry one with a good job and good home to offer, and what will the church say, knowing that she is rebelling against her parent's wishes and traditions? How can he lead a church when his own daughter fails to follow his will? Trapped and desperate to save his own face before others, he told his daughter to go and marry but they will not pay anything towards the wedding, and when she goes never to come back, she is not his daughter anymore.

This Pastor not only represents the Father to his daughter but also to the church. But not a single part of the Pastor's decisions was in line with the word of God in the parable of the Prodigal son, or indeed with His attitude towards the young man who was willing to give up all for the best treasure in the world – Jesus. He was willing to become poor in this world to become rich in the Kingdom of God. Even if the daughter was wrong and rebelling, is she not then the younger son in the parable, demanding the inheritance of the father before he is dead and going to do her own thing. Where does the parable tell us that the father argues, or manipulates, or tries to control the son by threatening if he goes to not ever return again?

I want to add at this point that actually the merchant who sold all to purchase the field of treasure of the pearl is in fact Jesus, and you and me are the treasure, the pearl of great worth... so much so Jesus set aside His Divine Nature in heaven, in search of you and me, to purchase us with His own precious blood. As the parable speaks to us as Jesus being the pearl

/ treasure, it also speaks of you and me, who Jesus was willing to pay the highest price ever, for our redemption.

It is our calling, not just to be children forever receiving His mercy and grace, but we are to become like the Father, giving out mercy and grace to others. How will people see the Father, if not through our own lives? The trouble is, we cannot give out what we have not yet received. If we have never seen the Father, how can we then reveal Him to others? This is not a word of judgement, or condemnation, this is a heart cry, because there are people in the church today who despite the many years of going to church, even serving God in ministry who have still the picture of a God with a beating stick controlling us through fear, having never had an encounter of the Loving Father whose love for us is unconditional. His mercies are new every morning.

I am not going to heaven because I am afraid of hell! I am going to heaven because I am in love with Jesus, completely beholden to Him for his unconditional gift of love on the cross for me, so that I may come home to my Father restored as His daughter, and part of the Bride. I want to correct what I just wrote.... I say that I <u>may come home</u> to the Father as in the future, but the truth is <u>I am home with my Father</u>, here and now in the present. The veil is torn from heaven to earth through the sacrifice of Jesus on the cross. There is no need now for a High Priest to commune on our behalf, the veil is torn and I / we have total access to the Father... I do not have to wait to be summoned like a servant to enter a room and His Presence, I have total access, liberty to sit on His lap with my head on His chest. He is my Father and I am His daughter. All that is His is mine...

The church needs to be re-united with the Words of Jesus, we need to see that we are wretched and poor and begin to hunger and thirst after righteousness. Jesus is Righteousness. We need to see that God is not angry with us, but is broken hearted because of the deception that has blinded His children into believing they are now perfect and no longer in need of His deliverance, healing and restoration. Oh that we could see how we have become the Pharisees of our day, and repent! He is gentle and kind, forgiving and merciful. He wants to set us free, He sent His son to set the captives free, the trouble is do we realise we are prisoners in need of deliverance and do we want deliverance from what is comfortable and enjoyable, maybe cute? The church is full of older brothers, self-righteous and proud of their dutiful faithfulness all the years, not like the younger son who ran off and squandered their inheritance... and yet they see not they have an inheritance which they do not choose to ask for... they choose not to use... and their love is a duty but not of the heart... and that is called religion! I come back to the words of Jesus when the disciples are angry over the extravagance of the sinful woman who broke a whole jar of perfume and poured it all over his feet. He said basically that she who is forgiven much loves much. **Luke 7:47.** The older brother also needed to be forgiven for an unrighteous heart but could not see it because he was blinded by his own good works of being dutiful. Who then of the two sons will love much... the one forgiven much! Who then will enjoy the depth of the Father's heart? The one who has been forgiven much, will also know the richness of such love. I not only am learning how to love and be loved as the Bride of Christ, I am still understanding the wondrous love of my Father, receiving the grace beyond measure for the things I don't deserve... but I am learning to love others with that same love... and I know I still have a way to go... but I am on the way! Jesus is the Way to the Father. The more I get to know the Father, the more I realise my own worth. In the second book "Rejoice... The Bricks Have Fallen" I wrote that "I longed to love and be loved in return". What I am realising beyond measure is that "I AM loved, and now learning to love in return...." for God first loved me!

He is my Father, and no matter what - I will always be His daughter. What is His is mine! Like Job who at the end of his life was richer than the beginning. He was rich and lost all, but at the end of his trials, he was a man of great wealth. Riches are considered often in terms of material riches but wealth is something more precious... it is a richness that money cannot buy. I am rich in Christ, and I rejoice in Him. Let the weak say "I am strong," Let the poor say "I am rich" because of what the Lord has done for me – Give Thanks!

Matthew 20:1-16; 15:3-20; 18:15-20

The First Shall Be Last.

The parable for a long time remained without understanding to me. I could read it and never grasp it, but I want to deal with it here following from the story of the Prodigal Son. It is to do with the older brother, and his jealousy.

He was jealous that his brother had dared to do probably what the older brother had wanted to do but never dared risking the loss of his inheritance. Although it doesn't say anything, I bet whilst he was working hard the fields that his brother should have been helping with, the older brother would be thinking about what kind of things was his brother doing instead. For sure in his heart he would have also travelled into the distant land through his imagination. Maybe he thought how glad he is now – because the brother has gone – truly everything will be his in the end when the father eventually dies, so imagine how he must feel knowing that the son has returned and his father has just slaughtered part of his inheritance to celebrate the younger brother's homecoming. The older brother cannot rejoice at his Father's generosity because all he could see was that it would be his loss.

Matthew 20:1-16

The parable now is that of a landowner who goes out early in the morning to hire workers for the day to work in his vineyard. He agrees a price which was one denarius. However a few hours later at the third hour it says, the owner goes out again and sees men waiting to be hired and he takes them and adds them to the workforce already in the field. Some hours later in the sixth hour the owner goes out again, and hires more men to work in the field. He offers them a wage that would be right. At the end of the day – at the eleventh hour he finds men still waiting having not been hired all day. The landowner sends them to his vineyard to work.

Now what happens next would never happen in this day and age. He calls in the last to be hired that had worked for only one hour, and pays them each a denarius. When those who had been hired in the first hour saw this, they are already in their minds thinking overtime, trying to calculate what they would be given if the last were given a denarius, but when they received their wages, they received also a denarius. Jealousy and self-righteousness rose up as they complained about their salary, how unfair it is that they who have worked twelve hours get the same pay as they who only worked for one hour. Let's face it at this point you and I would all do the same – start arguing our rights and fair play.

The landowner challenged them and reminds them that at the beginning when he hired them he offered them each a denarius to work the day – and they agreed the price. Why are they now angry because the landowner is a generous man deciding to give all the same regardless of how many hours they worked?

I think at this point of the man that is hanging on the cross next to Jesus, who asks Jesus to remember him when He comes into His paradise. Jesus tells him that this day he will in fact be with Jesus in paradise. In his last breath of life on the cross he repents through his recognition of his own guilt but of Jesus' innocence. He has lived a life of sin up 'til the last minute and gets to repent and he is promised paradise with Jesus.

However, for many of us, we have received salvation, and then had to live long lives being a good Christian. And what about me, one who received salvation but after 15 years, I turn my back on the Lord and walk away in rebellion, doing all the things that others have worked hard at not doing, even though temptation was there they worked hard not to fall. Is it fair that all receive the same reward as those who have lived a life of walking in godliness? Shouldn't those who have persevered the longest be the ones with the greatest reward?

Am I not the lost sheep that he leaves the ninety-nine for to bring me back? In these last days there will be many who come to Christ and will be anointed with all the gifts in measures we have only dreamed of, to collect the same prize as those who have been long-suffering and gone through many trials and tests.

I believe in the last days there are many in his church jealous of the way God is using others because they are willing to be used however the Lord calls, and not hindered by traditions and manmade laws in the church. The youth will be burning with new ideas that we would never have considered and now believe is outrageous, and yet the Spirit of the Lord will be upon them regardless of having done a Bible School training programme or not.

I believe also that the pensioners who should be at home by the fire with a blanket about their legs day in and day out waiting for the Lord to take them home, will instead rise up against that which is expected of them, with new life and calling despite age and health to be part of the last days army, willing to catch the **foxes** and go up to the mountain of spices with their Beloved, as he leads them out into the harvest.

But there will be those who will be like the older brother and be jealous of the late comers or the prodigals return to share in the inheritance that we don't deserve.... Indeed in these last days the wheat and the tares will be separated. The wheat is only recognisable because at the time of being ripe for harvest the head of wheat bows in humility, whereas the head of the tare remains upright and proud. Pride, and arrogance blinding them to the **foxes** they have allowed in to ravage the garden.

Whilst I was in India, my host family had a beautiful aquarium of fish in the kitchen/ dining area. In the tank, on my arrival there was a huge silver white fish – with beautiful fins like angel hair in the water, and about ten smaller fish black and golden. One day passing through to the bathroom, I was told one of the smaller fish was dead. The big white one had killed it. They tried separating it with a shelf from the fridge, but for some reason they removed it because it wasn't working, I think the smaller fish could swim through the wires and therefore back into danger with the big fish. I went for weeks without really paying attention to the fish, then one day I realised there were no other fish except the big white. I asked what had happened. The big fish was killing the others, so they removed the small fish into a bowl to safeguard them from the white... to find them dead in the morning, because there was not oxygen in the water. My question is – if the white one was the offending fish – the bully, the **fox** – why wasn't it removed into the bowl without oxygen and keep the majority in their home environment? Because it was beautiful! It is a picture of the church when we keep the one with the compromise because it is pretty and cause others to die.

Matthew 15: 3-20.

Here the disciples are discussing about things that make us unclean, because they had been accused of not washing their hands before eating, it was against the traditions of the elders. Jesus was angry because they, The Pharisees, were in fact willing to keep the traditions of men, holding fast to their cultural rules, whilst disobeying the word of God. Jesus rebuked them for not honouring their fathers and mothers saying that people honoured God with their lips only, whilst their hearts remained far from God. He said – they worship God in vain, for their teachings are but rules taught by men.

He goes on to explain, it is not what we put into our mouths that make us unclean, but in fact what comes out of our mouths. The food – whatever we put in our mouths will all enter the stomach and then be expelled from the body as a waste product. Only the non-waste is used to feed the vital organs what it needs to flourish and function.

There are some who hold to different traditions regarding what is right to eat or not. It is considered that pigs are not clean to eat – maybe because Jesus allowed the demons from the demon-possessed man to enter into the herd of pigs, sending them off the edge of the cliff into the waters. Yet – Peter received a vision that told him that everything is acceptable if given thanks for, allowing him to eat with the gentiles.

God is saying that we are concerned and teach of things that are irrelevant, because what goes into our mouths and stomachs will leave the body, however, that which is evil within our hearts are the things that come out of our mouths. It is of that which we have in our hearts from which we speak. People who are obsessed with vanity will always be talking of the body and how it looks and of sport or fitness in order to have control over the body. Those who have a love of money will always be talking of ways to invest it make it produce more and to revel in the things that can be bought with it – as a sign of their own wealth and success as they see it in life. These are examples, of **foxes**, because these are hidden idols that have replaced God and His word. Out of the heart comes murder (yes even to think it or unleash anger upon another), adultery and sexual immorality (from the things we have fed on through our eyes and ears either in the media or from others that have dulled our sense of godliness), theft as we look at what others have and covet what they have – be it theft of other peoples possessions, be it cars etc. or theft of someone else's wife or husband, false testimony telling untruths or lies, and slander (cursing others through gossip and negative talk of others). These are all **foxes** of compromise! They cause our hearts to be unclean, these are the things that can bring us to a place of eternity without the Father, when we love these above loving Him and His Word.

Isn't jealousy part of it? – Coveting what others have or are given, believing it should be theirs? Indeed these are the things that cause us to be unclean, yet we let them be because they are enjoyable in our lives, and focus on empty rules such as what to eat or not eat.

How to deal with compromise and sin? For most of us, we don't worry about it in other people's lives unless it causes them to sin against us, and then we are offended. Our excuse for letting others be, is because the word tells us not to judge others less we be judged. Paul talks about leadership in the church how it should lovingly restore those who are walking in sin. It does not say to ignore it. The problem will be that if we are with sin, then it is not realistic to go and deal with someone else's sin – forgetting our own, that would take us back to the word in Matthew 7 and the "tree trunk" in my own eye. However the last verse of that teaching does say... "First take the plank out of your own eye, and then you will see clearly to remove the speck from your brother's eye."

The word is clearly telling us that we are to help our brothers and sisters remove the compromising sin from their life, once we have removed our own. To do otherwise would make us hypocrites. Clearly if we don't want to remove our own, then we are less likely to want to remove others for them unless of course we are with a religious spirit that looks for fault in others and hides or is totally blind to our own sinfulness. How should one remove anything from an eye? – Very, very carefully! It requires for the person with the speck to completely trust the one who is going to help remove it – you don't just let anyone near your eye. It is a place of extreme sensitivity and pain, and a wrong action could cause a person blindness of the eye.

The Lord, as I have spoken before, had refused me to share a word with someone, until I was free from a religious spirit, because only then would a corrective word be received with the pure unconditional love of the Lord and without condemnation. To help others remove their compromise it needs to be done carefully and with love – not human love, but the unconditional love of God. We need to be like the Father, full of grace and mercy, loving, yet able to teach others the ways of the Lord.

Matthew 18: 15 – 20 talks of how to deal with someone sinning against you. First it says to go and talk with that person to let them know that what they have done is wrong. It says that if you do this and the person responds well – then you have won your brother or sister over into life. However, if they fail to listen, to take one or two others with you to establish witnesses as you try to win the person over. If the person still fails to respond, then it says to take it to the church, and if the person fails to listen to the church, then to treat the person as you would a pagan or tax collector. Basically it is not cruelty, but it would be to ask them to leave the church.

When I told of being in YWAM on a Discipleship Training Centre – and I confessed of my possible sin, they asked me to leave as it was contrary to what they believed and stood for. We are told that one bad apple in a basket can cause all the others to be bad. That yeast will spread into the whole bread. Sin if undealt with will spread throughout the church, because it is seen to be tolerated and then it becomes acceptable, and multiplies. They took it to my church leadership – by phone, saying they were sending me home, but as the church leaders prayed for me they believed I was called of God and asked instead for them to help me come to a place of healing and restoration, if I was willing. If I was not willing then I would be asked to leave YWAM. I was willing, I had been won over, mostly by my own church leader's compassion and unconditional love for me, willing to seek the Lord regarding the problem. It was however done in complete secret – only leadership were to know of it. It was love that covered a multitude of sin, but also knowledge of the incident to others could have been seen as toleration and allow it to spread further. My sin was that of Matthew 5:27-29. It was because of the leadership's willingness to help me come to a place of healing and restoration that I continued with my journey with the Lord.

It is of course a hard thing to do, and I saw it at the time not as loving kindness but of un-forgiveness and punishment, however I agreed to it – and it brought revelation and understanding.

Many churches are filled with compromise, because we have failed one another in dealing with sin as Jesus has taught. I am not writing to judge or condemn anyone, but rather to be as an open book, allowing others to see what the Lord is revealing to me of the inward condition of my own heart, to see the **foxes** of compromise, and together with Him, to catch them. As one who is openly removing the tree trunks in my own eye, the Lord is asking me lovingly to help you, to encourage you to remove your own specks. I cannot tell you enough that the Lord is not angry with us! He is not going to beat us with a beating stick, when we come to Him in recognition of our sin that He already knows about, He comes as the father of the prodigal, running to greet us and meet us with a kiss! Though we deserve a lecture – He gives us a kiss, not as Judas who betrayed Jesus, but in His Grace which is wrapped around us in His arms of love... and He slaughters the fatted cow ready to celebrate with the angels in heaven!!!!

Let us therefore not be jealous of the generous heart of our Father who bestows the same reward on the last as He promises to the first. Let us not be like the brother that is Jealous of the Father's grace that welcomes the lost home again, but rejoice in the abundance of His mercy and grace... but with humility come before the Lord and recognise we had taken our eyes off Him, and focused it upon the reward – the gift instead of the giver. In the Lord – His love is equal to all His children not favouring one above the other – to Him we are all his favourites, and no good works can benefit the size of the reward – it is not by the works but by our relationship to the Giver... and to love unconditionally as He loves unconditionally; praying for those that come after us, a greater blessing than we have known because of our great love for our brothers and sisters in the Lord.

Matthew 5:33-37; 18:18; 17:20;
21:28-32
Genesis 1:1-2

$\mathcal{L}et\ \mathcal{Y}our\ \mathcal{Y}es\ \mathcal{B}e\ \mathcal{Y}es.$

The Lord is placing a great emphasis here on the use of our words that we speak, be it as a promise or an oath made to the Lord, or the way in which we promise. Why such emphasis on the words that we speak? Every single word spoken will create life or death! We are created in the image of God.

"In the beginning God created the heavens and the earth. Now the earth was formless and empty, darkness was over the surface of the deep and the Spirit of God was hovering over the waters. **And God said**, "**Let there be light**", and there was light.... Genesis 1:1-2 (**NIV: 5**)

As God spoke the words, so it became!

So it is when we speak – He has given us the power to create or to destroy just by the words that we speak forth! It is an area that the Lord has had to deal with on two occasions in my life. When I was first saved – the Lord had spoken to me about getting rid of the language of the world, and I did obey cleaning my vocabulary up in every manner including topics of conversation. When I backslid as the prodigal – I also backslid into the language that I used. My, how the world had changed! Words, that I had never heard spoken publicly especially by women, were now being used as everyday normal language in conversation to each other. The word I am talking about is the "F" word. Hearing it spoken in almost every conversation with my colleagues at work – it soon became part of my own vocabulary, as I said before; I was on the slippery road to destruction.

As God was speaking to me again about it – I was shocked after I had returned to the Lord, how many people would use it from within the church. Shock! Horror! It truly had shocked me to hear it being spoken, but at the time I kept quiet. It was not used within the church itself, but in conversations over coffee after the service. One day however, whilst I was in the church hall, the service was over and people chatting together before leaving, when I heard it used by a church member. How is it possible that such language can creep into the church?

I remember meeting someone for coffee, a school teacher of English language and a Christian and asked her about it, as to what she thought of its usage in everyday language. Strangely enough she saw nothing wrong with it as it is used in a way to describe or to emphasise something being said. This word was about in the old days I know, and happen to know that it was a word used amongst men at work, but never in the presence of a woman, when I was a little girl growing up, and never before my mum or gran in the house.

The Lord had given a dream one night where I was preaching a word in the church and I remember saying clearly that His church (Bride) is in compromise! I clearly saw the whole preach, not once, not twice but three times. I knew that having seen it three times I was to write it down, and be prepared to share the word when the Lord opened the door. I had been preaching about the meaning of this word, so when preparing the message, I went onto the internet dictionary to look up its meaning.

Its first comment was that it was never used publicly but in code, and the first time was in the seventeenth century when it was used to describe what "men of the clergy" were doing to married women in a town called Ely in England. The action was describing sexual immorality, and adultery. It went on to speak of it being used as a descriptive word to express anger, and to intimidate causing fear. A certain 'F Buddy', is just a friend, with no strings attached to share sexual favours together as and when requested.

When I look at these examples, as born again believers we have to ask ourselves, what does the darkness have to do with the light? By accepting the use of this word into our vocabulary we have opened up to the **fox/ foxes** of sexual immorality, adultery and fornication, anger, intimidation, and murder to enter our hearts. The words that we use become life! Jesus clearly tells us that whatever we bind here on earth is bound in heaven, and whatever we lose here on earth is loosed in heaven. **Matthew 18:18.**

To bind and to lose, is done through prayer and the spoken word. Actually Jesus says that if we say to the mountain to move from here to there, it will move! **Matthew 17:20.** The power of the spoken word is like a two edged sword, and we can also read how the tongue is a small organ in the body and yet impossible to control it. **James 3:9.** We can use the words to curse or to be a blessing. Talking negatively about others and gossiping is cursing others and it is a sin.

King David cursed Mount Gilboa... **he said "O mountains of Gilboa, may you have neither dew nor rain, nor fields that yield offerings of grain....** "**2 Samuel 1:21(NIV: 5)** David was a thousand years before Jesus, and we are two thousand years after Jesus, and to this day three thousand years later, I am told that the mountains of Gilboa will not yield offerings of grain – it is barren land. The power of the spoken word!

Isaac, when his sight was failing him, was deceived by Jacob and his wife Rebecca in order to get the blessings that were rightfully belonging to his older brother, Esau. Once the blessing had been spoken, it could not be taken back again! Once the word was spoken – it became life! Jacob as we all know went on to become Israel. **Genesis 27:1-40**

Often I hear believers using the name of their beloved Jesus, in an exclamation when something happens that is shocking or surprising, or even God, but in truth no-one is actually calling on the name of Jesus or God the Father in prayer, it is just a way of emphasising what is being said. "I had a G-d awful day today!" First of all, there is nothing awful about our Father in heaven, to use such language is taking the Lord's name in vain and it is a sin.

Matthew 5:34-37. Jesus clearly is saying that we must not swear at all! **"Not by earth or by heaven, because earth is the Lords footstool and heaven because it is God's throne..."** As a younger person I heard many swear or promise something on their mother's or father's life or baby's life – all of which is wrong. **"... And you do not swear by your head, for you cannot make one hair of your head white or black, simply let your yes be yes and your no be no, anything beyond this comes from the evil one!"** (NIV: 5)

The Lord is calling us to clean up the words that we speak, or make oaths/promises to keep them. It reminds me when I was first saved some thirty three years ago. I was only a few months a Christian and not yet baptised, when I was offered a job in Spain as a nightclub manager. Not yet understanding the ways of the Lord, I was convinced it was a door opened by God, an amazing promotion with a great financial salary. I told the members at church who were my friends and they told me it was not from the Lord. I was so excited and wanted this so much I said that the Lord would have to close the door for me if it is not His will as I couldn't say no. Friends went to prayer, and a week later I received a call saying that the offer was off because of the Falkland's War. I was British, and the Spanish did not like the British because of the war. All rejoiced because God had closed the door. A week later, they recalled me to offer me the job! I said the same to my friends when they told me it was not from the Lord, and they all went to prayer. Again about a week later they told me the offer was closed, as the Spanish men would not agree to working for a female boss. All rejoiced because God had closed the door again! I received another call, and this time they were certain it was me they wanted for the job and they were coming to London to meet me and interview me but almost certain that the job was mine. This time, I told to my friends that they were not to pray. I said that the Lord was going to have to speak to me personally if it was not His will, otherwise I would accept the job and go to Spain. That following Sunday I was 'nodding off' as the pastor was speaking, when suddenly I received what seemed like a nudge on my shoulder, though no-one had actually touched me. As I awoke to what was being spoken the Pastor said; "When you make a promise to the Lord be sure to keep it!" He was obviously teaching from this passage. However with that one sentence, the Lord immediately reminded me in my thoughts of something I had said when I decided to give my life to Him. "I will not stop drinking or give up my friends, but I will not serve alcohol to others that I would be a stumbling block to others receiving the Lord." I was willing to be responsible before the Lord for self-control of not getting drunk, but I would not aid and abet others to break Gods word. I immediately realised that the promise I had made was contrary to the job offer I was about to accept. With some sadness, but in obedience, I called the people in Spain to tell them that I was not available for the job and please not to call me again. My friends greatly rejoiced, as I also did after I had told them, I felt I had passed a really big test, and I

had grown spiritually. I have never served alcohol behind a bar since that day. At the time I also had three jobs, one of which was serving in a wine bar in the evenings. I handed in my notice and left!

Matthew 21:28-32

Jesus tells a parable of two sons. The father asks each of them to do work for him. The first one says no, and the second one says yes. However, the first who said no, changes his mind and goes to do what his father had asked, and the one who said yes, actually did not do the work. The question is asked of the disciples who of the two sons' best pleased the father? The answer is the one who said no but then had a change of heart and did it as he was asked; there is a sign of repentance and a change of action. However the one who had said yes, had paid only lip service with no intention of doing what had been asked. This is also to do with giving a promise or an oath, which when we fail to keep it grieves the Lord, and it is considered as sin, but the one who at first had been honest and said no, suddenly had a change of heart. He pleases the father doubly because he was willing to speak the truth even though it was negative, he was honest to what he was feeling, but then there was also the added joy to the father of him doing a U-turn, which is repentance, and obeyed. The Lord also explains it as the tax- collectors of that day and such, who knowing they are sinners repent and turn, but the self-righteous and proud will be the last if at all to enter the Kingdom, heard to be saying the right words, but failing to act on them in their hearts.

The Father is looking always for the heart within. Nothing of the outer expressions of faith mean anything because what He is looking for is the true surrendered heart willing to walk in honesty and holiness, willing to repent and turn around.

In the previous chapter we have already spoken that unclean is not about what food you put into your mouth, but rather what comes out of the mouth; the spoken words reveal the true nature of the heart.

I was teaching some years ago as a motivational trainer. The teaching for the most was taken from the teachings in the Bible, but Jesus was never mentioned. The thing I taught was that we have to change who we listen

145

to and who we believe. We need to change the way we talk to others and way we talk to ourselves... because of the power of the spoken word.

I was awoken one night to pray for a sister in the church. I had no idea what I was to pray for but I had a real sense of urgency and danger. I prayed for approximately thirty minutes in tongues until I felt I had completed the task I had been woken to perform. The Lord then asked me to call her first thing in the morning to tell her. I called as I had promised the Lord, but she was not happy with my call, and I felt a bit daft because I couldn't tell her what I had prayed for – other than I prayed in tongues. She curtly finished the call as she had to drive to work. That evening I had a call when I was home from work from the sister. On her way to work that morning after I had called – she was involved in a serious traffic accident. Standing by her car, the police officer came to her to ask if she knew who the driver of the vehicle was. She said to him it was her. He looked in disbelief, it was impossible, the car was a total wreck and write-off, but when examined she did not even have a scratch or bruise on her – she should have been dead! I asked if I could drive to her house to pray with her and she agreed. On the way, as I drove, the Lord spoke to me that she had cursed herself. I asked her if she had wished herself dead. – She had! She repented for the words she had spoken over her own life! The power of the spoken word!

As I said I used to teach a motivational course, and I had been unable to see a fault with it because the truths being taught were totally in line with the Word of God. If people believed, they could achieve. If it's to be, it's up to me. Nothing is impossible. Of course we know at least two of those sentences can be found in the Bible. Most famous is "Nothing is impossible with God" – **Luke 1:37**.

Years later I was back with the Lord and He was showing me compromises in my heart. He showed me a book I had bought some time previous, because many were saying how fantastic it was and it changed their lives. It was a book about the power of believing and the words that we speak to create what we want in life. It is called "The Secret." I had begun to read it and did not continue, because actually I knew it – I had been a teacher of it. I had therefore placed it on the shelf with other reading books, to gather dust. Now the Lord was speaking to me about it. It is based on Biblical truth and therefore I had considered it to be true, but unless it is leading the person to the Cross of Jesus, it is a lie! The Lord was telling me that if

I take the Word of God out of context and use it – for example, nothing is impossible... and leave out God, then in essence I am saying nothing is impossible and we don't need God! Instead of it being a word of God It becomes a word of the devil that is encouraging others to be independent from God! Yet God is saying that without total dependency upon Him, not seeing Him first in all things, we are sinning. To believe that I can do all things, without God is about me being on the throne of my heart and not God. If the word of God spoken does not lead clearly to Christ, it is no longer the truth but a lie... and it is a deception of the devil. It is actually the deception behind the New Age movement.... "I will leave out the bit about God because I don't want to offend anyone, or Bible Bash people etc." In other words – I don't want to be rejected for mentioning the name of Jesus. The truth is that the people of God have become compromised in every way, fearing rejection, and accepting what the world has deemed acceptable through our non-believing governments. I had in fact been completely naïve, thinking that it was ok to teach it because it is what I believe in the Word of God. I did not realise at the time that to take the word out of context was a lie, and one day before the congregation I took that book and tore it into hundreds of pieces as I repented for being used of the devil to lead people away from God. Perhaps that day as I repented, without realising it, maybe it was the key that the Lord has been using to unlock the door of Independence, repentance activates the power of the Holy Spirit to set the captive free, to untangle the web of deceit about the mind, blinding us to the truths. And how many Christians are studying and teaching using psychology as their qualification to counsel others... and psychology is exactly what I just described – it is based on truths minus Jesus which makes it 100% a lie.... And with hearts wanting to help others we are leading people away from God instead of to God... teaching them to be independent of Him, saying we don't need Him because we can do all things and be all things without Him....

God is shaking the heavens and the earth in uncountable ways all over the world, as He said would happen in the end days. I am not preaching a time and a day – but I am preaching what the Lord has spoken to me. The Bridegroom is coming quickly, and it is time with haste for the Bride to be ready and waiting.

Let us together with the help of the Holy Spirit bridle the tongue, and tame it – train it to speak that which is Godly, of that which is pure, and noble, that which is of the things of God and not the things of this world. Let our tongues be a tool that releases healing and blessing, love and acceptance... to others but also to ourselves. We need to not only learn to love our neighbour but also ourselves... we need to see ourselves as the Lord sees us. The Father so loved you and me, he asked His Son to be the eternal sacrifice that would pay for our sin... Jesus' love for the Father and for us is so complete He willingly left the Divine Trinity to become flesh and live amongst us – perfect and without sin, to die in our place.... it is time we stop seeing ourselves with false vision of the world and begin to look with the eyes of God.... once we see ourselves in the truth we must continue to use our mouths only to speak truth. Truth only in part is a lie!

Matthew 6:5-8; 17: 14-21; 6:6-
18; 6:33; 7:1-2;
Luke 6:36-38 1
Corinthians 13;

How to Pray.

"And when you pray, do not be like the hypocrites, for they love to pray standing in the synagogues, and on the street corners to be seen by men... I tell you the truth, they have received their reward in full, but when you pray, go into your room, close the door and pray to your father who is unseen. Then your Father <u>who has seen what has been done in</u> secret will reward you, and when you pray do not keep babbling like pagans, for they think they will be heard for the many words. Do not be like them, for your Father knows what you need before you ask Him..." Matthew 6:5-8 (NIV:5)

Is God deaf? He is not! He knows the deep things of our hearts before we do, He knows the burdens that bring us to our knees in prayer before we pray them. Is God surprised when we pray? To the contrary; but yes He loves to hear our voices bringing the cares we have to Him in prayer. He loves to know that we acknowledge Him as the One who can help us in every area of our lives, and the lives of others that we pray for. He loves that we recognise right from wrong in our lives and although He has already forgiven us, longs to hear us come to Him with a contrite heart and say sorry to Him for the things we have done wrong and the intent of turning away. He loves us not only praying but talking to Him, words of adoration and love. He loves to hear us speaking to Him as a Father, and to Him as a Bridegroom and Lover of our souls, He longs to hear the unspoken words groans from within, knowing exactly what we are praying though we can't find the words to express. He loves us to speak to Him in the Spirit, He loves for us to be open to not only speak, but also He loves when we listen to Him, and long to Hear Him speak to us. But it is to Him we speak. It is for His ears.

I have experienced church life in abundance as I have travelled to many parts of the world, but I have found especially on the African Continent where everything is done on a microphone at full power so all the people from miles around can hear everything... the prayers and petitions, the spiritual warfare, the worship, the preaching, everything! I ask myself, is this not the same as standing on the street corners so that all will hear? Often the church buildings are shelters built with poles and tin rooves, to shelter from the rains when they come, and it is good... but the buildings even if they have walls of wood or iron sheets, they are not sound proof... however it is not about the construction, it is about the inability to use the microphones and speakers as they were meant to be used, and for whom are we using them?

Are we praying to God or are we praying to the people outside the church building so they hear what we are saying to our God for their gratifications or even an effort to cause change to their godless ways? Are we worshiping God, or are we performing for the people in the church and the surrounding neighbours? Are we teaching our congregations or trying to evangelise the neighbours from the inside of our churches? Jesus clearly "sent out" his disciples to evangelise, to preach the good news into all of the world. Have we become confused, that it says give unto Caesar what belongs to Caesar and to God what belongs to God? What do I mean by this?

First of all we are called to be worshipers. Who do we worship? God, and yet I have seen in many places the time of worship to be an entertainment. Christian artists, miming to their own recordings and performing – who for? It seems very clear it is not God. They are performing for the people, like it is a place to market their goods. Is not God worthy of our very heart, mind and body given in complete worship? They use their recordings from the studio (not just a backing track) so it sounds good, they want to sound perfect for the people. It is a performance! God does not truly care if we sing in tune or out, He cares about where and to whom our hearts are focused. Worship is not about the song or the dance, but the heart within, surrendered to give what is due to our God. The focus should also not be on the people at the front – the focus should be on the Lord. If the worship teams are attracting all to see them, then I am concerned. The worship team should lead a congregation into the presence of God, to seek God alone, not into a holy performance for God. Worship is all about Him and none of us.

I believe in dancing before the Lord, I believe in shouting and praising the Lord, I believe in the use of drama and the creative arts as an act of worship to the Lord... but it is to the Lord and not toward each other. One can always create another event to perform for the Christian audience, but let us not take that which is meant to be given to the Lord to be about ourselves.

He loves it when we pray together in agreement, so He loves corporate prayer as well as individual prayer, corporate worship, as well as individual worship, but God is not deaf! He does not need microphones, badly used, to hear His children. If we are misusing the microphones, then it is not for God – but for the people, which brings me back to standing on street corners or standing before all in the synagogues for all to hear and see how clever we are or how holy we are. And the misuse of the microphones is causing sickness and damage to the body when the decibel levels are too high causing deafness to those who come into the church building. How do I know that? I have irreparable damage to the ears because of the extended times in my youth in the nightclubs with too loud music, which at the time everyone thought was cool. Yes – the Lord can and does heal, but not always. Once again, have we brought the world into the churches, and instead of the sound system being a help to speak to large crowds it has become in some places an instrument of torture to the body, and to some degree a tool of exclusion to those who find the loud noises painful to the ears. It has also become a tool of control and manipulation where the people who have chosen not to go to church have to suffer prolonged hours of loud music, loud preaching, loud feedback from the system and speakers... and in some places, through the night when others try to sleep for their much needed rest before another long day of work. So let us ask ourselves, do we love? Do we pray with love and care for our neighbours who are lost, or do we control them, coercing the neighbours to hear, thinking they will respond positively to audible 'battery and assault' for hours upon end? Again I ask myself, if when we pray individually and seek Him in a quiet place and close the door as Jesus has taught us in the opening scripture, when we pray corporately is not the church hall or room the place of quiet seclusion with the church door closed to the people outside of the church. There are times when we need to close off from the world and seek His presence, and sometimes, that place of seeking is to sit quietly on his knee with our heads resting upon His chest and hearing His heart beat, or at His feet in quiet surrender waiting to hear His still small voice speak to us.

When Jesus went to pray he went to a quiet place, to listen to His Father. He only spoke what the Father told Him to say, and to know what the Father-heart is, we need to be quiet and listen. The people followed Jesus, to listen to His words. The people who wanted to hear, and therefore had open hearts to receive His Word, would go to where He was. Jesus spoke to multitudes, of five thousand and that was just the men, there were also women and children – and he taught about the Kingdom of God without a microphone. Wouldn't it be wonderful if church became a place known for the presence of God that covered and filled His children that when we left the church we were living lives so powerfully anointed with the Spirit of God, to love our neighbours in action, which would cause people to run to churches to experience His presence for themselves, because they like what they see in us? Yes we need to evangelise, we need to speak, but as you have read about the Prodigal son, you cannot force a person to love God. People need to love God because they cannot help themselves when they meet the unconditional love of Christ in action through His Body – His Bride – the Church. To control people to listen, will build up resistance, bitterness and hardening of hearts. To control is the same spirit of witchcraft and not of the Holy Spirit.

I had been working and ministering for long hours of the days, finding my bed at night with deep sleep that my body and mind needed during a week-long conference from mornings with appointments for one to one counselling and prayer, to teaching other groups in the afternoons to the evening full house teaching, plus continuous fellowship with the people in between. Tired and exhausted I went to my bed in the hotel I was staying, close to the church. At 10pm I was spending quiet time together with the Lord before sleeping when the sounds from the church were extremely loud and clear. I thought it will last thirty minutes maybe just for the worship, but no – it went from 10pm til 4am – everything – music, prayer / spiritual warfare and preaching on full sound in the middle of the night! As a believer, even I was angry. Angry that I was being denied my right to a night of sleep and rest before I worked another long day. Angry that I was paying money to stay in a hotel where I was unable to get the rest

I needed. I closed the windows, I put a pillow over my head, and toilet paper in my ears – and still the sounds were penetrating. In the hotel were workers from another country to do local work in the area, and so they worked every day 'til the work was finished so they could go home again to their families. How did they feel about their right denied, to a night of sleep to give the body energy and the mind a refreshing, to work and operate dangerous machinery for twelve hours the next day?

Maybe it was a 'once only' as an exception, but no – it happened regularly on a Friday night. I was told it was worship practice. Learning songs and singing together is learnt without microphones and if a piano is needed, it is not needed on highest volume like a disco blaring into the night air. I am sharing this for a purpose. It is not just one church, but a pattern I have experienced in different nations.

I was speaking this with another pastor, and he told me of a new church that had opened and every evening there was loud praying from the microphones for two to three hours. One of the teenage girls in the neighbourhood had come to the Pastor to see if he could do something to help. She was needing to do homework from school and to revise for exams, but every evening the noise was too loud and causing her to struggle with her study. It was not his church and the pastor did not feel he could encroach upon another's territory to speak of it.

The Lord teaches us that if we lived according to the first two of the Ten Commandments, the others would not need to be written. We are to love God before any other with all of our heart, mind and strength, and to love our neighbour as ourselves, which is meant to have respect, caring thoughts of well-being, thoughts of kindness and gentleness. However, we find a total indifference to the neighbours needs for sleep because of our own needs to be as such on street corners, showing how holy we are to be up all night praying and worshiping to our God! Some have said that the loudness is to help people not to sleep, but surely if they are tired – better let them sleep and those with the calling upon them to pray through the night do so without the encouragement of ear-splitting decibels as their encouragement.

I have heard that the government in a certain place is going to fine churches high amounts of money if they exceed certain sound levels. I was told that now the churches will have to comply. What is better, to walk in obedience because the government have enforced it into the law of the land, or, to walk in obedience to the Word of God because we love Him and love His Word? It's all a matter of the heart. Everything the Lord teaches us is not about the outward things seen but the unseen motives of the heart... these are truly the things the Lord is going to judge us on when we each stand before His Judgement seat.

This may not be the same where you live, however I think it can be looked at and see similar comparisons. If the building is sound proofed it is not as bad, so long as the congregation are not being caused injury from the level of decibels. The Word tells us through Paul's first letter to the Corinthians that without love, if we speak in tongues of men and of angels it is nothing but a resounding gong and clashing symbols! We can perform mighty miracles and fathom the mysteries of the world yet if we have not love, we are nothing. If we give all we have to the poor and surrender our bodies to the flames and not have love, then we have gained nothing.

Love is patient, Love is kind, It does not envy, it does not boast, it is not proud, it is not rude, it is not self-seeking, it is not easily angered, it keeps not record of wrongs... and now these three remain; faith, hope and love, but the greatest of these is love. People will know that Jesus is alive, when we love one another, not just the believing brothers and sister, but love all who Christ died for. We do not know who is yet to come home to the Lord, but we must treat all with the same unconditional Love of Christ. God sends rain upon the crops to be harvested and the weeds. He calls us not to differentiate between each other, but to be the visible image of Christ, His hands of blessings to those yet unbelieving. Without unconditional love and respect for our neighbours, my question is – are our prayers being heard or are they as clashing symbols and resounding gongs?

The gift of tongues is a heavenly language which for the most we do not understand but the Lord does. It is a language we use to the Lord in prayer, where the Spirit of God leads us to pray for that we do not know how to pray. It is not to be performed on a microphone for the entire world to hear, because it is not for them, it is for God. At times there is a prophetic utterance where the message is spoken out in tongues for the church, and there is in that instance to be a prophetic translation which God will have placed in someone's heart to bring understanding of that word. Otherwise the gift of tongues is a language between man and God. Not man and Satan, not man and man, but man and God.

There are times when the Lord may want others to know, like the time below, that they may know His love for them...

I was living as a missionary and sharing the room with two others. It happened that apparently I would talk in my sleep – not always, but often. One of the girls tried to record me in the night. One particular time, both of the girls were awoken from sleep to hear me speaking. Apparently I was seemingly praying for someone. They could not hear what I was praying, but they heard the name clearly, and the following morning told me. I was praying for a student doing one of the schools at the base. I knew of her and could recognise her, but I didn't actually know her. That morning as we all met for morning worship. I entered the door at the exact same time as the girl I had been praying for in my sleep, so I told her that I had been praying for her in my sleep in the night and hoped she was blessed. She burst into tears. Apparently she had been crying out to God believing that He was not hearing her cries for help and her pain. When I told her how both room-mates were wakened to hear me praying, not what I was praying but that I was praying specifically for her, she knew that the Lord had heard her every cry for help and indeed was with her in the pain. It brought her comfort. In this situation, no-one would have heard it in the night to report it to me who was oblivious of the Lord using me this way in my sleep, had the Lord not intended for it to get back to her personally.

In the chapter 'Let Your Yes be Yes, I told of another story when the Lord woke me in the night to pray for someone but did not know what I was to pray... I found myself praying in tongues until the need had passed... the results you have read for yourselves. However in both of these occasions the Lord had clearly wanted the persons being prayed for to be informed, otherwise they would have remained a secret act between the Lord and I.

The Lord also teaches us about fasting. It is considered to many, that it is to go without food in order to seek the Lord's presence and to pray for certain things. I have to say that where I have been involved in communal fasting, it was the fasting of food but vital water to the body was not fasted, and that was in a land where dehydration was not a huge problem. I was so surprised to be with my Ugandan son's Papa in the hospital because he was sick to find that he had been fasting for a long time not just food but water/fluids also. It is not me to suggest what kind of fast is right or wrong – that is for the Spirit of the Lord to speak to each individual.

Why do we fast? It was asked by Pastors at a leader's conference; "Which is the most powerful – prayer or fasting, to release the power and authority of the Lord to see miracles, signs and wonders?" A scripture that many quote is that of the disciples who could not cast out the demonic from the sick boy. Matthew 17:14-21

(NKJV: 6) "[19] Then came the disciples to Jesus apart, and said, Why could not we cast him out? [20] And Jesus said unto them, Because of your **unbelief**: for verily I say unto you, If ye have faith as a grain of mustard seed, ye shall say unto this mountain, Remove hence to yonder place; and it shall remove; and nothing shall be impossible unto you. [21] Howbeit this kind goeth not out but by **prayer and fasting**."

(NIV: 5) version does not quote fasting

[19] Then the disciples came to Jesus in private and asked, "Why couldn't we drive it out?" [20] He replied, "Because you have **so little faith**. Truly I tell you, if you have faith as small as a mustard seed, you can say to this mountain, 'Move from here to there,' and it will move. Nothing will be impossible for you."

The Lord was not referring to the demon being the difficulty, but to the disciples' unbelief. How do we deal with our little faith or unbelief, it is to get to know Jesus and our Father, and indeed the Holy Spirit in an intimate way, because when we know who He is, then we understand who we are in Him, and our faith will then be able to move mountains. The Word of God tells us that we need to pray and believe! Sometimes that which we need to pray for appears to be bigger than our faith. However it is not the act of starving our body that gives us power over the demonic, but that by using the time taken to eat instead to seek the Lord who has all authority and power in heaven and earth. It is nothing of us and all of Him, and when we get to understand the relationship we have in Christ and the fullness thereof, then we will pray and believe.

Basically we 'fast' that which is blocking us from hungering and thirsting after intimacy with our Lord. In a world of today, especially the western world but I believe it is the same all over the world in different levels, for example watching TV has become such a huge obsession that quenches our time and energies in seeking the presence of God in Intimacy, and filling our minds through the eyes, such hopelessness, and immorality which lead us away from the things that God has spoken to us. It could be our intense time used on Facebook and other Social Medias, internet games, it could be the music industry that we are so following and spending time listening to – yet never finding enough time to spend in God's presence. Is it our hobbies that consume our time and energy leaving little or no time to seek the face of our Lord?

Our source and authority as Christians does not come by 'doing' spiritual acts, it comes from the anointing that comes from sitting in the presence of Him who has and is all authority. When we spend time with Him, seeking His face, longing to know His heart, He is the one to give instruction how to overcome the enemy. Scripture tells us to draw near to God and the devil has to flee. We have in us all authority to overcome the evil one as born again Christians. It is not about how many long words we can pray, it is not by might or by power but by the Spirit of God.

So – what is hindering your belief? Take a fast from whatever it is, and instead use that time to seek the intimacy of God. He tells us, 'if you will seek Me you will find Me!' But we need to search with a hunger and a thirst... not half-heartedly, but with a deep longing to meet with Him. Maybe a church can suggest if people feel so led to join together in a fast to seek God's guidance and strategy for moving forward through a battle yet to be won. However – one man's fast may not be another man's fast. I believe the fast is determined by the individual and God.

There are times when Christian communities will pray and fast together, in agreement. They may not fast all the time but support each other as the Lord leads each individual. Jesus tells us that we are not to look in a way that others will know we are fasting, because it is between the individual and God. Yet I have seen it on social media pages for the entire world to see who is fasting, inviting people if they need prayers to send in their prayer requests. Indeed - ask if people have prayer requests to message you privately, but don't announce it to the world you are fasting, so people can see how holy you are. Something I find just so not in line with the Holy Spirit, is when a church leader will demand the people to fast, meaning food and some in places also water/liquid. Control is not a fruit of the Spirit of God – but is witchcraft. Let us not fall into the compromise of controlling others into religious acts, but let us gently lead one another into the presence of God to each hear for themselves what the Lord is asking of them to do.

Matthew 6:16-18

"When you fast do not look sombre as the hypocrites do to disfigure their faces to show men they are fasting. I tell you the truth, they have already received their reward..." It goes on instead to say use oil on the face so it shines and you look washed and clean so no-one will suspect you of fasting. It should only be obvious to the Father as it is written in verse 18. Because you do not receive the praise of man because of doing your fast in show to all – God will reward you for doing it in secret with Him alone.

When Jesus was talking about hypocrites He was talking about the Pharisees who wanted everyone to see them and respect them for their seemingly devoutness to Gods word, to be seen holier than thou, and yet Jesus tells us they were self-righteous and proud. I believe there is a Pharisee in every one of us, including myself, that needs to be caught and sent packing from the Lord's garden.

I recently heard a man of God preaching. He said if someone asks him if he fasts his reply would be; "None of your business, that is between me and God;" and I agree!

I am not saying we cannot fast together and seek His presence together – indeed we can, indeed we must, but let us not announce it for the entire world to see and hear. Fasting is about obedience to God, not a performance for others to see how holy we are, Let us learn to keep the things of God that are for God in the place He loves it to be – in private. It says to go into your room and close the door and pray. That is because He wants us to long for Him though He is unseen, and not to seek the favour of others for our spirituality.

He teaches us that prayer always starts with focus on who God is. A focus on His name. Hallowed be his name.... what is His name – names – He has many. We start by recognising Him for who He is, not about who we are, and in recognising who He is, we know everything we have need for is found in Him, producing faith in our hearts to believe for the things we ask.

Just as in the word He teaches us to Ask Seek and Knock, He teaches us to Seek first the Kingdom of God and His righteousness, because all other things that we have need of will be given to us as well. **Matthew 6:33** In the 'Lord's prayer' as we have come to know it, after Hallowing Gods name (to honour as holy with reverence), we are to pray for His Kingdom to come, and His will be done, on earth as it is in heaven. This is a time of intercession for others, for the governments and leaders of our village, town, and nation... for the lost to have their eyes opened to see the Kingdom of God, to recognise the spiritual battle and to do spiritual warfare for them. Something I will come back to later... or re-state something I have already written.

After intercession for others – for His kingdom to come, we can then ask for our own needs, the things we need on a daily basis. Notice God first, Others second, and self-last... yet how often we do it opposite, focusing on me, me, me, first, then maybe praying for others and lastly God – if at all we remember His goodness. Often our prayer is like a Christmas wish list... without thought of others even. Oh Lord we have so much to learn...

As we pray for our own needs – it says Forgive us our debts or sins or trespasses depending on your translation, AS we forgive those that have trespassed against us! Have we forgiven those who have wronged us???? Again I have spoken of this in the chapter of forgiveness. But I cannot stress enough, that to fail in forgiving others means that we too are not forgiven by Jesus, for as the measure we give to others it will be measured unto us. **Matthew 7:1-2**. Jesus is very clear on this teaching. **Luke 6:37-38.**

Now from **Luke 6:36**, Jesus tells a parable which I want to include with this chapter of prayer. "Can a blind man lead a blind man? Will they not both fall into a pit? A student is not above his teacher, but everyone who is fully trained will be like his teacher. Of course it goes on to teach us about judging the speck in others eyes whilst we have a plank in our own eye.

Can Satan cast out Satan? He cannot because a kingdom divided by its self will fail. **Matthew 12:22-28.** When we are praying for others either in forgiveness or intercession, if the Lord has shown us a speck in another's eye, we need to be sure first that our own plank is removed.

Quite often we have used the place of prayer as an open field for criticism of others before the Lord. God has not asked us to do this. In fact often, we when we have been wronged, we go into spiritual warfare to change them. Focused on all that is wrong with them, and yet Jesus focuses on all that is right with us, He does not focus on our dark places as in Song of Songs chapter 1 when I started the book. The Lord is clearly speaking to us that we are to pray for our enemies and to not only pray blessing but to love them! I know we have talked about this but we need to see it again in the context of prayer and you will see why soon. In **Matthew 6:43-48** Jesus tells us to be like our Father who is perfect, who has poured out the same love on all men the righteous and unrighteous.

God has given me a son who is not a believing Christian but a Muslim. The Lord specifically told me that I am to love him exactly the same as I love the believing children He has given to me... even if he never gives his life to Christ. This was a revelation to me though it shouldn't have been. Somehow in my mind I was thinking that Gods love is greater for those who have accepted Jesus as Lord. How can the Father possibly love us any greater than sending His own Son to die a cruel death on a cross for us? On the cross Jesus spoke out a prayer over all... 'Father, forgive them they know not what they do.' This is a blessing! A blessing of great love for all as He wishes than none shall be lost. For God so loved the World that He gave His only begotten Son that whosoever believes in Him shall not perish but have everlasting life. He sent His Son for all of us still in sin, because of His great love for us and His love does not change as I have written about in the chapter on 'The Prodigal Son'.

This is a huge challenge to us all in this day of great persecutions around the world and the terror that is being performed towards the Christians, yet the Lord is not calling us to curse our enemies but to pray for them in love and forgiveness. This is hard. But remember, if it is not hard, if it has no pain, then it is not forgiveness! This is how the Lord has asked us to pray.

That does not mean that we cannot pray by binding the enemy or losing the power of God, but it's to be done as we battle in the spirit for the souls of those still walking in deception and possessed by the devil, out of the unconditional love of the Father, that they too may find love and forgiveness at the foot of the cross through repentance. We are angry with the spirit not the flesh. Maybe even now you will feel some anger rise up in your heart as you read this, because the enemies of the cross "don't deserve to be forgiven." **Matthew 5:38 – 42** is teaching us about what was said in the past – but Jesus who has brought about the covenant of Grace tells us that it is no longer acceptable to give an eye for an eye, in other words to repay with that which they did to others. As Jesus did when He was wrongly accused, He did not try to escape from the injustice, but went peacefully (The peace of God that passes all understanding) through the pain and injustice with the love of God in His heart that all might repent and receive the fullness of Salvation. Are we ready to trust Him in the pain? Are we willing to be trained by The Teacher who has gone before us that we may learn of Him and become like Him? We will never be greater than the teacher, but we can be like Him, as we allow Him to transform us from glory to glory.

When an army is making its plan of attack on the enemy, does it announce to the enemy what it is about to do? Usually not, unless it is using a false plan as a decoy or they are trying to intimidate through fear. Usually an attack will be done in secrecy, to surprise the enemy and take the advantage to win. Often a special task force will be used who has been trained in specific ways of attack and maybe trained to endure longer and suffer through more pain, than the normal soldier. Such a task force will also be a smaller tighter knit team of people, who know each other's strengths and weaknesses and able to cover and support each other, whilst releasing each other into their specific gifting. Yet again what I have come to hear much of – is the attack in spiritual warfare is being made by all, and announcing to the whole world again over the microphones what is being prayed. God can know our every thought – however the devil cannot. He has to wait for it to be spoken to know what we are thinking. I believe the greatest form of corporate warfare is drawing close to Jesus in worship. Maybe working together with the special task force as in the Old Testament. The worshippers would go up front, and the fighting soldiers behind. I can remember in YWAM many years ago when half the group would be worshiping at the same time as the other half prayed in warfare... then they would switch roles as they prayed for different topics... it kept the people also fresh in prayer. It was good.

Yes we all have authority in Jesus name against the evil one – but at different levels. When I was only one week with a Bible after having visited church for the first time and not knowing anything, especially about spiritual warfare, I was confronted with a very drunk enraged boyfriend who was violent and uncontrollable 'til his anger spent. He stood over me with a carving knife from the kitchen, to tell me if he could not have me, then no-one else will get the chance, he was going to kill me. I had the small hand sized Bible hidden under my pillow, which I took out and held it before him and the poised knife, and looked him in the eyes calmly and said, "If you strike me you strike the Lord Jesus!" He dropped the knife and walked out of the room crying like a baby. I had never been taught that at the name of Jesus every knee must bow! The Holy Spirit led me as a week old believer. It does not however, qualify me to go from there directly to the devils lairs and high places, to tear down their altars. For me to do that, I need to first be sure I have rid myself in Jesus name through repentance of the planks in my own life, pride in me will only feed pride not rebuke it. I believe that those who are willing to humble themselves with a contrite heart in the secret place of the Lord, and together with the Lord catch the **foxes** of compromise, will indeed become better equipped to fight on the front lines. Not all fight on the front lines, even in the army there are people in supporting roles, each having been trained for combat, but each at different levels. **Foxes** ravage the fruit in God's garden in your heart, and make us vulnerable to attacks of the enemy because they have open doors to invite other **foxes** into the garden.

I once heard it said by a military leader, that the team is only as strong as the weakest link. It puzzled me for a while. I then saw a picture of a chain, and the links solid holding together a strong force.... But if one of those links in the chain is broken – when it is being pulled in the strongest force in battle the broken link will snap and the chain be broken and anything attached to the chain or being held in place by that chain can be lost or severely damaged. The chain is as strong only as the weakest link. If we are working in strategic battles against great strongholds and principalities... if one member of the team has not overcome the spiritual enemy they are fighting against, in their own life and closed the entrance for enemy to attack, through that person's open door the enemy will counter attack and in fact the spiritual force within will not disappear but will be fed and grow stronger. The spirit if witchcraft in the church is probably beyond belief, because people are trying to battle against the spirit of control and manipulation, (Jezebel) whilst the churches are being led in the same spirit. Satan cannot cast out Satan... instead he grows getting fatter and fatter. We wonder why many churches have so many people going through some bad times, repeatedly so. It is not God who is unable, but the devil who comes to steal and destroy, and has been given access and therefore authority because of an unwillingness to deal with the **fox** or plank of wood in our own eye, before engaging in trying to cast it out of the nation, the church, the neighbours, everyone else except me. Many churches especially here in Africa, it's like giving a child an artillery of machine guns, and they point and fire in every direction without plan, without training how to use the weapons, some shooting at their own people – brothers and sisters in the church under enemy attack from the prayers of other Christians, praying out of hurt and pain, bitterness, un-forgiveness, revenge, or just plain witchcraft... name it and claim it... people with zeal for the Lord but without knowledge and understanding.

Sometimes, the Lord may ask us to watch and not engage in battle – until He tells us... sometimes we think the seat of power is one place, but the Lord knows it is somewhere else. If we go for the small fish, it alerts the big fish, and can find ourselves under heavy attack. Warfare is not something we do without following the Captain... an army always follows orders, they do not make up their own orders – there would be chaos. Jesus is our Captain!

Prayers of the flesh – what are these?

It is like casting spells by using the words that we speak to become into being, but the things we pray for is according to our own fleshly desires or opinions and not after the will or way of God. From my own experiences I want to speak about this.

As a single woman for some years, every male I met, in my heart I was wondering if he would be my husband. I had not as yet surrendered my will – which I had spoken of in the beginning of this book. I didn't consciously know I had withheld it – it was a hidden compromise I had not yet seen or understood.

I met my husband when doing a drama on the streets of Copenhagen as part of an evangelistic outreach and had preached after the drama. I saw three men standing together, one of whom I saw like a spotlight was upon him, he was very handsome. I went to talk to them all but the one I felt drawn to spoke no English so we could not talk, however to my surprise I learned they were believers and attended the same church I was going to in Copenhagen.

Every time I saw him, my heart skipped a beat and I could hardly breathe because of the intense emotions I was feeling towards him. He however did not show any signs of feeling the same way about me. One day back from church, one of my team saw how flushed I was when I returned and asked why. I told her that I had seen the man again, and I couldn't control these emotions I was feeling within me towards him. I was head over heels in love with him regardless of the fact he showed no interest in me. She was from Korea and a prayer warrior. She said to me that she will pray for him to become my husband, and I said with great joy, that I would like that and thanked her. Approximately nine months from that happening, we were married. A dream come true! It was a disaster waiting to happen. There was great pain for both of us to follow, though I only realised my own pain at the time.

After the Lord had asked me to write the books, after I had returned from my distant land of rebellion, I was writing of that time and had gone to bed tired and exhausted. The Lord spoke to me in the night that I had forgotten to write about the Korean girl, praying for me that he would become my husband. I asked the Lord if it was important because it was only one sentence. He told me it was very important, so the following morning I returned to that part of the manuscript and wrote the sentence. Immediately as I wrote, the Lord spoke to me – Prayers of the Flesh. I asked the Lord what He meant by that. Clear and gently and without condemnation, He explained to me that neither the Korean girl nor I had asked the Lord what His plans were for our lives. It was a 'name it and claim it' prayer out of the fleshly desires for a husband. It is witchcraft, using the words that we speak which I have already said have power to create, according to my will and desires.

But you say that the word of God tells us in Ask, Seek and Knock of Matthew 5 that anything that we ask for will be given to us. The Lord then teaches us about how to pray – for **His** Kingdom come, **His** will be done on earth – which means His Will be done in 'my life', as it is in heaven. If my heart has not yet been fully delivered and attuned to knowing the will of God for my life, the plans He has for me to be a blessing not a curse, and the fleshly desires are still controlling a part of my will, then when I pray for my will, or my Korean intercessor is praying like the widow who keeps knocking on the door repeatedly until she is given what she asks for because of her persistence... for my will – what is sown in the flesh shall reap in the flesh. An avocado tree cannot produce a mango, and works of the flesh cannot produce fruit of the Spirit.

It is important to ask the Lord how to pray for issues, it is important if we do not know His will then to ask – and it shall be given. Do we bother in prayer to Seek Him in order to find out from Him what His will is for a person so we can pray accordingly? I am thinking of the verse at the beginning of the Chapter that talks of babbling like the Pagans. Of course it can mean lengthy prayers to be seen and heard and admired by others, but I believe it is also about praying out of our own fountain of opinion and flesh for what we think we should pray for instead of diligently seeking the Lords will to be prayed.

My husband told me he 'upped' his hours of praying from two hours, to three and then four hours because he was praying for me. When I asked him what he was praying for me, he told me it was for God to change me to be the wife I am supposed to be for him. He was praying his own fleshly desires of the person I should be, instead of lifting me in love for the Lord to develop within me that which He has called me to be. Praying prayers of the flesh is witchcraft, it is no different than a witchdoctor casting a spell over someone for whatever someone else has requested, and the person themselves has not agreed to. And the power of words become life! This is a curse by others.

It is interesting to remember from the Chapter on Forgiveness, of the woman who had been sick for 20 years, despite attending all the healing services and having the leader pray for healing. Had the prayers for healing been answered, she would still be walking around with a bitter heart towards her landlady and would never have learnt about the true meaning of Forgiveness, not being an optional extra but a compulsory part of carrying our own cross to follow Jesus. I didn't ask because I was better than anyone else, I cried for help because I didn't know how to pray for healing.

I myself had experienced a sort of indignation after many people had been praying for healing of the back problem and find no healing take place. It was also becoming hard for me when people were asking to pray for me. They prayed lengthy prayers of deliverance and healing... and with great faith to see fulfilment there and then, it is not a criticism of their desire to pray with faith to see me free from such agony, yet none to my knowledge asked the Lord what He was doing or how to pray for me, because if they had, He would have told them that I was needing to trust Him in the pain. It is good to learn how to pray for the sick or how to pray deliverance to see people set free, but the first thing we need to develop is how to hear the voice of the Lord speaking to us, directing us how to pray for matters. Jesus is the lord of Hosts – the one who leads us into battle, He has got the battle plan – strategies from the Father who sees and knows all things... ours is to hear His plan and to pray according to His will... like Jesus who said that He does nothing except that which He hears from the Father.

Many people will argue that we don't need to ask the Lord, because it is His will that all be healed. I understand the heart of that because of the compassionate love the Father has towards us, but I didn't see it in practice through the ministry of Jesus. Yes, everyone that we are told about through the eye witnesses of Matthew, Mark Luke and John were healed, however, at the pool of Bethesda found in **John 5:2-9**, there were many waiting around the pool waiting for the waters to stir, and yet it was only one whom Jesus went to, and healed. Because that man's heart was ready, and the Father had directed Jesus specifically.

I once attended a John Wimber conference. We had to choose which daytime seminar to attend, and I didn't really know, so I chose the healing seminar. My friend asked me if I had something that needed healing, which I hadn't thought about, I wanted to learn how to pray for the sick, but suddenly I said 'yes I do'.... I have bunions on my feet. She laughed at me wondering if I was serious enough to think the Lord would want to heal my bunions. Before the seminar, I prayed and said to the Lord, that if He wanted to heal them, I knew He could give a word of knowledge to the ones holding the seminar. The time came when they were going to pray, as others watched... the first word of knowledge was "Bumps on the feet". That was good enough for me, I jumped up like someone who had just won a bingo line shouting 'House'... and they called me to the platform for prayer. Sitting me down and placing my feet on another chair, I began to wonder how it will feel to have the Lord miraculously take away the bunions. As they were waiting on the Lord, someone said there was something I needed to be forgiven. I said – oh no – been there, and done that, I know the Lord is going to heal the feet. (I thought maybe the person was a novice...) They prayed again, and again she said I need to know I am forgiven. I was a little impatient (many people also watching) and I said – no really, I know I am forgiven, please pray for my feet. She then spoke again that there were two reasons I needed to know forgiveness. As she said 'two' the Lord revealed to me the two abortions I had before I was a Christian... and I burst out crying. But I knew I had been forgiven, it had been dealt with... the woman then said –'you have been forgiven, but you have not forgiven yourself!' To not forgive oneself is to say that what Jesus did on the cross was not sufficient and therefor continue to punish yourself, actually it is inverted pride... I didn't know, and I wasn't being sarcastic, I was totally blown away by the revelation. Oh healing came that day – but it wasn't my bunions... something far more important to the Lord. I asked her please what about my bunions? She told me that if I had already had an open plan for the Lord to minister – He will use it to get you into the place of receiving what He wants to give. I believe the spiritual healing is higher priority on God's heart... I was so thankful for the woman who asked the Lord how to pray, despite the word of knowledge about bumps on the feet that brought me to that place of further healing and restoration.

Lord teach us to walk not in the ways of man trusting in our own understanding, but to seek Your face, that we might seek you in the secret place to hear the beating of your unconditional love for us all, and teach us how to pray Your will, according to your wisdom and understanding of the plans You have for us all. Forgive us for our pride and arrogance that we perform for the people rather than in the secret place for Your eyes only. Indeed help us to walk in Humility, to come as servants in our prayer life, and that as we humble ourselves before your throne, You will empower us by your Spirit to cause mountains to move, cause the rain clouds not to rain, for the sun not to shine, to still the storms and the seas or whatever else seems impossible, possible for those of us in the Will of Christ Jesus. Lord I pray, join us as we catch the **fox** of witchcraft in prayers of the flesh, **foxes** of pride and self-centeredness, the **foxes** of hypocrisy praying for others to change and yet unwilling to change ourselves first. Have mercy on us we pray, and give us the gift of obedience, to trust You in the pain, as we choose to forgive the unforgivable and love the unlovable. May we become like the Teacher, may be become more like You. Amen.

Matthew 6:1-4; 6:19-24; 6:25-34;
Matthew 19:16-30; 25:14-30
Luke 6:38; 12:13- 21; 16:1-15; 16:19-31;
Luke 18:18; 21:1-4

Money, Money, Money.

Matthew 6: 1-4

"Be careful not to practice your righteousness in front of others to be seen by them. If you do, you will have no reward from your Father in heaven. ² So when you give to the needy, do not announce it with trumpets, as the hypocrites do in the synagogues and on the streets, to be honoured by others. Truly I tell you, they have received their reward in full. ³ But when you give to the needy, do not let your left hand know what your right hand is doing, ⁴ so that your giving may be in secret. Then your Father, who sees what is done in secret, will reward you." (NIV: 5)

I wanted to start with this verse as it follows from the previous chapter I have written, where everything God is asking for is to be done for Him and Him alone, to be done in secrecy. The righteousness would be good acts which come with faith... if we truly believe, then our obedience will produce good works, but it is not good works alone that can give us Salvation. I have heard it preached that the Hebrew word for righteousness is virtually the same word as for generosity. I am not a scholar in languages but something I know from God's word is that God is a generous God – He gives to His children, saying that we are to be like Him and give to others.

Luke 6: 38 Give, and it will be given to you. A good measure, pressed down, shaken together and running over, will be poured into your lap. For with the measure you use, it will be measured to you." (NIV: 5)

We have read of His generosity in the parable in the chapter of the prodigal son that the workers who were hired in the morning were paid the same as those who worked only one hour... and the workers of the day had been jealous and angry because of the Masters generosity to give all the same. The Fathers generosity is the sacrifice of His son, to pay our debts, His generosity is His grace. It is a gift which we do not deserve.

I have also heard it preached that there were always collection bowls at the synagogue entrances on the street, which were the collections on a daily basis for the poor. The bowls were shaped like a trumpet at the top, narrowing and then like a round bowl at the bottom, to prevent people's hands entering and take money out. When people would throw in their money it would make a noise when done hard. It was often done so people could hear that many coins were being put in because of the noise they made. It is where the saying "Blowing your own trumpet" comes from. Of course we use that term when we are boasting before others... and it comes from this time when the Pharisees amongst others wanted people to know when they have put money in for the poor!

What did Jesus have to say about this? Well in line with everything so far discussed, it was to be done in secret, so much so that it said don't even let your left hand know what your right hand is giving. The Lord once again is talking of the heart attitude.

I will be honest, in the western world I am accustomed to a plate, or a covered plate being passed to collect the offerings where you can place your hand in covering what you are giving. In the Baptist church where I was first saved they had a cloth bag on a stick, so it didn't make a noise either. Later it became that church members would have envelopes they could place their offerings in to keep the giving secret.

In Africa they have large baskets at the front of the church and people get up to put the money or chicken or sugar cane or rice into the basket, but I have also witnessed something else. A member of the church would stand and share of the special needs, it could be to pay the electric bill or it could be a specific collection for someone in need. They say how much they need, then ask for givers, and one time it was a family needing to get to the hospital and also for the bill for urgent treatment. I went up to the front to give a note which was folded and not visible for all to see but to my shock and horror the pastor unfolded the note and announced how much I had given before the whole church. I felt embarrassed and also something in my spirit was very uncomfortable. I witnessed something similar in a different church, so it wasn't something just the one church did. This time I refused to give until after when the service was finished, rather than have it announced and used as a way to bludgeon people to give. I have also experienced a very controlled manner of giving of the offerings, after first the tithes have been collected. The amount of the note being given is mentioned and those giving that much stand and take their gifts... then next lower note amount is mentioned, and people giving this then rise and walk forward, and so-on 'til the smallest amount is called forward. It means everyone sees who gives what amount, it is a public scene. I had mentioned my concern of this to my host and I believe my complaint of this way of collecting the offerings came back to the pastor, because on the microphone the next week he made a public announcement that this was biblical and that he was closer to the bible than the one disagreeing with it. He stated he was as the high priest who examines the offering being sacrificed... but again I disagree with that because Jesus became our High Priest and He alone is to see and know what our offerings are. Money given in this way becomes the same as blowing the trumpet, although he says we are all a family and nothing is hidden within a family. Do not misunderstand, this pastor is not demeaning in any way the large or the small, for he calls it out according to what each have been blessed with, so it is not done with intent of embarrassing those who give little. After this offering people have returned to their seats, having given their tithes and then offerings, and then on the way out all are to pass again by the front table on the way out to leave a love offering... and this is done at virtually every meeting, be it the morning service or the afternoon Bible study or the mid-week Bible studies. I have not come across anywhere in the Bible where it announces what is being given for all to see and hear... but the Lord does speak of doing the charitable works and giving is one of those, to be done in secret.

Of course there is the story of the couple Ananias and Saphira in Acts 5, lying about the amount they received when they sold a plot of land withholding some in secret for themselves. It was however something which the Holy Spirit had brought to Peter's attention... otherwise he would not know... God has not told all landowners that they must sell their land and or possessions to place it at the feet of the pastors for it to be distributed out... it is something which had been instructed by the Spirit. They had been obedient to sell the land, but they had not been honest about the amount and they both lied. Again it is back to Obedience is better than sacrifice... it is a matter of the heart.

I have always loved that parable in **Luke 21:1-4**, where the rich man placed in a large amount – visible to Jesus, but the old lady put in a single small coin. Jesus says – she gave the most! The rich man had given just a small part of a vast amount, but the old woman had given everything she had! It was not the amount that blessed the Lord, but the generous heart from which it was given.

Jesus goes on to talk about storing up treasures in heaven. Again He is speaking against storing up the things of this world and what money can buy, because the things of this world cannot be taken with us when we die, and neither can it buy us into the Kingdom of God.

Matthew 6:19-24 "Do not store up for your selves treasures on earth where moth and rust destroy, and where thieves break in and steal, but store up for yourselves things in heaven where moth and rust do not destroy; and where thieves do not break in and steal. For where your treasure is, there your heart will also be... (and continues to talk of light and darkness)... **No-one can serve two masters. Either he will hate the one and love the other or he will be devoted to the one and despise the other. You cannot serve both God and money."** (NIV:5)

Luke 12:13-21; Also in this parable, Jesus Condemns Greed.

13Just then someone spoke up from the crowd and said, "Master, You should tell my older brother that he has to divide the family inheritance and give me my fair share!" 14Jesus answered, "My friend, you can't expect Me to help you with this. It's not My business to settle arguments between you and your brother. That's yours to settle." 15Then speaking to the people Jesus continued, "Be alert and guard your heart from greed and always wishing for what you don't have! For your life can never be measured by the amount of things you possess!" 16Jesus gave them this illustration: "A wealthy land owner had a farm that produced bumper crops. In fact, it filled his barns to overflowing! 17He thought to himself, 'What should I do

now that every barn is full and I have nowhere else to store more? ¹⁸I know what I'll do! I'll tear down the barns and build one massive barn that will hold all my grain and goods! ¹⁹Then I can just sit back surrounded with comfort and ease. I'll enjoy life with no worries at all!' ²⁰"But God suddenly spoke to him saying, 'What a fool you are to trust in your riches and not in Me. This very night the messengers of death are demanding to take your life! Then who will get all the wealth you have stored up for yourself?' ²¹This is what will happen to all those who fill up their lives with everything but God!" (TPT:2)

This is without need of explanation, the words of Jesus are clear, and yet the western world spend millions of pounds or dollars on homes, cars, and possessions, on expensive soft furnishings not to mention jewelled collars for their dogs and complete outfits costing thousands of dollars. It is completely out of proportion and then you see how the people in the third world live, with hardly money for a bowl of rice to eat or a glass of water.

Indeed I know people in the western world who have been generous giving to others and helping those in need and in return the Lord has blessed them with more as said, pressed down, shaken together and running over. God blesses a cheerful giver. If everyone gave to those in need instead of filling up their own barns, the world would be a richer place.

The Old Testament is very clear on looking after the widows, the women whose husbands are dead with no-one to provide for them, and the poor. The West, once again is very good to pay someone else to look after the elderly, and the governments have been left to look after the poor and the widowed, so people see their share from work as their own and indeed will store it up for their own good - after all they worked for it – they put in the extra hard work.

The church in the beginning was a place of sharing all things, trusting in God who already knew their needs, and provide for them.

Matthew 6:25-34

Jesus tells us not to worry about anything as worrying cannot change a thing. He teaches us that the birds of the air do not worry about what to eat, and the flowers don't concern themselves about a thing – likening our clothes to the lilies of the field. The Lord knows we need these things, if He will provide for the birds and the flowers how much more will He provide for you and me.

This is a big area for me, linked with the independent spirit, and trusting God for all things, to be totally dependent on Him. Of course God has given us gifts and talents that we can use to earn an honest wage, it is not that we should go around begging from others if we have the chance to work, but it is not to put what I can do before the Lord. Not that long ago, the Lord asked me to give up my flat and sell my possessions to be obedient to the call He has placed upon my life. For the last twelve months He has been showing me fear, fear of ill health, fear of lack of finances. Where there is fear there can be no trust. If a husband or wife fears their spouse being unfaithful, it is because there is no trust. When the Lord asked me to trust Him in the pain, He has been working to show me that His perfect love casts out all fear. The truth remains also for finances. There are some who totally disagreed with my decision at my age to do what I am doing. I am sixty years old and should be focused on living a comfy life, and paying into a life policy and insurances and pension funds so when I reach sixty five or sixty seven I think it is now before I reach my pensionable age, I will be able to live still a good life. When the Lord was challenging me to step out of the boat and trust Him, at that time I had to choose between what friends thought and what God was saying. The Lord was so clear in speaking to me; I chose to take the step of obedience. It was in that step, He has been revealing the areas of fear – **foxes**, and teaching me to catch them and evict them from the garden. I continue to say – I am not writing this book as one who is perfect, on the contrary, I am being taken by the master Fox Hunter, to teach me how to catch **foxes**. We are doing it together.

It is hard to trust. My family may have had two incomes when I was little, but my mother somehow knew how to lose the family fortunes if ever there were any. In my marriage, having opened a joint bank account, I was in fear when my husband spent virtually the contents of the account on a sheepskin coat in the middle of summer at the beginning of the month, leaving virtually no money for food for the rest of the month. His answer to me was basically that now I will have to fast and lose weight. Such things happening cause you to take care of yourself because no-one else will do it for you. I created another account in my name and transferred an amount every month for food and household needs and emergencies that he could not touch because it was in my name. I was a survivor, and a survivor often becomes independent in order to survive.

I will be honest I thought selling my things would be difficult emotionally, but it was not. It happened within a month, and without doubt with the blessing of the Lord. Am I a joyful and generous giver? It is something I am learning to be. I am willing in some areas of my life to give without question, but financially it is a lesson I am learning.

We know what the Bible has to say about tithing, from the Old Testament, where one tenth is to be given to the Lord – the church, but I believe the Lord is looking for us to give out of our hearts over and above what He is asking, because He tells us that the measure in which we give will be given to us... back to the heart of free will instead of plain obedience in the exact amount He told us to give and nothing more. I guess this giving would be looked as offerings and love offerings.

Clearly the words of Jesus are telling us not to worry about anything, not even about tomorrow. Someone was preaching and said, do not put off giving tomorrow what you can give today. Giving of course is not just about money, but the Lord is clearly talking of money being a god – contrary to the first Commandment to have no other Gods before Him.

Matthew 19:16-30... The Rich Young Ruler.

This rich young man came to ask how he can get eternal life. In Matthew it says what good thing can I do to receive eternal life, however in **Luke 18:18**, it is written that the man called Jesus 'good teacher', whereby Jesus asks why he calls him good because no-one is good except for God. Hereafter he asks the young man in both accounts if he knows the Commandments. When asked which ones, Jesus tells him about not to commit adultery, murder, steal or bear false witness or lie, honour your father and mother and to love your neighbour as yourself, to which the young man told Jesus he had kept them all! Jesus then tells him to go and sell all his possessions and give the money to the poor then follow Him. He told him that by doing this he would have treasure in heaven. The young man was very sad because he was a very wealthy man. Jesus said to the disciples after this man had left that it was difficult for a rich man to enter the Kingdom of Heaven, because often those with money make it to be the God they serve and love money more than they love God. Idolatry in the first degree.

I love what He says though it puzzled me for a long time as a new believer... It is easier for a camel to pass through the eye of a needle than for a rich man to enter the Kingdom of God. Of course it is impossible for a camel to enter through the eye of a needle. These days in my slightly older years I find it hard to pass a sewing thread through the eye of a needle – though of course that is to do with my own eyesight. Why would God say that, other than to express the impossibility, **but that with God all things are possible**, and there are rich men and women who have learned to love God before their wealth? A missionary who some years later was to become a friend of mine, was visiting the home church from India, and stood to tell a story for the children. She described that in India – in the old days when there were walls built around the cities, there was always a small oval headed door, and was set into the large wooden gates. People arriving by camel at night after the large gates had been locked shut to prevent attack, would first have to get off the camel, and unload all the baggage being carried on the camel, and then the camel would have to enter through the gate on its knees. In India they called this small door – "The eye of a needle". What a wonderful picture of how we can enter into the Kingdom of Heaven, on our knees of humility, and stripped bare of all baggage. So no possessions can enter through the door with the camel. We cannot take our wealth and lavishly furnished palaces or houses with us. All of these things will either be destroyed by the moth or rust – they are temporal and of no heavenly use. Despite this word, how so many start off with good intent, but as the wealth increases, it usurps the place of the Lord. I don't have to spell out the **fox** here. It seems very obvious.

The last part of Jesus teaching here I think is very strong. Though it is not just about money, but about all forms of idolatry... **"Everyone who has left houses, or brothers or sisters, or father or mother, or children or fields for <u>My sake</u> will receive a hundred times as much and will inherit eternal life. But many who are first will be last and the last will be first."** (NIV:5)

Clearly the Lord is showing us that even our family members can become greater than the Lord – another form of idolatry. He is a jealous God, and though He wants us to love one another and our family with an unconditional love, it must not be greater than our love for the Lord our God. I also realise that it is not how we start with the Lord but how we finish!

When I was at the beginning of my return as the prodigal, I can remember crying out to the Lord wanting to be the Fenella I was before I had married and all had gone wrong. I wanted to be the missionary that prayed for the sick and cast out demons as I did in the past; I saw her as the perfect Christian. I received a word – it was so clear... "Can bread become wheat again, or wine become the grape again? No, forget the things of the past, do you not see that I am doing a new thing." Of course the Lord teaches that we cannot put new wine into an old wineskin, because it will tear and will lose both the wine and the wine sack. **Matthew 9:17**

The wine sack was a bag made from animal skin. When wine was poured into it as a new skin, it would absorb the wine and stretch the skin. The practice would be that when the skin was empty it would be steeped in water and the skin would shrink back to the size when it was new, so when new wine is added, it will stretch again. If the skin is not shrunk back and fresh wine poured in, then the skin will continue to stretch and burst because it has no more stretch in it. God was telling me the past is finished, and He is preparing a new skin to hold the fresh wine of His love. Of course five years later the Lord has been revealing that I was far from the perfect Christian, and the more I became aware of my own wretchedness and the **foxes** within the garden, the more I was glad that I was not to be the person I was before. I share this because some of us start out really on fire for the Lord, but we lose our passion, and the light goes dim. Others may be late comers to Christ, living a terrible life of sin, but at the last hour, turn and repent, and their inheritance is the Kingdom of God. It is not how we start the race that matters, it is how we finish! All ten virgins were dressed ready, but only half of them were found with oil for their lamps, the others in the end missed the boat so to speak, because whilst they were gone to get more oil, because it had burned up and finished, the Bridegroom came and took those who were ready and waiting. I do believe that the oil is not transferable, in other words we cannot attain Heaven living off someone else's relationship with the Lord.

Luke 16: 19-31

Parable about the Rich man and Lazarus. Lazarus was a beggar who sat at the gates of the rich man, waiting for the crumbs from the rich man's table to fall. It says that he was so poor and his needs were great, he had sores on his body that the dogs would come and lick clean for him. The time came when both men died, and the rich man went to hell and was burning there. He looked up and across a gap, there he saw Lazarus with Abraham. The rich man asked Father Abraham to send Lazarus to dip his finger in the water and to feed it to him to cool him down from the agony of the fire. Abraham reminded the once rich man, that during his time here on the earth he had many fineries that he enjoyed whilst Lazarus had none, receiving only the bad things in life. Now in the after-life, Lazarus has the good things of eternity to comfort him, and the once rich man has the bad.

I think this is the only time where it is recorded that Jesus speaks directly of someone in hell, who happened to be rich and totally unconcerned for the poor of this world. The word of God is very clear throughout, that the followers of Christ will have the same heart for the poor as He did. When Jesus was found, it was always with the poor and needy or the sinners such as prostitutes and tax collectors. In fact in **Matthew 25:31-46**, almost at the end before He is arrested, Jesus is trying to inform of the things that will happen in the last days, he talks of separating the goats from the sheep - the sheep to His right and the goats to His left. He says to those on his right – the sheep, to come forth because when He was hungry they fed Him, and when He was thirsty they gave Him water to drink, He was a stranger and they invited Him in, when he needed clothes they clothed Him and when He was sick they looked after Him. When He was in prison, they visited Him.

Those as sheep seemed confused asking when did they visit Him and do all the things He had just said. Jesus replied that when they did it to the very least of the brothers of His, it was done unto Him. Jesus goes on to say to the goats that as much as they did not do such things for the least of Jesus brothers – they did not do it to Him, and were told to depart from Him, to eternal punishment.

God is the God of unconditional love, who, if anyone hears His word and obeys, will receive eternal life, as the Bride of Christ, and to reign together with Him, but those who have had wealth and their time in this world, and did not use it to share with the poor the orphaned, the widows, and the sick and the downtrodden and the unrighteous of this world, will not be fit for the Kingdom of God.

Luke 16:1-13 The Story of the Dishonest Manager

Jesus is clearly talking in this parable about honesty and good stewardship. The manager for the estate was mismanaging the money, and when the master hears of it, he calls in the manager to account for everything, and that his job had now been terminated. Knowing he was to be without work, he panics and plans how he can find favour with others by continuing to cheat his employer. He uses a term that he can't dig... which could refer to the fact that he is used to an office job and cannot go to work the fields, however the original Aramaic word used was to say that his misdeeds could not be hidden...

¹⁰"The one who manages the little they have been given with faithfulness and integrity will be promoted and trusted with greater responsibilities. But those who cheat with the little they have been given will not be considered trustworthy to receive more. ¹¹If you have not handled the riches of this world with integrity, why should you be trusted with the eternal treasures of the spiritual world? ¹²And if you've not been proven faithful with what belongs to another, why should you be given wealth of your own? ¹³It is simply impossible for a person to serve two masters at the same time. You will be forced to love one and reject the other. One master will be despised and the other will have your loyal devotion. It is no different with God and the wealth of this world. (The word used here is "mammon" which is money personified as a god that is worshipped.) You must enthusiastically love one—and definitively reject the other!" (TPT:2)

Especially in verse 10 as he explains the parable, those who are given little and are trustworthy with that will be given more, but whoever is dishonest with the little they have will also be dishonest with much. In other words He tells us if we are not trustworthy handling the wealth of this world, then who will trust us with true riches? The riches of heaven...

and then it says if we are not trustworthy with others property, who then will give you property of your own?

I want to just say at this point it does not just mean about money, I think also as property especially rented property where the tenants have no respect for the building because it is not their own, allowing it to become in great need and cost to the owner for re-decoration. I have heard terrible stories of house owners who have had tenants from hell, causing great damage to the property. Failing to keep it clean, allowing all kinds of spills to the carpets that in the end the carpet is beyond cleaning, but needs to be ripped out and replaced... furniture being broken because children have been allowed to jump all over it for example, burn marks on the wooden tables because of fallen burning cigarettes, or hot cups and plates left to mark the wood, or children scratching the tables thinking it is fun to write their name in the wood. If someone borrows a friend's car, and allows the children to jump in and out of it playing, when it is not their own car, or indeed any other kind of borrowed or rented item, it is wrong! I live in a place where it seems expensive items such as mobile phones are allowed to be played on by small children, who fall and break the glass.... no care for such items thinking they can be replaced so easily. We live in a world where we are helped to communicate across the globe within seconds and for many these are tools to help business and in case of emergency, yet they are allowed freely to be used as a toy by the small who have not yet learnt the value and cost of such things.

I am aware whilst living in Africa, that nothing has a 'value' to children. I had bought a brush – long handled and an extendable handled broom for cleaning the ceiling in corners etc. Within twelve months the brush handle had been broken and not a few months later the extendable brush broken and the brush laying discarded in the garden. They have toys to play with, a large garden, animals etc.... but still they had to play with items bought as tools not toys. No-one thought to say sorry, or even tell of the damages. To buy these two items does not break the bank, however, in the western culture, we would buy such things and they would last a long, long time... the brush head would wear out before the handle. Western culture tends to think by taking care of things we can use money elsewhere instead of keep having to replace broken items... but here it doesn't seem to be part of anyone's thinking. One day I found the young boy crying in the living room, and asked what was wrong. His baby sister had been playing with a toy he was given for Christmas, and had already within days broken off the leg of the toy. He was heartbroken... I tried to use this to explain how it feels when I had bought things to keep the house clean, but they had been misused and broken. It is not about the money as such – but trying to teach good stewardship. Items for the house, that normally in the west would last for years, be it buckets and wash basins, seem to break and get damaged within such a short time... but they do not have the money to replace them. Is there a spiritual principal here to be learned to see some of the poverty turned around into blessings of abundance?

We need to teach and even to be taught about good stewardship.

On stewardship I would like to add here that our children are not ours. We have been made caretakers of infants that we will instruct and teach them in the ways and of the love of God, so they will grow to make right decisions. I believe often children are considered a disturbance of the things we need to do. We yell and scream instruction, but rarely do we give the time to lovingly teach by example. I see often the duties of the home become more important than the care and discipleship of the young. Keeping dangerous objects out of reach from small children is a huge thing in Europe, but in Africa I see knives left lying on the floors where the babies can pick them, often by the blade, try walking with them in hand... needing only to stumble as they do learning to walk, and fall on the blade piercing the body or even cutting off a finger, or deep wounds, and then hearing parents say – they learn by their mistakes! No, they are to learn by our care and instruction, making sure 'til they are old enough to understand, dangerous objects are kept out of reach. We are stewards of these precious young ones... we need to see the value of each and every one and know that we will be held accountable. Our role as mother is higher than our role as dishwasher and house cleaner. As parents we need to understand that more energy and time is required to teach – disciple our children when they are young... and fathers your role is higher than any other. We see many fathers involved in church ministry, but the children never see them. The fathers have time to take care of others in the church but not with their own children. What is it worth that we spend a lifetime preaching for others to be saved, and find our own children did not because they never understood the truth of who God is, based one their own father was never there or showed any interest.

The truth is, we believe that what we work for is ours. It is a lie of the devil. Everything we have comes from the Lord, and it is given to us as stewards to take care of it and use it wisely. The gifts and talents that we have enabling us to work and earn living, first come from the Creator who gave us all that we would need for the purposes He had ordained for us since the beginning of time. We have all had a choice to take care of the talents, to train them to be better and therefore reap more of the blessing – but what we were given we were given from the Lord.

Matthew 25:14-30

The parable of the man who was going away and entrusted his property to his servants and gave them talents of money according to their abilities to take care of 'til he returns. One who was given five put the talents to work and gained five more, another was given two talents, and gained two more, and the master called the good and faithful servants who had been faithful with the few things that now they can be trusted with many and to share in the master's happiness. But the one who was given only one, did nothing with it other than to bury it until the master returned and he gave him the one talent back. The master was angry with this last one calling him wicked and lazy, because he could have at least put into a bank to make interest for when the master returned.

What has God given to you in gifts and talents? What have you done with them, have you trained them and put them to good use that made them increase for the master when He returns? Or have you thought that the Lord is a hard task master reaping where He has not sown, therefore give him back only what he first gave you? Everything He has given to us – was and is for the purpose of the Kingdom of God to come, here on earth as it is in heaven. What have we done with what He gave us? Have we put it to good use to accrue for ourselves a comfy lifestyle, surrounded by fine things, costly holidays, expensive cars, and when the King returns you give Him the original talent back, having kept the profits for yourself and your rich friends?

It seems to me that of all the sins and **foxes** in the teachings of Jesus, the group he is harshest towards are the rich, proud and arrogant, who have no cares for the poor, sick, needy, prisoners, or strangers, who are self-absorbed in all the pleasures of this world and building their own little kingdoms of self.

Matthew 5:31-32; 19:4-9
Luke 16:18

 Divorce

Matthew 5:31-32

"It has been said, 'Whoever divorces his wife must give her legal divorce papers. 32 However, I say to you, if anyone divorces his wife for any reason, except for infidelity, causes her to commit adultery, and whoever marries a divorced woman commits adultery." (TPT: 1)

"Furthermore it has been said, 'Whoever divorces his wife, let him give her a certificate of divorce.' But I say to you that whoever divorces his wife for any reason except sexual immorality causes her to commit adultery; and whoever marries a woman who is divorced commits adultery" **(NKJV: 6)**

Marriage is a binding and sacred agreement, not just between a man and a woman, but between man, woman and God! God takes very seriously when we make an oath, a promise, for he is faithful and fulfils His promises to us, and expects the same of us to Him, and one another. Marriage is not just a partnership of business. Two people can partner in a business and remain two, however in marriage there is a sealing of the Spirit where two become one.

This is a big one, and what I write may offend – it is not intended in any way to do so, and once again, I am writing this as a divorced woman! I am not condemning anyone – because whatever situation you are in whilst reading this, I believe the Grace of God is covering.

Let it be said once again, when I married in 1990, I was intent on doing so despite what anyone else thought about it. I truly thought at the time it was from the Lord, it is only with hindsight and the Lords healing and restoration, He has brought me to a place to see that it was my will and not His. It went wrong after eleven days, when I was given the option of continuing the marriage or continuing to serve in the mission. I could not do both. I am not condemning my husband in any way – for the Lord has revealed much to me since, however at the time I was blinded by my own pride and rebellion. The marriage was a disaster, and although we remained together in total for seven years, it was a living hell and I think it is safe to say that for both of us, though at the time I thought I was the only victim in the marriage. Having planned my suicide as a form of escape, and the Lord's hand that kept me from doing it, again it is documented in the second book Rejoice... The Bricks have Fallen... Enough was enough! I could not take any more of the control and manipulation. Often he had suggested going out to have sex with someone so as to give me the freedom to divorce, and instead of accepting his offer, I argued back that I thought it was unfair that he should get to have all the fun, and I would go out to give him the freedom of divorce. Word of warning – beware of the words that you speak!

I filed for divorce, and it was all in place, but he refused to divorce me on the grounds of his faith. I could not understand that for one moment, because if his faith had meant anything, then he would have loved me as Jesus loves the church, not through control, manipulation and fear. I was divorcing him not on the grounds of sexual immorality but domestic violence – emotional abuse. During the time I waited for it to go to court, I fell in sin. As such, I was then – although separated, according to the word of God in adultery. My husband was now free to divorce me... but he wouldn't. It was agreed that we can wait two years of separation and then the divorce would go through regardless. Again I will not go into the story here, but eight months after the court hearing to which my husband refused to attend, the man I was newly involved with, died. Following his death, I received news that my husband was now willing to divorce me... I was free. I met my husband a year later when I went to Denmark, and we were amiable and friendly with each other, and he told me then that he had heard of the relationship I was in, and refused the divorce so as to protect me, because he did not want me to marry him. When he heard of the death, he released the divorce papers and it went through immediately. He actually proposed to me again, suggesting that it was

God's will for us to be together and we should re-marry, but I could not go back into what I had suffered behind closed doors, hidden from all.

In my heart I believed I would find another to marry – it happens all the time, people divorcing and re-marrying in the church, and living happy lives. I began seeing someone from my workplace, not a Christian, but a kind man. The Lord had also asked me to step back from ministry in the church that I had been involved in because he wanted to do something in my life. He was about to show me the **foxes** of anger and bitterness in my heart. I was already in rebellion being in a relationship with a non-believer secretly and serving in the church, I was on the slippery slide seemingly without any control to stop...

I had decided to call my mother-in-law on a specific day when their football team was playing against England, expecting to find everyone sat around waiting for the match to start. No-one was there but her, my father-in-law had died. She told me that my husband had re-married, a woman from the church whose husband had left her for another woman. She told me that they have a baby girl. When I said previously that I have murdered many times in my thoughts, this is when it began. I was not angry he was re-married, but the child hurt me. I thought I had been pregnant twice in the marriage, and he prayed over me casting out demons! I hated him for that because it made me feel ugly and worthless, yes also insignificant. That night began recurring dreams of hatred where I saw my husband on the floor on his back, and I with my stiletto high heels using them like a knife to his stomach. (I want to add at this point as I am in India, that the goddess Kali, which is the same as Jezebel, is pictured with her foot on the stomach of a man on his back under her total control with cutting objects in her hands wearing a necklace of men's severed heads around her neck – she is a man hater, and I am seeing the connection of this for the first time as I am writing now. The Jezebel spirit of control and manipulation at this time had not yet been revealed to me.) For sure in my heart at this point I was in total hatred towards my husband – hence the link to **Matthew 5: 27-30**.

There was no way I was in a position to forgive... and no-one suggested that I should as far as I remember. I hated him with every beat of my heart and he deserved it – that is how I felt at the time... and this was the turning point when I shouted out to God in anger, that if that was the best husband He could give me, I would go out and find myself a better one! That was my moment of complete insanity so to speak, when I turned my back in outright rebellion, with one thing in mind, to find another husband.

I was desperate! Desperate to love and be loved. I searched high and low, but no-one matched up to my desire, and the one that I wanted – the non-believer, didn't want to marry me. I went through another time of planning my suicide, I was sick twice with work related stress, and then when I was hoping to marry a descendent of a Pharaoh from Egypt, I became seriously sick. It was expected I would be in a wheelchair for life, and I moved to live in Malta because the weather would be better for my condition... and the search continued to love and be loved. I cannot tell to what depths I stooped to in those angry years, but I can say, there was nothing good in me... I know!

I met and found someone who loved me and proposed. We were set to marry, I had the dress, we had booked the honeymoon and paid for the venue, when suddenly I came to my senses, and realised I didn't love him, I was only in love with the idea of being married. To everyone's surprise including my own, I cancelled everything including the relationship just seven weeks before the wedding! The wedding was planned for the end of June, and it was November that year when I was beginning to consider the possibilities of returning to the Lord. It was a time when the Lord started connecting me with long lost Christian friends; it was the Lord wooing me back. My come-back was three months later in the February of the following year. I believe Jesus was the one who had opened the eyes of my heart to begin to see again.

Two years after my return to the Lord, in 2012, suddenly, whilst reading my Bible, I came across the scripture written by Paul in the letter to the Corinthians. I had seen it many times and probably never read it, skipping over it – I don't know, but this time it was like there was the brightest spotlight shining upon the scripture to read. Paul wrote about Married, Single, Widowed and Divorced. He clearly wrote that it is not the will of God for a divorced person to re-marry. It is adultery. He also clearly states that "the Lord says, not Paul". I am not going to review it further here because the Lord wants me to focus on His words.

You would have thought that this scripture would bring anger and pain back towards God because I still hadn't found a husband, but instead, I began to cry pure tears of joy! I realised that the reason the Lord had not given me another husband was because I would have been committing and causing the new husband also to commit adultery. I had been asking why for so long... Why had my marriage been such a disaster? Why did I not have another husband? At least now He had shown me His word, and that for me to marry again would just be heaping more sin into the fire that needed to be put out.

Before I go further with this – you may be a divorced person re-married, and you are feeling angry towards what I have written. Please stay with me and follow through with me. I believe that where we have been misled and unknowing of the truth I believe that is where the grace of God is. This is not the end of life as we know it – there is nothing that can separate us from the love of God and His forgiveness when we come to Him with a contrite heart. Remember Samson who was one of the Judges of Israel, used of God, he was an adulterer! So was David with Bathsheba with the added sin of murder to his list. God's grace was with them. It does not give us permission to willfully sin, but if you are remarried, I believe that you are forgiven, though I do believe that He would have us come before His throne of grace and acknowledge what His words actually say, asking Him to forgive us for hidden rebellion in our heart as we did not know what we were doing. (I say this because Jesus from the cross spoke out to the Father on behalf of all us; "Father forgive them they know not what they do." He understood that mankind was blinded, walking in deception. (Someone who is deceived does not know they are deceived, because they are deceived)) What it does – it will stop the accuser from coming in and bringing about condemnation, and the Lord may reveal other areas of hidden rebellion that are hindering you from moving into the deeper relationship that you long for, and release the fullness of God's grace.

If you are divorced and in a relationship with a view to getting married, I would suggest to you both that you both come before the Lord with an open and surrendered heart to know His will... not in false humility as I have already described earlier in the previous chapter, but truly willing to hear what the Lord says to you. and a willingness to obey.

Let me continue with my own story on this matter. I had already closed the door maybe eighteen months earlier. I had closed the door by surrendering my desire to be married after the Lord had shown me in a dream of being in the lions mouth and it was about to close. It was sometime in the months of November/December 2010. I spoke of it earlier in the book. I repented, and as if then the Holy Spirit went to work in my heart to heal and restore, to later bring me revelation and understanding. There are many people who felt they should challenge me on this matter. When I was writing the Rejoice books, and writing a chapter about this revelation, sharing it with someone to ask for their feedback on it. The feedback I received was that it was seemingly legalistic. That may well have been the case, because during that time the Lord had not yet revealed to me the religious spirit within me, of which legalism would be a part, so it could have been in the manner in which I had written it. That chapter was for the third book – yet to be published so I left it for a while and prayed over it several times. Because of it – I put the book on hold.

Others challenged me saying that the penalty for adultery was death, and as my husband is remarried he is as such in adultery and therefore would have been dead giving me freedom to re-marry but for the fact we are not barbaric people putting people to death anymore. I thought about this – and this also doesn't ring true. I have mentioned the woman found in adultery and Jesus who could have stoned her because He was sinless refused to do so – rather pardoning her of her sins. He asked her where were they that condemned her, and she said there were none because all had walked away. He said; "Neither do I condemn you, go and sin no more!"

Jesus did not come to destroy or to kill; He came to give life in abundance, through the forgiveness of sins. Therefore my husband is not dead because Jesus paid the price for him, me and each and every one of us. Therefore my husband is still alive, and so according to Jesus' word, I do not believe I am free to re-marry:

Matthew 19:3-9

"Is it lawful for a man to divorce his wife for any reason?" 4"Haven't you read the Scriptures about creation?" Jesus replied; "The Creator made us male and female from the very beginning, 5 and 'For this

reason a man will leave his father and mother and live with his wife. And the two will become one flesh.' 6 From then on, they are no longer two, but united as one. So what God unites let no one divide!" 7They responded; "So then why did Moses command us to give a certificate of divorce and it would be lawful?" 8Jesus said, "Moses permitted you to divorce because your hearts are so hard and stubborn, but originally there was no such thing. 9But I say to you, whoever leaves his wife for any reason other than immorality, then takes another wife is living in adultery. And whoever takes a divorced woman in marriage is also living in adultery."(TPT: 1)

Luke 16:18

18 "It is wrong for you to divorce to cover your lust for another wife— that is adultery. And when you take that one you have lusted after as your wife, and contribute to the breakup of her marriage, you are once again guilty of adultery."(TPT: 2)

[18] "Whoever divorces his wife and marries another commits adultery; and whoever marries her who is divorced from *her* husband commits adultery." (NKJV: 6))

These words by Jesus as recorded by Luke are very clear that the Lord himself is saying that remarriage after divorce is committing adultery, though the translation in TPT seems to attach it to divorcing because of the desires to marry another causes adultery.

From the beginning it was intended that only death can separate what God has put together. Paul clearly communicates this that a widowed person is free to re-marry but only to a fellow believer, it is unlawful to marry an unbeliever – to be unequally yoked. To be divorced means we can be free from living with the spouse, but in God's eyes what He put together in marriage cannot be broken except in death of one or the other.

I am divorced and to be honest I was the adulterer, and if anyone marries me it says in the last part of verse nine that he would become an adulterer. I believe that it is permissible to divorce because of sexual immorality only because we are with hardened hearts, stubborn people, but it does not say that it is permissible to re-marry.

I continue to look at these words of Jesus, saying that except for immorality. Immorality here is not specified as sexual immorality and therefore violence of either emotional or physical can come under that term... if I found my husband was a bank robber or a murderer such things are also immoral – am I at liberty to divorce for those reasons too? Because I was the adulterer having a sexual relationship whilst I was separated from my husband and not yet divorced, does it mean that my husband was the victim and therefore free to re-marry? His new wife was the victim in her first marriage – was she now free to re-marry.... And that the guilty party such as I am not? And what of forgiveness and grace? I heard an amazing preach by someone that was so convincingly good to say it is ok to start again with another marriage. He said in the Old Testament, God divorced Israel, and that is why He hates divorce because of the pain involved in such a separation. He talked with such great compassion and love for the people who married young and it was disaster, are they then intended to live the rest of their life paying a punishment because of their early mistakes... or the wife who was being beaten daily who finally divorces and is given the chance to find love and happiness again in a new marriage... or a husband whose wife is repeatedly gambling all the money of the family away.... Indeed such sad stories and he talks of God's love and grace. He talks about the history behind the questions asked because of two views about marriage and they wanted to know which one of them Jesus supported... and I have seen this twice, and both times there is something in me that says "looking for loopholes", "**foxes**". I do not know...

I recently had a vision regarding marriage. I was in a kitchen, and before me were certain ingredients: flour, margarine or butter, sugar and eggs. All were measured to exact proportions required to make a "Victoria Sandwich Cake". There was a mixing bowl of marriage (a public declaration of commitment for life between one man and one woman) and a whisk (the intimacy of consummation through intercourse).

In the mixing bowl of marriage the four ingredients were beaten together with the whisk of sexual intimacy. Once the marriage was consummated through intercourse, there were no longer four ingredients, but one combined wet mass called 'cake dough'. The act of consummation had changed its complete form, and now it was impossible to separate the four ingredients, because four had now been blended into one mass. This mass was then turned into a cake tin and placed into the oven, Gods sealing of the covenant.... And when the mass was taken from the oven, it was no longer a wet mass, but had been transformed into a soft sponge cake. Totally impossible to distinguish the four separate items blended in the beginning from it's now changed consistency. Four had become one... the cake now can never be separated again... if cut it just becomes fractions of a whole cake. It will always be one cake.... When cut, through divorce, it will never be two cakes but two halves of one cake. It is only when death takes out the other half that the half remaining is now one cake... but one cake cannot mix with sugar flour and eggs again.... In other words just as the combining of the ingredients is a miracle so is the miracle of separation through death... the one remaining is no longer two but one again, and therefore free to remarry.

The truth of the matter is, this is not about my husband, what he has or has not done. It can be said that as I was the adulterer he is free, and his new wife was also not the adulterer therefore they are free to remarry... but it does not change the fact that he and she are still only half of two different cakes, so because death has not occurred to free them – are they still in adultery? Why... because they are still only half a cake except through death. I am not judging them or anyone else because there are many voices speaking on this matter with different perspectives of God's grace, and I know the Lords love and grace is with us. Contrary to what some believe, I am not condemned as a divorced woman and an adulterer, because of repentance the Lord remembers not the sins He has forgiven. It says he remembers them no more, and the Father sees not what I was, but sees the robe of Jesus' righteousness about me – the Robe of Righteousness. So if God can do that for me – He can do it for all – including remarriage... but as I said earlier, this is not about what my husband does... **This is about me and God.**

This is about the relationship that has grown between us. In the beginning of the Song of Songs the story of the Shulamite, it is all about what she is getting from this relationship with the Bridegroom. She loves all the love and devotion from Him. She is first in this relationship for what is in it for her! Later he comes to her, she is as such in her nightdress, and He asks her to come with him, He needed her to be with Him in His darkest hour, but she hesitates to open the door saying, haven't I already turned from the old ways and given myself to you, is it not enough? Many of us in our Christian walk are in that place. Basically living an ok good life, going to church, doing all the things a Christian should be doing... being kind to all, but not willing to go the rest of the way, not willing to give up certain pleasures for the sake of the One they say they love. The story continues about how she is transformed by His suffering love, to become in the Image of Him, His Equal, His Bride. Yes it starts off as selfish love – what she can get from this relationship, but it ends with her wanting to give the same as she receives. She is so totally in love with her Beloved, she has willingly caught the **foxes** of hindrance and is completely His, and He is hers, giving to Him all of her love. It would not occur to her to do anything in disobedience, or rebellion... the two have become one heart, what may have seemed a sacrifice of catching a cute **fox**, soon became to be no sacrifice at all, but rather a willing gift of her unconditional love to Him. In the light of His love, nothing can be compared, nothing else desired of this world. His will becomes her will. The Bride of course is the Church, for sure the five virgins ready and waiting with oil in their lamps and the wick trimmed back, it is you and me individually and corporately.

As I am being transformed inwardly by my Perfect Valentine, having already caught many **foxes**, with more to go no doubt when the Lord's timing is to reveal them to me, nothing is as a sacrifice anymore. I want more of His love; I want His fruit to flourish in our vineyard of love. I could no more look for loopholes in the word to feed my desires of the flesh. This is not about anyone else, but the Lord and I. Knowing that the word clearly says that I am still married until death do us part, I know I am not free to re-marry despite what any may say. I know what my Lord and Beloved says – and it is enough for me. Obedience is better than sacrifice. The Lord says if we love Him we will obey Him. How then can I do otherwise? How can I agree knowingly to sin even though grace is available? He forgave us because we knew not what we were doing; **but Now I Know!**

I have shared with you my open heart on this matter. I stand to judge no-one; I compare myself with no-one. It is about my relationship with the Lord in accordance to the revelation He gave me as to why He had not given me another husband.

I recently saw the film called "Courageous", which I think is such a wonderful film. The father who is working hard, with a wife and two children suddenly loses his young daughter in a car accident.

He is distraught with pain and asking many questions of why! He starts to delve into the Word of God about what the Father has to say about being a husband and a parent. It causes Him to repent and make a new covenant with the Lord. Others however think he is being hard on himself because he was a "Good enough" father. He looks and says that "Good enough is not good enough!" That is the relationship with the Lord that I am talking about. The Shulamite says – I have already changed my lifestyle since I was born-again, is that not 'good enough'? The answer lies in the statement that says there is still a lot of "I" on the throne, yet to be surrendered, because when our relationship with the Lord denies self so that the Lord's will be done... then it is not about what others do and seemingly get away with, but with total commitment to the Lord and obeying His commands.

If you are single reading this male or female, it is the same for all, I urge you to be certain that it is the will of God before going ahead in marriage. Do not enter into marriage lightly as I did, with rebellion in your heart. The Lord revealed to me that my marriage happened because of prayers of the flesh... which I have already explained. 'Prayers of the flesh' is witchcraft!

If you have already given yourselves to each other sexually before marriage, I pray that you will consider all that you have read so far, knowing that sexual relations outside marriage – which is 'til death do you part, is sin, and an open door for the enemy to attack and make captive, and ask the Lord to forgive you. You are already attached to one another through a soul tie, of immorality. Ask the Lord to break that tie between you through repentance, and place the relationship back into the Lord's hands and refrain from any further sexual activity. I suggest you receive some biblical counseling on this and also about marriage. Truly before getting married, know that it is for life! Life is too short to waste it in wrong relationships based on hidden motives such as rejection, unbelief, rebellion. It may seem right for the short time, but if it is not the will of the Lord, it will leave deep wounds that need to be healed. It all takes time. Healing and restoration is a miracle of God's handiwork, something that no human can perform. If I can spare anyone of any unnecessary pain and pitfalls, this is one of them! I am not against marriage – no! My warning is about marrying the wrong person for the wrong reason. I believe that when Jesus is our everything, and we can find the fullness of all we need in Him, it only enhances the marriage, because you are not expecting each other to fill unmet needs... that is the role of the Lord to heal and restore filling us with all of Him, and therefore you are free to be a blessing – a gift of unconditional love to each other in every way.

If you are planning in your hearts to divorce I pray that you will first think seriously of what you have read. Where there is infidelity the Lord through Moses gave permission because of our hardened hearts to divorce, but I also know that God is able, to forgive and heal and restore. I believe it takes two surrendered hearts to the Lord for this to take place, as one must be willing to forgive and forget as Jesus, the other must be willing to repent – to turn away from the things they are doing wrong... but I will go further to say that I have found that the things I hated my husband for, the Lord later revealed to me were also in me, and that I must have as such tormented him also, but I was blind to my own sin and only seeing his. That is why it takes two surrendered to the Lordship of Christ... because in all honesty there is no-one good except God, so we are all in need of forgiveness. Where divorce is inevitable, because I would never expect someone to remain in a marriage that is violent and abusive, though it seems unfair that such cannot find happiness in another marriage, it is between **you and the Lord**. I cannot personally say it is wrong, but I can say **draw close first to the Lord, let Him bring healing and restoration, let Him fill your needs and hopes and dreams, and from a surrendered place in His all-consuming love, be led by His Spirit. It is between you and the Lord**...it is not about what others say is ok or not ok, it is about **you and Jesus** and the relationship you have with Him.

Matthew 16:6-12; 23:13-34
Luke 20: 45-47

Leaven Bread

I had ordered a book about the Religious Spirit, because I was living in a land of religiosity, with little personal relationship with God. I thought it would help me to be able to share the gospel better if I understood. What a shock I was in for. As I began to read the first page, it stated something like: You have probably bought this book with someone else in mind, but I am sure to say, that this book will speak straight into your own heart!!!!!!!

I shared this story back in Chapter 6, so there is no need to repeat it again here, but to say it had an amazing impact upon my life, and the things still to come.

A religious spirit counterfeits the activity and power of the Holy Spirit! Its' objectiveness is "holding to a form of godliness, although they have denied its power" 2 Tim 3:5 (NIV:5)

and we are told to stay away from it... *"avoid such men as these"*

Matthew 16:6-12

[6] "Be careful," Jesus said to them. "Be on your guard against the yeast of the Pharisees and Sadducees." [7] They discussed this among themselves and said, "It is because we didn't bring any bread." [8] Aware of their discussion, Jesus asked, "You of little faith, why are you talking among yourselves about having no bread? [9] Do you still not understand? Don't you remember the five loaves for the five thousand, and how many basketfuls you gathered? [10] Or the seven loaves for the four thousand, and how many basketfuls you gathered?

[11] How is it you don't understand that I was not talking to you about bread? But be on your guard against <u>the yeast of the Pharisees and Sadducees</u>." [12] Then they understood that he was not telling them to guard against the yeast used in bread, but against the teaching of the Pharisees and Sadducees. (NIV: 5)

Leaven (yeast) is what puffs up the bread! Leaven is Pride. Once leaven gets into bread it is most difficult to remove **– as is Pride**

EVERY ONE OF US IS SUSCEPTIBLE TO THIS AND SHOULD CHECK OURSELVES. We cannot deliver others from it if we are not free from it ourselves. Pride is part of a Religious Spirit and doesn't need to listen to the voice of God, but presumes it knows God's opinion and what pleases Him. In which case, we won't then be open to correction or rebuke from others. It is important we ask God to shine His light in our hearts and reveal to us if there is any of this lurking within personally... because we can only deliver others in as much as we ourselves are free. Satan cannot cast out Satan. (Matthew 12:22 – 37)

I started to look into the life of the Pharisees and Sadducees – in as much as what they believed. Well of course, they were well learned of the first five books of the Bible, which is the Word of God to the Jew. By the age of five they had learnt to memorise it by heart! They knew the Word of God! Inside and out – they had memorised every word written! And yet – they did not recognise Jesus when he came, and they refused his teaching. They presumed they knew the word and did not need correction. They presumed they understood the Law, and were sure that they were living out all of it in their lives, at least in a way others would see. They were full of pride, and their pride in knowing the Word, presumed that they did not need to ask God his opinion, but that they knew that also. Pride and arrogance – a Religious Spirit.

A religious spirit is zealous for God and things of God – so isn't that a good thing? Well as we have covered in previous chapters, God is not interested in the outward appearances, but rather the heart motives. The hidden sins others don't see. A religious spirit will therefore be focused on good works, and sin, but will often bypass the Cross of Calvary. Of course the Jews rejected Jesus as the Son of God – the awaited Messiah, so they definitely rejected the Cross and all it accomplished for us in establishing God's Grace. So there is no presence of God's Grace, God's strength made perfect in our weaknesses. It is focused on the outward performance as seen with the eye. It is based on the Law, and upholding all of the Ten Commandments, which can be said there would only need to be two: The greatest commandment is to Love Your God. The 2nd is to love your neighbour... if we upheld these two – we would actually fulfil all the commandments because if we love the Lord we will not love idols, and if we love our neighbours we will not steal from them, commit adultery or murder etc.

I have already written in a previous chapter that Jesus came to fulfil the Law not to abolish it.

If the Grace of God is missing then it all becomes works of the flesh – what I can achieve, and nothing about the empowerment of the Holy Spirit... and works of the flesh are dead works, no matter how good they are.

Matthew 23; Luke 20: 45-47

There are eight "Woes" spoken by Jesus to the teachers of the law and Pharisees regarding their religiosity.

Matthew 23:13

13 **"Woe to you, teachers of the law and Pharisees, you hypocrites! <u>You shut the door of the kingdom of heaven</u> in people's faces. You yourselves do not enter, nor will you let those enter who are trying to.: (NIV: 5)**

A religious spirit will cause those who truly seek intimacy and a deeper relationship with the Lord to be threatened, and others hindered by the preaching of a false gospel message that would allow the flesh life to continue without challenge. The cross and repentance do not exist to the religious spirit because that was only the door of salvation, and all our sins are forgiven - so we don't need to repent anymore – we live in grace!... But this grace that is preached is a false Grace. The religious spirit perverts grace by saying because of it we are forgiven and therefore Jesus loves us as we are, so there is no need for repentance and change. It did not exist for the Pharisees of the day because they rejected Jesus as the Messiah so the cross does not exist. Just live outwardly a pious life... good works are all you need, and yet Jesus tells us if we choose to follow Him we must deny ourselves and take up our cross every day. Other ways is by opposing personal prophecy, denying God speaks through dreams and visions, fervent prayer, speaking in tongues, praying for the sick, singing that song, going to that church, raising hands, dancing in the sanctuary and so on. Less obvious but still a strong form is not being supportive of your church's leadership. So rather than getting behind the vision and helping, for example, the religious spirit refuses to cooperate. The religious spirit prefers to dodge responsibility, argue, complain, debate, and otherwise avoid helping the cause, and frustrates the plans of God. Indifference is a vehicle for a religious spirit to hinder God's plan for the church. All of us must beware of the religious spirit who shuts up the Kingdom of Heaven. The word **indifference** also describes the way I felt towards the Jewish people. It was not as such a strong dislike or hatred, I felt no malice or ill intent toward them, in fact I had compassion because of the way they had been wrongly treated BUT I saw them of no interest to me. It is vital that we realise that all nations, all tribes, are loved and precious and of interest to our Father, and He longs for NO-ONE to perish but that all should be restored to the Kingdom of God as sons and daughters. Only a religious Spirit would be exclusive.

A religious spirit will cause scriptural truth from being taught, and oppose anyone who is trying to walk in obedience through criticism or making fun of your spirituality or your relationship with Jesus.

Luke 20: 45-47

45 While all the people were listening, Jesus said to his disciples, 46 "Beware of the teachers of the law. They like to walk around in flowing robes and love to be greeted with respect in the marketplaces and have the most important seats in the synagogues and the places of honour at banquets. 47 They devour widows' houses and for a show make lengthy prayers. These men will be punished most severely." (NIV: 5)

When you see the robes and fancy suits it's time to say "Let the show begin!" It is a time of entertaining the crowds with a performance of perfection with even solo performers miming to their own records. I mentioned it earlier in Chapter 15, performance and entertainment is all about us, and the things that make us feel good – its focus is on the flesh being satisfied and receiving gratification, instead of denying self and the focus being on meeting with the Living God and giving unto Him all glory honour and praise! I am not talking about performances which are specific like dramas and dance, which tend to have a message attached, and can be used as a form of worship and evangelism / teaching.

The Spiritual leader or speaker will arrive in style escorted by their 'sons in the faith'. After the service no-one can leave the meeting place before the leader has departed... protocol, and respect, pomp and ceremony, whilst Jesus stands at the door knocking to come in... and the speaker / leader is protected from talking with the people after the service, rushed off first before the rest of the congregation can leave.

Matthew 23:15

15 "Woe to you, teachers of the law and Pharisees, you hypocrites! You travel over land and sea to win a single convert, and when you have succeeded, you make them twice as much a child of hell as you are. (NIV:5)

Such people are in search of bottoms on seats, for their own personal gain and recognition. There will be fervent religious activities for the congregation, with no time or space for personal time with God and a reliance upon the leader to spoon feed the Word, instead of encouragement to read the word for yourself and seek God's presence. They will take the place of Jesus as the 'High Priest', and they will have lots of Praise and limited time in Worship, lest you hear from the Lord for yourself.

Such teachers will use the Word of God to control you. Some ministers will cause you to believe you cannot exist without them. As such you become hooked on them, either in counselling or advice or the delivery of the word... you just can't get enough of them and an unhealthy soul tie with this religious person is formed.

A religious spirit is head knowledge (theory) and no heart knowledge (practical experience) of the Word of God. Scriptures are banded about out of context, or as flippant responses to situations they don't know how to handle. "By His stripes we are healed" is truth, but when spoken out to people in sickness and pain without love and compassion, it can be received almost like a slap in the face, causing the one who is sick to feel guilty if instant healing is not experienced. In fact a religious spirit will make you feel guilty for being sick in the first place. I remember a church movement in Scandinavia that was preaching that you cannot be sick as a Christian. It seemed for a long time that there were many miracles taking place, only that some years later it came to be known there had been a lot of rehabilitation centres set up for Christians who had tried to commit suicide. They were sick and had faked healing, but could not live any longer under this oppression to be perfect. This is a religious spirit – perverting the truth of God's Word. Not everyone is physically healed. Everyone who we read Jesus ministered to and the disciples were healed – because these are the testimonies of faith, but there were many around the pool of Bethesda, waiting for healing when the waters stirred, but there was only one person by the pool that Jesus healed. Jesus heard the Father's heart and obeyed.

Religious people make promises and vows / oaths to God and others publicly, usually to be seen to be generous and compassionate, but often do not fulfil those promises. It's a kind of 'selling' technique, making false promises for what is being sold, in order to get money in the offertory plate, and they love to split hairs discussing the Word.

Matthew 23: 16-22

[16] "Woe to you, blind guides! You say, 'If anyone swears by the temple, it means nothing; but anyone who swears by the gold of the temple is bound by that oath.' [17] You blind fools! Which is greater: the gold, or the temple that makes the gold sacred? [18] You also say, 'If anyone swears by the altar, it means nothing; but anyone who swears by the gift on the altar is bound by that oath.' [19] You blind men! Which is greater: the gift, or the altar that makes the gift sacred? [20] Therefore, anyone who swears by the altar swears by it and by everything on it. [21] And anyone who swears by the temple swears by it and by the one who dwells in it. [22] And anyone who swears by heaven swears by God's throne and by the one who sits on it. (NIV: 5)

This is where the gifts of the Spirit are sought after more than the Giver of the Gifts. They will place emphasis on material things rather than upon the spiritual purpose for which they were to be used, for example building a new church costing lots of money when the hearts of the people remain in ruins. A religious spirit cannot take someone else somewhere, where they have never been themselves… a plank in their own eye trying to take out a speck in someone's eye

Matthew 23: 23- 24

²³ "Woe to you, scribes and Pharisees, hypocrites! For you pay tithe of mint and anise and cumin, and have neglected the weightier matters of the law: justice and mercy and faith. These you ought to have done, without leaving the others undone. ²⁴ Blind guides, who strain out a gnat and swallow a camel! (NIV: 5)

This is a picture of the average church today that is busy making the outside of the cup look clean by religious works but never deals with matters of the heart. They go through all the ceremonies, have the best sound equipment, chairs, buildings, etc. But all of the external ceremonies cannot clean up the corruption of the inner man. The religious will substitute reality with ritual, faith with formality and true worship with liturgy and form. They worry about the food that goes into the mouth, but fail to understand that it is what comes out of the mouth that defiles a person. The Pharisees would pull their ox out of a ditch on the Sabbath **Luke 14:5**, but were furious when someone was healed **Luke 13:16** on the Sabbath. They cared more about the religious keeping of rules and traditions more than they did about people. People can play football any day of the week and go swimming – but not on a Sunday or drive a car. People can be part of leading worship expressing love and devotion, then have sex with their partner with whom they are not married… or beat their wives, or cheat through the company books… convict others of un-forgiveness, whilst harbouring bitterness and un-forgiveness toward someone in their secret heart.

Matthew 23:25-26

²⁵ "Woe to you, teachers of the law and Pharisees, you hypocrites! You clean the outside of the cup and dish, but inside they are full of greed and self-indulgence. ²⁶ Blind Pharisee! First clean the inside of the cup and dish, and then the outside also will be clean." (NIV: 5).

Extortion is the word used in the King James Version for greed, which means a predetermined plan of action with the intent to steal from someone. Jesus said the Pharisees were so full of excess that they had lost the ability to control their lust for more. Today we have modern religious merchandisers who steal from the people of God so they can lavish themselves with excess.

I was shocked when I learned that people who go to a minister of the faith for prayer will be 'treated' like at an emergency ward at a hospital. I think it's called "triage" where everyone coming in will be interviewed and placed in a waiting order where the most urgent case is prioritised and seen to first. This is good in the case of sick people because it could save someone's life to be seen immediately, however the type of triage I have heard of is dependent on the size of the note (money) in their hand. Does it only happen in Africa? I don't thinks so. But the Word of God says freely you have received, freely give. Yes a minister is worthy of his wages, but this is not about being paid for a job, it's about paying for preferential treatment. I cannot see how a minister of God can charge to pray for the sick and needy, it is all part and parcel of His job description and it goes against everything the Kingdom of God is about.

Maybe this does not come under greed and extortion, but what about the husband that commands his wife to submit to his every whim because he is the head of the house and that's what the Bible teaches for wives to submit to their husband in Ephesians 5:22. Oh, I have been here, where my husband said I was not to eat because I would get fat, not to speak, not to allow visitors without pre-arrangements into the house. I wrote about it as the control and manipulation, but it is so the religious spirit that uses scripture to blackmail and threaten. His hours of praying for me to change went from two hours to four because I was 'refusing to submit' to him as the Bible says I must, because I wanted to eat like everyone else. Actually he once told me that now I am married – I am born-again in him!!!! Such a perversion of the truth. This is not to blame – he was deceived... just as I have been deceived in many things. The Passion Translation by Brian Simmons, reveals that going back to the original Aramaic language in which it was written, the word means to be tenderly devoted to. The Greek translation is to submit. I have noticed that as the scripture is used against the wives, rarely does the husband see the Word that follows telling him to love the wife as Jesus who laid down his life for the church.

I was helping a couple in a marriage dispute that had arisen. There was a trust issue, and clearly the husband did not trust his wife to do what he thought was right. He was willing to change <u>when</u> she had proved she was trustworthy. This however is not what Jesus did for the church, because whilst we were all sinners and not trust worthy, He first laid down His life unto death, not knowing if we would receive such a gift or not and change. Truth is – I believe, any husband who is willing to deny himself because of such great love for his family, the wife will not be able to resist from being tenderly devoted to him, and therefore surrendering to His leadership.

The same applies to the scripture that women should wear a head covering forcing all women to wear hats or scarves in the sanctuary of the church, which later in the chapter Paul actually says that a woman's hair is her covering. In the past I had learned that women found in sexual immorality would have their heads shaved as a sign to all of their sinful ways. During the times of war between Ireland and England, one of the punishments if a girl was found in a sexual relationship with a soldier of the opposite side, her hair was shaven and then tar was placed on her head and feathers. It was done to shame the woman publicly. So for a woman to be bald was considered to be shameful, but hair is her covering.

There are some Christians who promote their businesses as 'Christians' who use it to manipulate clients and customers to trust them, whilst they rob them or cheat them no differently than the world in order to line their own pockets. Or Christians who hide money from the tax man in dishonest ways, paying people cash and not putting it through the books. It is all the Religious Spirit that works with Jezebel to manipulate and control.

Often the churches where money has been lavishly used to build either pretentiously to the sky like building their own towers of Babylon, or used to make the building so beautiful and pleasing to the eye, and yet there is no sense of God's presence in the place. A misappropriation of funds, where the hearts and lives of the poor and needy in the neighbourhood is less of a concern than the outward beauty of the building called church... where everyone is found to be in their Sunday best, with Sunday best smiles. Such buildings are built to attract those who are rich to place their gold and silver in the church offertory plate and the minister's pocket. It can be argued that the Gospel needs to be presented in a way to attract the rich, for they are also in need of salvation. My reply to this is: Blessed are the poor, for they shall inherit..... In other words, the story of the rich young ruler tells us that he was obedient to the law except for the first and most important of all the commandments – to have no other gods before him. We do not use a god to bring a god into the church... less we all fall into the sin of worshiping mammon. I was told once that we need to prepare a gospel that speaks intellectually to the learned... I ask why? Jesus did not. He spoke one message for all there were not different versions for the rich, or the intellectual, the poor or the not so clever.

Matthew 23:27-28

"Woe unto you, scribes and Pharisees, hypocrites! You are like whitewashed tombs, which look beautiful on the outside, but on the inside full of dead men's bones, and everything unclean. In the same way, on the outside you appear to people as righteous but on the inside you are full of hypocrisy and wickedness" (NIV: 5).

When people looked at them they saw good and righteous men of God, but Jesus called them dead, full of hypocrisy and iniquity. He then went on to say that they were full of uncleanness, which means they were full of impure motives and lust. No wonder they wanted to kill him! (Releasing a murdering spirit of anger)

There are some who burned with the love of God, and felt led to train to be a minister of the Word, but when they finished their training, they had lost all their passionate love for Jesus and instead became legalistic, and carnal. I remember many years ago meeting a young man who was so in love with the Lord - so it seemed – part of a huge evangelistic outreach at a summer concert known for its use of alcohol and drugs. I found this young man beautiful and it seemed he had a similar interest in me. I went to visit him for a holiday to find that he was not worried about having sexual relations outside of marriage. I found that he also had a friend who from time to time would come and share sexual favours. He was at theological college training to be a priest. I learned much later that the sin in me attracts itself to the same sin in others like a magnet. But I am highlighting that Bible or Theological College isn't always the answer. The religious spirit has perverted so many parts of the church subtly to violate the truth that sets the captive free, and instead binds up the congregation in stronger chains than before. This happens when we embrace Christian theology / philosophy but fail to embrace the founder of Christianity – Jesus whether in college or not.

Matthew 23:29-34

[29] **"Woe to you, scribes and Pharisees, hypocrites! Because you build the tombs of the prophets and adorn the monuments of the righteous,** [30] **and say, 'If we had lived in the days of our fathers, we would not have been partakers with them in the blood of the prophets.'** [31] **"Therefore you are witnesses against yourselves that you are sons of those who murdered the prophets.** [32] **Fill up, then, the measure of your fathers'** *guilt.* [33] **Serpents, brood of vipers! How can you escape the condemnation of hell?** [34] **Therefore, indeed, I send you prophets, wise men, and scribes:** *some* **of them you will kill and crucify, and** *some* **of them you will scourge in your synagogues and persecute from city to city..."** (NIV: 5)

Here is also reference to the sins of the fathers. There was no repentance for the sins of the fathers, and indeed an obvious transferral with each life producing its own sin and transferring it on. They were professing that they were not like their fathers, as I had of my mother and father, and yet what I had not seen was the same sin but in a different way in me, far more subtle and as such hidden from the obvious ways of my parents, yet never the less the same spirit. Jesus taught that there was a murdering spirit, whereby they honoured the prophets of old, but killed those yet to come, including Jesus. They were honouring the prophets that their ancestors had murdered, but the same hidden spirit was now murdering those such as John the Baptist, Steven would later be along with the other disciples, after they had murdered Jesus.

Christians who walk in this religious spirit will be easily angered. Cain was the first born of the Religious Spirit – he killed His brother out of jealousy revealing the murdering spirit. His offer to God was unacceptable works of the flesh, where Able's was that of the blood. Jealousy and hatred of a brother leads to murder – if not physically – in the heart – and the Lord tells us that even to hate in his heart – God sees it as murder committed!

Today we are seeing great atrocities of murder in the name of different religions, not only Islam, and Hinduism, but also within the church itself, where the searching heart for intimacy with Christ is rebuked and if possible, destroyed, celebrating the great names of the past but crucifying the names of today that seek the relationship that brings transformation and empowerment to the inner heart which is the true meaning of revival. It has been heard all around the world that a personal relationship with Jesus is not healthy... from a famous spiritual leader. And leaders who were renowned for their personal relationship with Jesus, are one by one renouncing it to follow the other leader. It seems totally impossible to see such once honoured men of faith suddenly become one with the ones who murder the Holy Spirit that brings the intimacy of Christ.

When we are focused on the outward performance of one another, there can be no room for mistakes, and we find judgement, condemnation and criticism. It is the one thing I thanked the Lord for in my first church thirty four years ago when I was saved. I used to dress – if you are old enough to remember, like Olivia Newton John, when she had just had a make-over and the sweet innocent had been vamped up into smouldering and sexy, wearing lycra leggings and close fitting tops, with a headband – as if from the gym. Actually one of the attires I wore to church was white lycra stretch legging – like spray on flesh, with a backless t-shirt, and therefore no bra, with over the knee leather boots. It is still the one thing the then assistant Pastor, still remembers. I would paint make-up thick and colourful onto my face. It was clothes more for the disco / nightclub than for church... but no one judged me. Not one person told me I should dress otherwise in the house of God. I was accepted by all as I was.

'Jesus take me as I am, I can come no other way. Take me deeper into You, make my flesh life melt away. Make me like a precious stone, crystal clear and finely honed. Life of Jesus shining through, giving Glory back to You.'

I am covered over with the Robe of Righteousness that Jesus gives to me. I am covered over with the precious blood of Jesus and He lives in me. What a joy it is to know, my heavenly Father loves me so – He gives to me – My Jesus. When He looks at me He sees not what I used to be, but He sees Jesus.

I had mentioned the story of when I saw myself in the mirror for the first time since I was fourteen years old, beautiful without make-up, so I remained without, and dressed up in a beautiful summer skirt and blouse, with a straw hat – like a fine lady – to go to church. My dear sister came to me that day after church to tell me she was rejoicing because her prayers had been answered... and when I asked what her prayers had been, they were that I would see myself beautiful without make-up.

She and others never told me not to wear this or that, but accepted me the way I came – praying for me of course, not to change me to be like them, but for the love of God to show me how beautiful I am the way He created me to be, and to relax in that. When God answered that prayer, it was my desire also to change the way I dressed. God had already been at work in my heart – because I had already bought the new outfit – it was hanging in the wardrobe... never been worn before. It was feminine and modest, not brash and flirty. Had there been a religious spirit in the church, they would have had someone take me aside and tell me not to come wearing such clothes... but their love for the lost was greater than the rules and regulations. They knew that when I had an encounter with the living Jesus, He would change my heart through the work of the Holy Spirit.

In Zechariah – the Word says "Not by might or by power, but by the Spirit of God." That is the difference between the Holy Spirit and a Religious Spirit. The religious tries to charm, manipulate, persuade, coerce through power and might in the flesh and mind, rather than allow the Holy Spirit to do the work within the heart. My husband was a 'charming man'. It was used as a compliment but the truth is he was a false picture – it was an outward beauty but did not reflect the condition of his heart. He was a work in progress, just like me, and though I do not condemn, the truth is, such a spirit is poison and destructive – it tries to murder the personal relationship we have with Christ to bring us to conformity of man's plans and indeed independence from God.

A religious spirit will say if you don't do this you can't do this.... A religious spirit will say you must wear a hat to church on Sundays, and you must not wear jeans but a suit and tie. The heart of God will say – come wearing what you have – it's your heart I am interested in and not the way you cover it in your finery.

The religious spirit will lift up those who are in a position to benefit themselves, so giving preferential treatment to those with money, seating them in special seats, whilst those who are poor will be sat somewhere in the back where they are not seen.

There are two foundations that the Religious Spirit is built upon – FEAR and PRIDE. A Religious Spirit seeks to have us serve the Lord <u>in order to gain His approval</u> BUT we already have our approval through the cross of Jesus. Doing good works or reading, praying, fasting do not make us more approved and accepted by God.... we have been accepted through the blood of Jesus and His righteousness – not our own – for we are not righteous outside of the blood of Christ.

The Religious Spirit bases relationship to God on personal discipline rather than the sacrifice of Christ. Motivation could be either Fear or Pride or BOTH. Deliverance from this spirit is usually a long process, which is why the Lord gave Jezebel 'time to repent' **Rev 2:20-21.** We should not tolerate the practice of it in the church – but we should allow someone who ministers in it a time to repent and be patient with them – because of the long process involved.

<u>**1 Samuel 3:13 – 14**</u> Eli served with zeal because of his own guilt as an irresponsible father to his sons. Guilt in our lives can stir us to be zealous hoping it will atone for the other failures.... but there is only one atonement for our sin and guilt – and that is the cross of Jesus! It is through the Grace of God – nothing that we can do to earn it – it is a gift freely given and totally underserving!

Pride seeks the highest standard of perfectionism for God's Glory through works of the flesh, which is directly in opposition to the Grace of God. It then pushes standards further upon a person that the Lord has not required.

For example, the Lord may ask us to pray to him 10 minutes a day... and as we become blessed by being in His presence we don't want to stop after ten minutes... so out of our love of being in His presence we tally longer with Him. When we end up praying 2 hours a day – it is not because of fear or pride – but out of LOVE.

I have seen a video that someone wanted me to see. **I was repulsed by it**. It was supposed to show a vision someone had received by God. The vision was that in heaven he was taken up and saw houses of all kinds, some like big mansions, others like small huts, some finished, some not, some nothing more than caves, and when he asked the Lord what this was, he was told that these were the houses in the New Jerusalem. Each were being built according to their works here on the earth. If you fail to read the Bible everyday – there are less building materials in heaven for your heavenly home, but if you pray many hours a day, read your Bible much, give good gifts of money to the church, and do good acts of faith – you will receive many building materials in heaven to be built a wonderful new home. Then it went on to talk about hell. I couldn't watch anymore!!! It was completely false to the Word of God that says Jesus has already prepared a place for us!!! It is finished! It has not been built according to our abilities and performance, but on the grounds of what Jesus accomplished for us – His Righteousness, not our own self-righteous acts! This for sure was a message straight out of a Religious Spirit – from the Tree of Knowledge of Good and Evil.

Perfectionism will stifle true maturity and growth. The Lord will lead us slowly up the mountainside – but when we fall or slip – there is no condemnation – only the love of God willing us to try again. He doesn't count how many times we fall – He is cheering us on by not giving up the desire to get it right.... so He loves us when we fall and when we achieve – the same love – He could not love us more than He already does – because He gave His best – His OWN SON for us!!!!! His love cannot be earned, it is unconditionally the same for all. Oh such love!

We do not become perfect in order to serve – if we did – there would be no-one serving!!! We are all a work in progress – still on the way. Perfect obedience should be our goal – but it is only attainable if we abide in the One who is perfect! – Jesus. We are perfected or changed by doing His will, and we are joined to Him and His strength. His strength is made perfect in our weakness and therefore His Grace is sufficient! We must correct our mistakes – that is how we learn but it is a correction that frees us – not enslaves us... no condemnation in Christ Jesus.

Fear and pride is a deadly combination. People bound by this go through deep anguish and remorse for their failures which will result in repentance but will simply be self-punishment and further attempts of sacrifices of the flesh... good works – doing penance! Then they will become so proud of being a better Christian than others that they become un-teachable and unable to receive reproof. It will become very difficult to rid – because when you confront the pride it will hide behind the fear – and the fear behind the pride.

Counterfeit Discernment is a manifestation of the Religious Spirit. Such people love to see what is wrong with others instead of focusing on their positives of what God is doing in them – and help them along. It will tear people down, not build them up because this is rooted in the Tree of Knowledge of Good and Evil. Even if they discern correctly – it will still be of evil fruit because of the spirit in which it is delivered. God will always deliver such in Love – which will be to build up a person not to see them defeated. No-one should give a judgement or criticism about another person or group UNLESS we know that the one who is bringing it truly loves that person or group and has made an investment of service to them!

Criticism holds forth an appearance of wisdom but it is pride in one of its lowest forms. When we criticize someone – we are elevating ourselves as better than they.

Jezebel Spirit is primarily witchcraft.... but works in close harmony to the Religious Spirit. The two feed off each other. Jezebel was married to Ahab – King. He was a weak King – and Jezebel was controlling, manipulative and domineering. This spirit usually gains its influence by seduction and by making political alliances. It will always need to be close to the centre of power – it will appear to be submissive – but it will usually manifest a strong controlling spirit and shameless presumption of others.

People think that only women are subject to this spirit – but it is not true – though maybe more women than men manifest characteristics of this spirit.... but some of the men are more powerful – especially in political arenas.

Any woman who does not submit to her God given role – will take on some form of this spirit. Any man who does not take up his God given role will either become a weak leader like Ahab and allow his wife to control and lead and do its destructive work – or will succumb to the aspects of this witchcraft that are manifest in the control and political spirits. To be free from this – is to return to our God given roles – this includes being content with our present positions without striving for influence until God gives it. (King David refused to take the Kingship until God rightfully gave it to him and he was given true spiritual authority) People who demand a title recognition for their position are self-appointed most certainly – and are in the spirit of the flesh. It doesn't mean that women can't work and men if they so choose to be home with the children, if it is how some choose to live their lives. Maybe the woman has a better paid job affording the family a better life style, but it should still remain that the man is the head of the family making the final decisions. Of course a good partnership would allow both the wife and the husband to suggest the steps required, but the God-given role would be if there is no unity of decision, the man as head of the family should make the final.

A religious spirit will put more emphasis on the sacrifice, perverting the command to take up our cross daily... therefore putting more emphasis on our own sacrifices than on the Ultimate sacrifice by the Lord Jesus. King Saul as found in 1Samuel 15, emphasized that his disobedience was because he wanted to offer the livestock as a pleasing sacrifice to the Lord.... It was out of a religious spirit, because if His heart had been in truth for the Lord, the sacrifice of His heart would have been to obey the word of the Lord. Obedience is better than sacrifice. Then king Saul makes another excuse for his disobedience saying it was because of fear of his people, and then wanted to repent of his violation of God's word, but Samuel then told him as he had rejected the Word of God, God had now rejected him as king over Israel. These were serious consequences for disobedience.

The first time I went out as a missionary the Lord had asked me to sell all my things, to pay for the mission school I was first to be part of. I did it with joy and the Lord blessed it by multiplying that which I was asking, as people gave. However years later when I was angry with the Lord because of the awful marriage I thought He had given me, I remember saying to the Lord... "I sold everything and left my family for You and then you give me this?" Suddenly my eye had been placed upon the self-righteous acts... what I had done for the Lord. I don't know when the change had taken place within my heart, but slowly and surely a religious spirit had grown that had taken my eyes off what the Lord had done on the cross and focused instead upon my own good works, which was not how I had seen it initially.

We are called to live a disciplined, self-sacrificial life - but it is the spirit which lies behind the motivation that will depict the fruit produced. If it is a heartfelt/ heart led relationship with God, through all that Jesus accomplished and nothing of self – then the fruit will be that of the Holy Spirit... not in comparison to anyone else, not according to good works, purely based on the Grace of God that empowers us to walk in obedience through humility and repentance. If however what motivates is the need for recognition, the need to be seen better than everyone else... if you only see the faults in someone else and none in your own life, that is motivated by perfection in yourself and that of others, the fruit will be that of the flesh – a Religious Spirit.

Even if it is small in our lives now, undealt with will become like a huge tree, better to chop it down when its roots are still small and manageable, and to pull up the roots.

God has been teaching me to love others, as He loves. He looks always for the best in others, sees what we are destined to become – not focus on the things we have been, that is why our sins are forgiven and NO LONGER remembered by God. Our sins are buried in the seas of Gods forgetfulness and a sign that says no fishing! I know that if I am sharing that which the Lord has been revealing to me, it is not that I am better than anyone else, but rather that maybe by sharing my places of failure it will give hope to another that all things are possible with God, and that His Grace is more than enough to meet us at any place in our life. His hand is not too short to deliver us from a religious spirit, or any other, my life is a testimony to His amazing grace, that forgives all things, hopes all things, delivers all things, and restores all things. His love is so unconditional towards each one of us... He loves me – and I don't deserve it, but I rejoice in His relentless love, His unfathomable, and too marvellous for words, incomprehensible, amazing, all-powerful, priceless and unfailing love.

John 15:1-17;
Matthew 11:21; 20:20-28; 23;
Luke 9:23-27; 19:44
1 Samuel 15:22

A Question of Independence.

John:1-8

¹"I am like a sprouting Vine, and the farmer who tends the Vine is My Father. ²He cares for the branches connected to Me by lifting and propping up the branches that are fruitless, and pruning every fruitful branch to yield a greater harvest. ³The words I have spoken over you have already cleansed you. ⁴So step into life-union with Me, for I have stepped into life-union with you. For as a branch severed from the vine will not bear fruit, so your life will be fruitless unless you live your life intimately joined to Mine. ⁵"I am the sprouting Vine and you're My branches. As you live in union with Me as your source, fruitfulness will stream from within you, but when you live separated from Me you are powerless. ⁶If you live separated from Me, you will be discarded like shrivelled up branches that are gathered up and thrown into the fire to be burned. ⁷But if you step into My life in union with Me and if My words live powerfully within you—then you can ask whatever you desire and it will be done. ⁸When your lives bear abundant fruit, you demonstrate that you are My mature disciples who glorify My Father! (TPT: 3)

When I started this book, it was in Song of Songs, and talking of the vineyard of God's love within our hearts. Jesus again here talks of being The Vine, and we, you and I its branches. The fruit of the vine is of course grapes which are a fruit I think most people in the world know of, as the fruit which grows in clusters, and are often taken to people who are sick because they contain vitamin C and are considered fruits to help healing in the body. They are also the fruit which is used to produce wine.

The wine is the symbol of Jesus' Blood used in the sacraments of Holy Communion. Wine is made from the flesh of the grape being pressed to expel all the juices. Just as wine is poured out of a bottle, so the Blood of Jesus was poured out for us at Calvary, which the Lord asks of us to drink often in remembrance of Him, along with the eating of the bread – a symbol of Christ's Body broken for us on the cross.

When I moved to live in Uganda, I took with me a vine. The Plant was two but only one survived, however it began to grow so quickly we all marvelled at how fast the vine grew so long, that we placed rope around the front porch of the home, and trailed the branches back and forth to create a wonderful canopy. I had always wanted such a vine, and now I had one. My family were also very excited because they had never seen this plant before; they had only experienced the fruits that were imported into the country. They kept asking me, when will it have fruit? Of course I had never grown it before but I did know from friends who grew vines for a wine company on the island of Malta, that they were never allowed to grow as I had done, because the plant only produces the fruit if it is kept cut back, or pruned. It is true that eventually the long vine will produce some fruit but it will not really be sweet and good to eat because all the energy of the plant is going to producing the long branches and its leaves. I asked another friend if she knew how I could take a cutting from the main vine so as to produce new plants, this time to focus on the produce of fruit. I followed her instruction, and out of three that I tried, two were successful. Now we would learn to keep the vine trimmed back, forcing the fruit to be born.

The instruction I received was that the new part of the vine was to be bent down into the soil where there is a joint on the branch, and to leave it covered for two to three weeks with watering, to encourage the joint under the soil to produce roots. Once the roots have taken, the vine can be cut from behind. I did it as said, and after cutting the back I noticed all the vines from the growing end begin to wither. I was discouraged, but my daughter kept watering. They had still been receiving the life source from the main vine, now they had to learn to take its new supply from the ground through its newly developed roots. Two survived and have been replanted. Now the vine has to be kept short to make it produce new branches and eventually fruit.

It is like parents who have children, they nurture them and train them in the ways of God, 'til that day comes when they too will leave the family home. You have prepared them planting the part of you that is the flesh of your flesh, into the soils of the Word of God, and watered it with the Holy Spirit through prayer, now trusting for the child to grow its own roots, and then you cut the spiritual umbilical cord to watch it grow for itself. Sometimes it looks like the new adult life is withering, but with prayers - Holy Spirit watering, the child begins to soak up from the soil for itself, to produce the fruits of the Lord in their own divine relationship with Jesus – the Bridegroom.

I am interested in the fact that the vine has to be cut back in order to produce fruit. Year after year the vine will produce but it must be cut back to encourage the fruit to grow. It would seem that the more the vine is cut back the better the fruit that is produced. It is the same with our spiritual life in Christ.

We have been grafted into the vine, and so long as we are attached to the vine we will grow and grow and grow with God as the source, however we can grow for many years without pruning and we will produce long vines and canopies of leaves but no fruit. Jesus talks in Song of Songs that the fruit of his vineyard is being destroyed, therefore He is focused on the fruit and the harvesting of that fruit. If a tree fails to produce fruit after a few years it will be cut down, and another planted in its place. A tree without fruit is no good... its fruit is the sign of its worth. It says that a bad tree cannot produce good fruit, and a good tree cannot produce bad fruit. The fruit is hope fulfilled, it is what we plant the tree for in the first place.

So the first question I feel I need to ask is what kind of vine are we? Are we one that is just growing longer and longer through the years producing a canopy of leaves, but failing to produce fruit? If we think that our lives are enough in Christ, after all we are still attached to the vine, enjoying this world and all it offers, going to church on Sundays, even Bible study in the week, but unless the Word that is preached and taught causes us to respond to the Word and let it prune us, cleanse us... then we indeed just remain a canopy of leaves... beautiful and yet without purpose – no fruit.

Song of Songs 5:3 tells us that the Shulamite – Bride to Be, has surrendered her life to Him and exchanged her old ways – laying them aside like an old garment to wear the new garment of His righteousness. Is that not enough that I appear to all to be good? The garment is the outward appearance, but Jesus is appealing to her inner heart of intent... though she appears to be fully His, she is not... she still has to understand and experience the cross in her own life. We are to be united with Him in both his death and His resurrection. We like to accept resurrected life without crucifixion. The pruning is Gods discipline – His discipling, and He disciplines those He loves.

We can be Christians for many years believing that all we have to do is accept Christ through the sinner's prayer, and be good. The problem with that is that no-one is good but God (Luke 18:19), and it is by His Spirit that He reveals to us all that is not good – not from the outward appearance, but in the inner heart. The Holy Spirit does not condemn us, but the truth is we have taken our measuring stick from the world, and when it says that which is not acceptable according to God's Word, is now accepted in the law of the land or even the whole world as it seems now to be, we go with it. So we cut out the still quiet prompting of the Holy Spirit, to listen to the OK's of this world who is now calling all that was wicked in the eyes of the Lord, now to be good. We measure our Christian life by how many times a week we go to church, or to house-group, bible study, prayer meeting, worship practice, over-night meetings, evangelistic outreaches.... we count up all the attendances and also how many people got saved, and feel good as a Christian. People from within the church seem to congratulate us by our attendances, and our performances... but Jesus is not concerned how many times a week, or how many lives got saved... (Of course he is overjoyed with people getting saved) but when He looks at me He is looking to see if the Word is causing fruit to grow in my heart? Are we allowing the Word of God to prune us back?

A time of pruning is a time of preparation for the Lord to empower us in new ways for ministry and we are all called to ministry in different ways. This is not just for those we see as pastors or preachers etc... we all have been called! (Remember Steven was set aside because of his anointing, to wait tables. It was his place of ministry, and he was later stoned to death because of the anointing upon his ministry.) It means that God is requiring from us new levels of surrender as well as fresh crucifixion of the flesh. A time such as this can appear to be a time of testing, even of humiliation... like the way I have written about in Chapter five. To be honest – it has been such a time for almost sixteen months since the start of the back problems and the Lord preparing me to trust Him in the pain. I think of 2015 as a year on my bed of thorns! It feels sometimes of being a time of complete emptiness and ineffectiveness, but I know that the Lord is deepening my dependency upon Him and Him alone. He is pruning in such a way that it will produce an abundant harvest in the time to come. It means that for some they will see me and judge me, perhaps condemn me because despite the many prayers I have not been healed totally. It is a time where we are weak, and the Lord says "My grace is sufficient; My strength is made perfect in your weaknesses." In our weakness during this time it is not only the people about us that see, but also the devil – powers and principalities, who will use it for their purposes to draw us away from the work God is doing... because that is what the Devil does, he lies, robs and destroys and this is where we are tested.

Jesus reproved His disciples for their jealousy and selfish ambition, He rebuked the crowd for their unbelief, complacency and failure to discern the times... such a rebuke is for the church today in this late hour before the Bridegroom returns for His Bride. Jesus was grieved by the hardness of hearts, pride and lack of compassion in the "religious people" of the day. For many in the Church today it is the same, where complacency has replaced the fire that once burned brightly, and religious outward acts are the measuring stick for goodness, while the heart within is defiled by the things of this world. We are like whitewashed tombs He says. All of the above were opportunities for pruning, but not all people will allow the Master to do His work. He will not prune us without our permission. He reveals what needs to be pruned, but it takes for us to accept and repent for the pruning to begin.

Jesus tells us that we will also bear fruit. The proof of the tree is the type of fruits we produce, and there is a list of the fruits of the Spirit found in **Galatians 5:22-23** love, joy, peace, patience, kindness, goodness, faithfulness, gentleness and self-control. Against such things there is no law. The fruits of the Flesh or Acts of the sinful nature are also listed in **Galatians 5:19-21** – sexual immorality, impurity and debauchery, idolatry and witchcraft, hatred, discord, jealousy, fits of rage, selfish ambition, dissensions, factions and envy, drunkenness, orgies and the like. It is not a completed list. By its fruit we can discern the tree, whether its roots are that of the tree of good and evil knowledge, or the tree of life!

Jesus is the Tree of Life, and to bear His fruits we must be rooted in Him.

Why then is this a 'question of independence'? We live for the most in a world where independency is considered a good thing, being able to care for one-self and not being a burden to others always requiring help with this and that. I have said before how having my driving licence gives me the freedom to buy a car and be able to drive myself where and when I need to. It helps me plan times of departures better for punctual arrivals, be it for interviews, getting to work on time, meetings, appointments, luncheon or dinner engagements, or any other programme planned in the course of a lifetime. It is not a sin to be able to drive oneself or even to be a good manager of time; I would see it as commendable because it shows respect for others too. Sometimes it is the hard and difficult times that cause us to develop new abilities to do things we couldn't do before, so even something good can come out of something bad. As children, we will learn skills along the way that will benefit us when we leave home either to be married or to live a single life independent from our parents. Our parents have instructed us and supported us in what they believe to be right all our growing years for such a time when we will be able to stand alone on our own two feet, raise our own families, and it is good. So what is wrong with being independent? We can do all of the above and still be dependent on the Lord. We can still be following His guidance for the things we are to do with our lives, after all He is the Author and Perfecter of our faith, He created us for the sake of fellowshipping with us. We were created in His own image that we can communicate with Him intimately, and still do all the above things independently but according to His will... the problem is when the independent lifestyle brings about independence from the Lord. Every vine is rooted but the question is who is supplying the energy to keep the vine growing... it is either the Lord, or the Devil. The truth is if we are not dependent on the Lord then we are dependent on the Devil. It really is that black and white! Whose garden are we growing in?

The Lord had showed me in Chapter five, that my independent spirit meant that I didn't have to wait for others, wait for buses in terms of having my own car, and He showed me that not willing to wait for others could also be a sign of not waiting for Him. Let me look at the fruit of the spirits again and see which ones **were NOT present** in my idea of being independent and owning my own car: **love, joy, peace, patience,**

kindness, goodness, gentleness and self-control could all be missing or in lack because of the independent spirit. Lack of love for others - to be unwilling to wait, lack of joy and peace, because waiting will cause me to be irritable, lack of kindness and goodness to others due to the unwillingness to wait and possible selfish ambition, and if I became irritable I could have a lack of self- control as I lash out at others verbally.

I had offered a lift to someone, taking them to church on the Sunday because the buses were not so reliable and I lived nearby. I told the person what time I would pick them up at the pickup point. It was always my routine and plan to leave home without breakfast or coffee to arrive early and find parking, then go to the nearby cafe for hot coffee and croissant before the service. She arrived late by about five minutes. The following week she was late by about fifteen minutes, and even up to twenty minutes. I was angry. One day it was terrible rain so I drove to her home so she didn't have to make the journey in the wet, and still she was fifteen minutes late leaving her front door – so had I waited at the pick-up place she would have been almost thirty minutes late. I can surely say that I was lacking in love, patience, kindness and goodness! Even though I drove to her home which could be considered kindness and goodness, my heart was far from thinking thoughts of love but my own selfish interest for breakfast and hot coffee. I am not saying that she was not in the wrong, because I truly believe she was, without consideration for keeping another waiting, making an agreed time and not keeping it – not just once but consistently, but that is truly between her and the Lord... worst is what it shows me, that I was far from a benevolent attitude of love and grace (but in a distant land in my heart). We ended up having a disagreement, about a different matter, but I used all of the above as an additional arrow of condemnation when the opportunity arose. The Lord had to prune back this branch, to teach me how to be loving and gracious, forgiving, merciful, and patient.

Have I learnt the lesson yet? No not fully! I am in a place where now I have no car, and rely many times on others. Someone tells me they will pick me up at a certain time, and I am always ready and waiting, but they can be up to an hour late in arriving or longer. Maybe I have to learn patience as I am being kept waiting. The Lord has as such cut back the branch for circumstances to produce the fruit within me that is lacking. Many people say to me it is a question of faith, and if I believe, I will receive a car. Whilst

I will say that the Lord is able to provide all that I need, He is also able to use the lack of such things to produce a fruit within me that will be sweet to His taste. I am in Him, and I know that He knows my needs. Sometimes the things I need are not the things I ask for, but rather the things that the Lord sees that I need, which I am blinded to, so as to produce the fruit He is longing for within me.

Jesus is the source and energy of my life, and so long as I remain in Him, the Gardener – The Father, will continue to cut me back and show me the things that are preventing the fruit to grow. As I allow Him to prune back or cleanse me of the things that are still of this world, slowly but surely He will produce a fruit in me that will be pleasing to Him. As I also close the gaps in the fence to my garden, and catch the **foxes** who love to devour the fruits He has produced, so then my vineyard will become a garden of His delight, with fruit in abundance for my Beloved to feast upon. In **Ecclesiastes 10:1** the **foxes** are as little follies... that defile a person who appears to be wise in God, like flies in an ointment. The flies that fall and die in the ointment will putrefy and cause the ointment to smell bad, but it will also defile the ointment that would otherwise have brought healing. Such follies or foxes that will ruin the fruit of His love are: foolishness, <u>pride and arrogance</u>, exaggeration and self-importance, <u>lack of patience</u>, **a spirit of independence**, a negative and complaining spirit, speaking critically of others, slander, anger and bitterness, laziness and time wasting... speaking too quickly and worldly thinking, self-defensive and being over sensitive, neglect of prayer. I have learnt how crafty my own flesh has been – like a **fox**, hiding the independent spirit behind a mask of religiosity... appearing to be godly but using scripture out of context to give me permission to be independent. **Foxes hide**!

I promised I would by the end of this book let you know if I am now free of this spirit. Well I cannot yet say for sure, but one thing I can say is that I am understanding it, and seeing it now for what it truly is...

I had been led to look through some material sent by a friend, but because it was two hundred pages long I had put it off. As I skimmed through it, suddenly I saw something that seemed to be standing out. It was in a chapter about New Age. It seemed strange to me because I have never (I thought) been involved with New Age. The thing I saw was in fact a company name... as I pondered this name wondering why I know it, suddenly it came to me. It was the organisation that had produced the "Motivational Training Course" I used to teach. I had already recognised three years ago that this teaching had been wrong and repented. I have already mentioned it in the book... but this time I got to see something very clear.

In Chapter 5, the Lord spoke to me that **He had been working to unlock the door** that He was now inviting me to open up to Him for Him to clean... the room of Independence. I had not really thought about what He had been 'working at' to unlock this door. It seemed suddenly that this was a huge room with a door that was heavily locked and not easy to open. Then I started to see that the Hidden Iniquities that the Lord had been showing me, for which I repented, happened after I had repented three years ago for teaching lies through the Motivational Course.

The Spirit of Witchcraft – Control Manipulation and Domination was the first huge one, so to speak, because of the manifestation... followed by Racism, Anti-Semitism and Vanity, but revelation of the Religious Spirit was first. I suddenly saw each one like a locked door before a door... **a vault within a vault.** Repentance for the teaching of lies, opened a door to then look at the next vault door – Religious Spirit, then Witchcraft. When that was opened through repentance and the breaking of a generational curse, deliverance took place...revealing the next vault, Racism and Anti-Semitism, and then the next vault of Vanity. It's like each vault door had a guarding spirit, which had to be removed in order to open up the vault door.... Hence the words "I have been working at unlocking the door to this room..." This room – this Spirit would appear to be the Big One that all the others had been masking. When the door was finally opened again through repentance.... (Every door was opened through repentance), the Lord showed me inside this cold dark room of independence, was also hidden anger and insignificance.

What was I teaching that says its New Age?.... I know I have mentioned it earlier, but I feel the need to repeat. I had been very certain when I went to train first –(I had to participate in the course first before being allowed to facilitate it), that I would not allow anything not of God into my life. I relaxed because it had Biblical truths.... **Nothing is impossible** (with God), **I can do all things** (in Him who strengthens me), **If it's to be, it's up to me.** Not a biblical verse but in essence if I am to change the way I am walking away from God – and instead walk toward God, it is me who has to make the decision. It is true – I have the authority to make that happen... so I was very comfortable with it, I just was not able to complete the sentences in brackets because we were not allowed to evangelise in the work place. What the Lord showed me is that when you take Jesus and the Cross out of the sentence, it is saying that we don't need God. I can do all things and nothing is impossible... then go on ahead and show how to make it happen by renewing the mind.... But not with The Word of God, but by visualising the things I want to happen, and speaking out the words in the form of affirmations.... Why... because the words that we speak have power to create (because we are created in the Fathers image). It is the same as prayers of the flesh – witchcraft, fuelled by "I don't need God, I can do all things, and nothing is impossible for me to achieve – so who needs God? – I am capable of achieving everything on my own!" I had been teaching total Independence from God! I was explaining this to someone, and he said – well they are half-truths! That is the voice of the devil... because there is no half-truth. If it is taken out of its context, and if Jesus and the Cross is removed, then it is no longer truth – but a lie! There are no grey areas here it is either right or it is wrong, there is no 'on the fence'. We are either drawing people to the Lord or we are driving them away. I suddenly saw this spirit of Independence as the spirit of Anti-Christ.

Forgiveness had been the cornerstone almost six years ago to regaining territory in my heart back to God. Learning to forgive and to love was taking me down the hallway that had been a secret passageway to deliverance. When the Lord gave me revelation of the wrongness of teaching the Motivation Course, repentance then activated the unlocking of the doors - dealing with the "Guarding Spirits" at each level / door to what was like a vault within a vault .... Unlocking the way in to the inner hidden chamber of my heart harbouring the spirit of the Anti-Christ... it was the Independent Spirit that was dictating my desires I Want... I Need... which is why they need to be crucified with Christ – nailed to the cross.

I was recently talking with a friend, who having been through an incredible time of healing and restoration for three months as the Lord ministered to her through the Book: Song of Songs... she said to me that despite knowing that Jesus is her Perfect match, she was still feeling lonely...

I mentioned that we need to crucify the flesh desires of our hearts – including the desires for a husband in this case. She said – during her time with the Lord she had seen her desires nailed to the cross, but the loneliness had not gone away. I suddenly found myself saying that when Jesus was nailed to the cross – it was not the nails that killed Him. Nailed to the cross His flesh / body was still alive, and still suffering terrible pain. The final battle Jesus had to overcome was that of the mind. In His time of excruciating pain he could have looked down at everyone in scorn and bitterness, anger in His heart, for doing what they did though He was innocent – without blemish.... Bitterness and disappointment could have settled into his mind knowing that Peter who said he would go with Him even to prison and death, was nowhere to be found because he had denied even knowing Him... AND... Despite His cry to the Father – 'Why have Thou forsaken me...' He still kept His heart and MIND on the will of the Father... and He spoke out 'Father forgive them they know not what they do'. His last battle was of the mind... and he was crucified where???? At Golgotha – the place of the skull! The same place where David killed Goliath – in the forehead – the skull... the house of the mind! Why had the Father as such turned away as Jesus was on the cross? Because He is Holiness itself and cannot communicate with sin, and the sins of the world were upon Jesus, all that separated us from God – Jesus took because of the Father's and His great love for you and me.

Once we have taken the step of obedience that takes us to our cross, things don't immediately die... the feelings don't suddenly change. I remember having to forgive my husband, and I kept remembering in my mind with flash backs of the pain and hurt... I felt the pain resurface and the anger and bitterness stirring, but suddenly I found myself saying; "Get behind me Satan, I have forgiven him, he is forgiven." I cannot remember how long it happened before suddenly I didn't get any more flash backs and although I can remember, there is no pain. I remember because it is part of the testimony of Gods amazing healing power. I do not remember his sins with malice and continue counting, if it was not for the amazing testimony I have through it all – I am sure it would be as with Jesus – in the sea of forgetfulness not to remember again. I shared with my friend the need to pray out when the loneliness manifests, to pray the same, "Get behind me Satan, Jesus is all I need, He is 'my sufficiency'!" In fact I had a picture, when I was writing it, of Satan at the foot of the cross looking up at the fleshly desires nailed to the cross with a sponge to bathe the hurting wounds, dressed like 'Florence Nightingale', in a nurses uniform, looking compassionate and caring. His words were such as, "Surely, He understands your needs, and would God truly deny you the things you so desperately long for if He loves you? Let me take the desires from the cross and nurse better your wounds from the nails... surely the loneliness is the sign of what God really wants for you to have, because He loves you."

Lucifer wanted Independence from God, and wanted all the worship and praise, power and dominion that is God's alone. Now to get all the worship he craves for, he feeds us with the same independent spirit, that we have no need for God, and for many of us, we are without realising, bowing down and worshiping Satan, doing his will obliviously thinking we are our own masters. In some ways I looked at the spirit of vanity and didn't see it to be a huge thing, but whilst placing it together I realised it is not just about looking nice in the mirror (and let us not forget that Lucifer was very beautiful), it's very roots is in pride, self-exaltation, condemnation and judgement based on the outward appearance whilst failing to value a person for the heart within... and when put like that – it also sounds a lot like a religious spirit.

I have made a diagram of how I see the Lord has been leading me step by step, at the end of this chapter, identifying and catching the **foxes** that have been ravaging the fruit of His Spirit. He has led me to reveal the **Fox Lair** in my garden. – But I say "no more!" I have banished the foxes and sealed the entry points. The fruit is growing, I know it is growing. What was once a cold dark room within a room, is about to be a Holy Spirit furnace of the Lord's love, and the fountain of life shall spring forth... as His Paradise garden is being restored. It is about to be a place where His lovers will come to feast, and drink and drink and drink.

Song of Songs 5:1

[The Bridegroom King]
I have gathered from your heart,
My equal, My bride,
I have gathered from My garden
All My sacred spices—even My myrrh!
I have tasted and enjoyed

My wine within you.
I have tasted with pleasure
My pure milk, My honeycomb
Which you yield to Me.
I delight in gathering My sacred spice,
All the fruits of My life
I have gathered from within you,
My paradise-garden!
Come all My friends—
Feast upon My bride!
All you revellers of My palace—
Now feast on her, My lovers!
Drink and drink, and drink again
Until you can take no more—
Drink the wine of her love.
Take all you desire, you priests!
My life within her
Will now become your feast! (TPT: 4)

Jesus laid down His life for us, and He has called us to do likewise for others. We do not need to go to the cross as Jesus, who became the Perfect Sacrifice once and for all time, but Jesus still has called each and every one who believes upon His name, to take up his spiritual cross and follow Him. (**Luke 9:23-27**) In other words we are to live 'a life laid down' for others that they may drink from the overflow of His life now within us... somehow in my ears it rings a different tune to an 'Independent Life'. I also know that if I am to deny myself so that Christ may live in me, I cannot do that alone and independent of Him. I need the fullness of the Holy Spirit within me to empower me, strengthen me, guide me and teach me the ways of Christ. I have learnt that without Christ, during the time I was the prodigal and left my spiritual home with my Father, there was nothing good in me. Without Christ I am wretched and good for nothing. I know that the only way forward is together with my Perfect Valentine, who loves me, and is willing to help me to become more and more like Him, to be His Equal, His Bride. He doesn't ask of me then leave me to achieve it alone, He instead walks besides me, strengthens me, empowers me, loves me beyond measure drawing me closer and closer into His presence and love as He is restoring my soul. He asks only that we be willing to repent, and He does the rest! "............. We will do it together!" Song of Songs 2:15

In some ways the closer He draws me to Him, I realise there is so much of Him yet to learn, His love and His Person is infinite. My mind cannot comprehend the fullness of all that He is, His mercy and grace towards me compels me to follow Him.

9"I love each of you with the same love that the Father loves Me. Let My love nourish your hearts.10If you keep My commands, you will live in My love, just as I have kept My Father's commands, for I am nourished and empowered by His love. 11My purpose for telling you these things is so that the joy that I experience will fill your hearts with overflowing gladness! 12"So this is My command: Love each other deeply, as much as I have loved you. 13For the greatest love of all is a love that sacrifices all. And when a person sacrifices his life for his friends, this great love is demonstrated. 14"You show that you are My intimate friends when you obey all that I command you. 15I have never called you servants, because a master doesn't confide in his servants, and servants don't always understand what the master is doing. But I call you My intimate friends, for I reveal to you everything that I've heard from My Father. 16You didn't choose Me, but I've chosen and commissioned you to go into the world to bear fruit. And your fruit will last, because whatever you ask of My Father, for My sake, He will give it to you! 17So this is My parting command:

Love one another deeply!" John 15:9-17 (TPT: 3)

Verses 10 and 14, both speak of obeying His commands. His commands are the teachings of Jesus in the New Testament. He fulfils the law, He is not cancelling the laws of Moses which were and are seen as outward virtues, but He takes them beyond... to the heart! My question is now "Do we love Him?" If we love him – truly love Him, we will obey. Obedience is better than sacrifice! **(1 Samuel 15:22)**

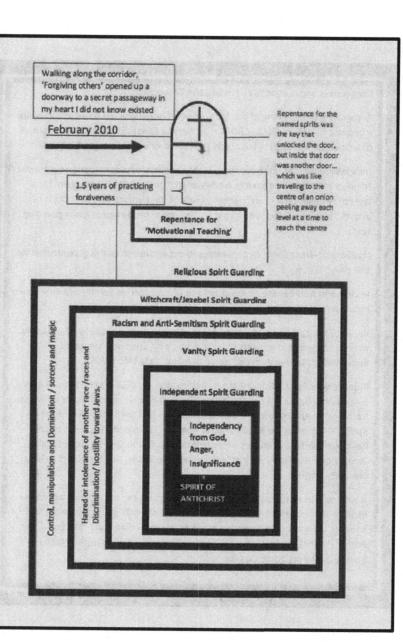

Forgiveness opens door to all healing and deliverance...

Recognising the teaching of the Motivational Course was not based on scripture – because "TRUTH – JESUS/CROSS = LIE " at the time I did not see the relevance of where this was leading but it was the first layer of the independence spirit

Religious Spirit is as you have read, so deep with a murdering spirit unbeknown to me, and takes a long time to be delivered from... and I can see again it is a layer of recognition and willingness to repent, that unlocks the next chain of events... opening a door into a room with a **room inside again, and a guarding spirit.**

Jezebel and Witchcraft: Repentance and deliverance from this generational sin and own... leading to

Racism and Anti-Semitism: Another form of a murdering Spirit – one only has to remember the Gas Chambers of World War II... leading to

Vanity: I thought this was a small spirit – then realised it is the Spirit of Lucifer, who was beautiful in appearance, puffed up with pride and arrogance demanding to be worshipped... to be like God. EXTREME PRIDE

Independent Spirit: Thinking it was nothing big...SURELY it's good to not be a burden on others... but the truth is spiritually it is to not need help or guidance from God... entering into the dark cold room to find the **Seat of Antichrist Spirit**... Harbouring **No Need for God, Anger – (The Murdering Spirit of Cain – Religious Spirit)**, and the lies of **Insignificance**... supporting the need to be Independent because I am not loved enough to belong and for others to help me... pity pity me!

A vault within a vault with layers of spirits guarding the strongholds within the vault. I had no idea, I could never have for-seen it, BUT JESUS my Deliverer, knowing the work of redemption required, He looked and said "My Equal, My Bride" He sees the finished work... still in progress... Not by might, Not by Power, but by My Spirit says the Lord!

I Know Your Deeds!

I cannot ignore the Words of Jesus through the revelation given to John whilst on the island of Patmos. Out of interest, Patmos means 'My Killing.' It was a place where John's flesh as such was put to death. As the Lord asks of us to take up our cross daily, it was in this place, where any selfish ambition was dead, the place of 'my killing', became the place of Gods Glory manifested to John in revelation of the last days, of things seen in the throne-room of God, and details of the New Jerusalem to come. Let this be an encouragement to us, that as we lay down our lives, we are ushering in the glory of God, where His Presence fills the Temple. As we draw closer to Him, there the devil has to flee! He calls us into the Chamber of Chambers, otherwise known as the Holy of Holies, to share with us the secrets of His heart. As we die to self, we live in Christ and His Glory within us is becomes like a bright light in the darkness of this world, as a beacon of life to those who are perishing, lighting the path home to The Father, through Jesus who is 'The Way The Truth and The Life'. It is at this point of time the words written by Isaiah become reality and prophecy fulfilled, when the Bride of Christ, has caught the **Foxes** and is adorned in Purity and Holiness...

"Arise, shine for your light has come and the Glory of the Lord is upon you. See darkness covers the earth, and thick darkness is over the peoples, but the Lord rises upon you and His glory appears over you. Nations will come to your light and kings to the brightness of your dawn..." Isaiah 60:1-3 (NIV: 5)

In the early part of the vision, John receives words to the seven churches. I believe these are words to us today, they are not physical churches in these places, but they represent the whole church.

1. To the **Church of Ephesus**. He speaks of the things they have done well in verses 2-3 of their perseverance, enduring hardships and they refused to tolerate wicked men, and tested those claiming to be apostles but are not... but verse 4 tells of the things the Lord holds against them. What could his problem be with the people, who have endured...

They have lost their first love!

The first love, is the passionate desire for God, to desire His presence above all else, to talk with Him because you love Him so much, to be ever available seeking Him out just to hear His heart beat. This love has a trust and total dependency upon Him. He created us for fellowship... that is why we are created in His image, so we can communicate intimately with each other... heart to heart, face to face. The one thing God held against them was their lack of personal fellowship with Him. It is not the good works – commendable as they are, but they had lost their First Love. He tells them to remember the great heights from which they have fallen and to repent! If they fail to repent He will remove the Lampstand from its place. I believe Jesus is the Lampstand... if I am correct then this is serious!

2. To the **Church in Smyrna,** again He speaks of the good things, although the things mentioned according to the fleshly ear seem bad, such as afflictions, slander and poverty and yet they are rich! He encourages the church to hold fast and not to be afraid of the things yet to suffer, of imprisonment and persecution even unto death, but to be faithful even unto death and He will give the crown of life.

3. To the **Church of Pergamum,** He speaks of despite living where Satan has his throne, they have remained true to His name..... **"Nevertheless, I have a few things against you. You have people there who hold to the teaching of Balaam, who taught Balak to entice the Israelites to sin by eating food sacrificed to idols and by committing sexual immorality. Likewise you**

also have those who hold to the teaching of the Nicolaitans. Repent, therefore!

The story of Balaam is that when he was asked to prophecy defeat over the Israelites, he could not because the Lord had prophesied victory through His blessing over them, however Balaam knew a loophole to remove the blessing of God. He suggested that the local women entice the men to lay with them and to eat the foods sacrificed to idols, this would remove the blessing of God and therefore defeat would come.

I do not know as such where people of God in this day are **enticing believers into sexual sin**, however, I believe where church leadership turns a blind eye to it, allowing it to happen within the body of the church, unchallenged, I will suggest this could be a message of warning. May the Lord have mercy, for if repentance does not come it says the Lord will come against them with the sword of His mouth! The teaching of the 'Nicolaitans' is as such a false doctrine and a leadership that dominates through hierarchy – producing carnal and fleshly superiors creating "rank" in the otherwise Divine brotherhood, all of which DESTROYS fellowship, creates division and strife, and fosters envy and it promotes a False grace, it is what we know as prosperity teaching, where grace is freely given and the 'cross and repentance' are missing from the message.

4. To the **Church of Thyatira** again He speaks of the good deeds of which He knows; of love, faith, service, perseverance, and that it is all greater than that at the beginning.

"Nevertheless, I have this against you: You tolerate the woman of Jezebel who calls herself a prophetess. By her teaching she misleads my servants into sexual immorality and the eating of food sacrificed to idols. I have given her time to repent of her immorality but she is unwilling. So I will cast her on a bed of suffering and I will make those who commit adultery with her to suffer intensely unless they repent of their ways. I will strike her children dead, so all the churches will know that I am He who searches hearts and minds and I will repay each of you according to your deeds."

I do not presume that any church has a prophetess called Jezebel. This is speaking of the leaders and people of the church who have a

Jezebel Spirit. I have written about it earlier and this spirit **controls and dominates through manipulation**, it is **witchcraft** and it allows or even entices **sexual immorality**. Though it is often seen strongly in women, it is not just women, but men can also be strongly affected by this spirit, usually used to feed selfish ambition. Anyone who commits adultery with this spirit will suffer intensely! These are strong words to the church!

5. To the Church in Sardis,…. **"You have a reputation of being alive but you are dead. Wake up! Strengthen what remains and is about to die, for I have not found your deeds complete in the sight of my God. Remember therefore what you have received and heard, obey it and repent! But if you do not wake up, I will come like a thief and you will not know what time I will come to you."**

I for sure do not know specifically who this is speaking to, although part of me looks to the charismatic movement that sees itself as being alive. I have spoken earlier about hearing it said, when challenged regarding a word preached by Jesus, that I was told that Pentecostal tradition will not change, it's the way they always do things. It was about an outward zealous heart, but within, pride and arrogance that makes their traditions higher than the Words of Jesus. It could be that the churches promoting the manifestations of Christ, look to be alive because of miracles (which the devil can also duplicate) and yet their hearts inwardly are dead. I am not saying this is how all charismatic and evangelical movements feel, or all Pentecostal leaders, it could likewise be about churches that are State-run churches, filled with nominal Christians so the church looks alive, but the hearts of the people are dead. The Catholic Church has the largest following of the Pope in the world, looking to be very alive. In whatever scenario, and those denominations I have not mentioned, we ALL need to check our hearts and minds, for it is here which will tell our state of alive or dead. The worldwide church has indeed been sleeping, all denominations. Suddenly when the governments start to support non- Christians and persecute the Christians, it is a wake-up call to everyone. Churches have recently been highly outspoken against the people who do not believe in Christ, and yet have tolerated the church who fails to be Christlike! The Church has been nothing but hypocritical for so long, preaching one word, yet living openly another, prostituting itself with the pleasures of this world. No wonder the world turned away from the church, but I believe the church, through the beginning of persecutions on all levels, is waking up. It is coming to a time where every believer will need to truly decide which side of the fence they are on. There is no sitting on the fence – we are either followers of Christ, in the fullness of His word, or we are not. If we are on the fence so to speak we are not followers!

6. To the **Church of Philadelphia**, He has seen their deeds, and they have remained faithful despite having little strength, keeping to His word and not denying His name. They have kept His commands and endured patiently, therefore He will keep them from the hour of trial that is going to come upon the whole world to test those who live on the earth...

7. To the **Church of Laodicea**... **"These are the words of the Amen, the faithful and true witness, the ruler of God's creation. I know your deeds, that you are neither cold not hot. I wish you were either one or the other! So because you are luke-warm – neither hot nor cold- I am about to spit you out of my mouth. You say "I am rich; I have acquired wealth and do not need a thing." But you do not realise that you are wretched, pitiful, poor, blind and naked. I counsel you to buy from me gold refined in the fire, so you can become rich; and white clothes to wear so you can cover your shameful nakedness; and salve to put on your eyes, so you can see. Those whom I love I rebuke and discipline, so be earnest and repent. Here I am! I stand at the door and knock. If anyone hears my voice and opens the door, I will come in and eat with him and he with Me...."** (NIV:5)

We are in a world of materialism, a world where we consider the things we have, be it possessions, healthy bank accounts, good jobs, good qualifications and certificates of this world... and we say we are rich. We see everything about us to be the works of our own hands, the work of our long years studying to become qualified, the money in the bank because of my clever mind and ability to save and invest through long hours of hard work... and we forget that nothing belongs to us, it all belongs to God, it was Him who gave us the abilities to be used for His Kingdom purposes, but we have transgressed from that to take ownership of all, and consider ourselves rich and not in need of God, we have done well by ourselves, totally independent, not requiring Him. The deceived will say – 'God has enough problems in the world to sort out, I am one less to waste His time and energy because He has given me the ability to sort it myself'. It is a lie of the Devil! God created us to be involved with Him and be dependent on Him in every area of our lives... He has given us the abilities to use for the purposes of His will... therefore He wants us to spend time with Him every day, to hear His heartbeat, to listen to His plans of how He wants us to use and increase our abilities for His Kingdom, not to make our own plans and ask God then to bless them. Jesus tells us we are deceived – spiritually blinded... all that glitters is not gold! In fact the true gold of heaven has been refined in the refiner's fire – which has been offered to each one of us. We believe we are dressed in fine clothes, but the Lord sees us naked and shameful. He offers us clothes of white – purity and holiness found only in the blood of Christ – His Righteousness!

I believe that the 'cold' are the self-confessed sinners of the world who do not believe in the Lord and don't pretend to. I believe the 'hot' are they who are hot for the Lord, who are passionately in love with the Lord and willing to lay down their own lives for the sake and purposes of the Kingdom of God, out of love and obedience, not duty. So who are the 'luke-warm'? I believe they are those who have confessed Jesus as Lord, yet walk in compromise and rebellion, prostituting themselves with Satan and the things of his world to satisfy the lusts of the flesh. I read once that the things that entertain us – ENTER us!

Why would God prefer us to be cold and unbelieving than luke-warm? I believe because there is still a hope that the unbelieving will see and believe! There is still a chance of them to repent and come to salvation, and indeed in the last days – many will! Like the one beside Him on the cross who asked to be remembered, having confessed Jesus was without sin and he deserved to die... Jesus promised he will be with Him in Paradise. We think our many years as believers will bring us through, but I know that the first shall be last and the last shall be first. Some of the first have lost their passionate love for Christ as I had, maybe through heartaches and pain becoming embittered with God, and have been tempted by the lustful passions of this world, be it sexually, materially through possessions and wealth, musically, physically to have the body beautiful, drunkenness and lack of self-control of the words and language used. We are entertained by immoral movies and TV series bringing sexual immorality, demonic manifestations – also in children's cartoons and movies, and violence into our homes, we love music and performers that promote adulterous relationships, or again demonic alliances... then go to church on Sunday and with the same mouth and defiled hearts to sing our praises to the Lord! This is I believe 'luke-warm.' The luke-warm are those who confess Christ yet are not satisfied by Him alone. They are the religious people who know the commandments and appear to be upstanding in the community doing good works, but in their hearts they are like the Pharisees and the Scribes of Jesus time, like whitewashed tombs. The House of the Lord (His Temple being our hearts) lies in ruin.

Am I free from the above? No – I am still a work in progress as the Lord leads me to catch those **foxes**! The diagram in the previous chapter reveals that which the Lord has shown me to date... of which I have repented... (there is still room and time as long as I have breath for Him to reveal more – I am not saying that it is an exhausted list) and the Lord by His Spirit will do the cleaning out, meanwhile it is still my responsibility to prevent holes or doorways back into my heart for the **foxes** to re-enter. How do I do that? By drawing closer in intimacy with the Lord, seeking Him to overflow in abundance His love and grace, remaining in humility lest I should fall. I was visiting a friend once who had numerous films. Many I just couldn't watch... I saw how they began and realised the Lord's voice was telling me no-way! However there were still some that crept passed the still quiet voice. One specific series of films I found so enjoyable... but how is it possible that I can be watching the film and encouraging the ones committing the crimes to escape and not get caught by the police. The characters are what I would call loveable rogues. The truth is there is something loveable in every one of us, because we are each and every one created in the image of God, but what has Obedience got to do with Disobedience? Righteousness with Unrighteousness? What has Light got to do with Darkness? What has revenge got to do with God's Word that tells us to walk the extra mile, to bless and not to curse? What have the people of God got to do with the works of darkness? If I allow for those films to remain lurking within me, then my heart becomes tainted with the lies of the devil; that rebellion to the Word of God is OK. We don't just watch a movie, we are normally absorbed by them. I love to watch films, I don't watch TV because like many in the past I was hooked onto all the soaps as they are called, and realised I could not control it, so I got rid of the TV stations, removing the aerial... but I love to relax with a good film... and I have to admit that as I pursue my relationship with Jesus, longing more for His Presence, there are fewer films available to me to watch. I have mentioned elsewhere in the book, that comedy is also a problem. I have realised if I/we laugh at something which is immoral but spoken about in humorous form – the fact that I/we laugh at it – the compromise has entered me and it's OK.

I look to the seven churches and see something of most of them in the things the Lord has been speaking to me about in my own heart. The truth is God's Word! It is the same Yesterday, Today and Forever! It cannot change to meet the passing trends of our modern-day freedom revolution that says all is acceptable. Though the Word tells us to believe on His name and be saved, there must be another deeper meaning of the word believing. Demons believe Jesus is the Son of God and shudder – but they are not saved!

This is my cry, deep from within – "Lord, search my heart, and renew a right spirit within me. Cast me not away from Thy Presence O Lord, and take not Thy Holy Spirit from me; Restore unto me the Joy of Thy Salvation, and renew a right spirit within me. Have mercy on me O God, according to Your unfailing love, according to Your great compassion, blot out my transgressions; Have mercy on me O God, according to Your unfailing love. Wash away my iniquities, cleanse me from my sin, and teach me Your ways O Lord and empower me by Your Holy Spirit to walk in them. Fill me O Lord with Your redeeming love, and clothe me in Your purity and holiness... Draw me ever closer to You my Lord, the Lover of my soul, that You alone fill my every need, that my desires are met in You... Smother me with Your kisses, breathe Your life into mine... that I may run away with You into Your cloud filled chamber and drink of Your love - more intoxicating than wine, 'til I can't take anymore. That the two of us become one; one heart, one mind, one spirit... bound together forever as Your bride, Your beloved, Your favourite, Your Equal."

I cannot finish here – but to mention that to each Church there was a finishing word....

1. He who has an ear, let him hear what the Spirit says to the churches. **To him who overcomes**, I will give the right to eat from the tree of life which is in the paradise of God.

2. He who has an ear, let him hear what the Spirit says to the churches. **He who overcomes** will not be hurt at all by the second death.

3. He who has an ear, let him hear what the Spirit says to the churches. **To he who overcomes** I will give some of the hidden manna. I will also give him a white stone with a new name written upon it, known only to him who receives it.

4. (not all had fallen to her teachings, and not learned of Satan's so called deep secrets) "I will not impose any other burden upon you. Only hold on to what you have 'til I come. **To him who overcomes** and does my will to the end I will give authority over the nations – He will rule them with an iron sceptre, He will dash them to pieces like pottery just as I have received authority from my Father. I will also give him the morning star. He who has an ear, let him hear what the Spirit says to the churches.

5. "There are a few in Sardis who have not soiled their clothes. They will walk with Me, dressed in white, for they are worthy. **He who overcomes** will, like them, be dressed in white. I will never blot out his name from the book of life, but will acknowledge His name before my Father and His angels, He who has an ear, let him hear what the Spirit says to the churches.

6. "I am coming soon. Hold on to what you have, so that no-one will take your crown. **Him who overcomes** I will make a pillar in the temple of My God. Never again will he leave it. I will write on him the Name of MY God and the name of the city of My God, the new Jerusalem which is coming down out of heaven from My God; and I will also write on him My new Name. He who has an ear let him hear what the Spirit says to the churches."

7. "Here I stand at the door and knock. If anyone hears my voice and opens the door I will come in and eat with him; and he with me. **To him who overcomes** I will give the right to sit with Me on my throne, just as I overcame and sat down with my Father on His throne. He who has an ear, let him hear what the Spirit says to the churches."

All I know is that I long to be **one who overcomes**! 'To overcome' demands activity and not passivity. "Lord I hear what you are saying, where my spiritual hearing is impaired in any way to hear all You say, heal me my

God, that even the softest whisper will be heard in the deepest part of my heart, and I am totally surrendered to Your Word."

The truth is, the Lord knows all of our deeds, and many of them are commendable and good, but there are areas of our lives that are not yet surrendered to His will. There are **foxes** of compromise to be caught, and the walls in our 'Garden of Love' to be closed and sealed, preventing the **foxes** return.

Will you catch them? We will do it together.

Prisoner of Love!

The Fox hunt is to bring us to a point as we can read in the Song of Songs chapters 7 and 8... It is our destination and purpose for this journey... and the chapters I have written are to inspire you to seek Jesus in person for yourself that the Holy Spirit will reveal to you as He has done to me, the hidden foxes of your heart. It is not a book that judges anyone or condemns, and even examples I have used of the things the Lord has shown me, it is only to show or illustrate how **foxes** can look. The chapters are not a complete list, they are with a view to draw **you** personally back to the Word and Commands of Jesus, and allow Him to help **you** catch the foxes that are ravaging **your** fruit that Jesus so hungers after. I will be honest, had I known anything of the condition of my heart in the beginning, I would have been desperate feeling like the hopeless case... it shocks me to see the diagram, and yet it excites me in Christ, to understand that despite all the darkness within me, He still says, "and yet so beautiful!" And despite all of this in my heart – He has still used me along the way... and He will continue to, as we continue together.

In the beginning, the Lord ignited our hearts, to seek Him. He chose us – we did not choose Him. He had sought us out and wooed us with His love. When all we could see was our own worthlessness, our sin and shame... dark in comparison to His great light, He spoke to us; "Yet you are so lovely! Like the fine linen tapestry hanging in the Holy Place."

I want to point out again that in the Old Testament we can read of how particular God was in the building of the tabernacle. He was specific about the materials used, of the fabrics used for the curtains, for the priest's garments, wood for the seat etc. God was not interested in 'any old building' for His residence. The curtain between the Holy place and the Holy of Holies represented Righteousness, and would only ever be seen by the High Priest, who once a year would enter into the Holy of Holies – God's Presence to offer a sacrifice to God on behalf of the people. If the priest was not found acceptable before God, he would be struck down dead, so the priest on this day would wear a bell so others could hear him performing the duties, and a rope around his leg. If all went silent, they would know he was dead, and would pull him out by the rope on his ankle, in case God's wrath would fall upon them if they went into the sanctuary to carry him out. I repeat this because it is so important to understand the way the Father see's us. When Jesus died on the cross, that fine linen curtain was rent or torn from top to bottom. In other words God tore the curtain from heaven to earth, allowing all who receive Christ to enter, because when we become born again, we are covered with the Righteousness of Christ. Jesus in us IS the High Priest. Jesus is the fine linen tapestry. In Christ we are free to enter into God's presence, not just once a year but all the time. In Christ we have become family – sons and daughters to the Living God, and sons and daughters have access to the father without appointment or being summoned. Because of Jesus, because of His sacrifice, He covers us in Righteousness, beautiful like the fine linen curtain... Oh how priceless it is... because of Calvary, despite all I know that is within me that is yet dark and shameful, because of being born again and inviting Jesus to become Lord, The Father sees only Jesus' Righteousness. (This does not mean we do not continue to catch the **foxes**, it means that He alone knows our hearts. Though we are not yet perfected in Christ, He knows the longing in our hearts to be like Him, to have more of Him.)

My daddy, when he was sick before he died, was living with my sister. He would always sit with his arms resting on the dining table at the window, so he could look out into the garden during the day. He had asked for an apple tree to be planted. My daddy watched every day to see the tree grow. He knew when there was a new bud about to break with leaves unfurling into visible life... he watched with great joy in his heart as the tree entered each natural stage of life it had to go through for the promise of fruit to become a reality. When flowers appeared on the tree it was the sign that the fruit was soon to come... and oh what joy when the flower had been blown away and the small round of the apple was in sight. The fruit was visible... it was not yet ready but it was there – growing. He watched it with every passing day slowly explode in size, knowing that inside there was a process at work that would make the hard ball become soft and fleshy with a juice so sweet to taste, however he knew that if he tried eating it before time it would be hard, and sour causing stomach pains once digested... so he would wait with anticipation. So long as the fruit remains part of the tree it will grow to maturity and ripen ready to eat.

We are like that fruit on the tree. First of all the Father is watching us intensely with such delight and anticipation knowing exactly what we will become. He knows the beginning and the end! As we are born again into new life with Christ, we are like the tiny hard ball of fruit... but as the fruit gets bigger and bigger it is maturing and ripening. If we are eaten too early we are hard and sour, and yet the stage of this apple's growth is perfect. It has not reached perfection, but in every step of the way it is perfect for its stage of growth. You and I have not yet reached perfection in Christ... but when He sees us right now, at whatever stage of growth we are in Him, He sees us with great joy and delight. He knows the **foxes** within me that are preventing the fullness of fruit to be harvest, but as I say yes to catch those **foxes**, He helps us, empowers us, because the fruit of His love in our hearts is what He is longing for.

What I love is that in **Song of Songs 2:3** the Shulamite describes her Bridegroom King as 'the most fragrant apple tree that stands above all others'. Trees in the Bible are often used figuratively to describe people... and Jesus, who became man, is above all others. His love is greater than any earthly love and there is no-one like Him... He stands above all the rest! As I am in Him, then the fruit of my love will become the refreshing fruit for others to feed upon at my time of ripening. The apple tree is a similar picture of Jesus as the vine and we are the branches... so long as we are in Him we will bear fruit... but I see that I am the fruit of His love, just as I recognise that I am the Rose of Sharon and the Lilley of the Valley... beautiful, precious, radiant, His equal, His bride - seen without flaw in His eyes.

Remember in Chapter 2 when she is love sick for Jesus, drunk in His kisses that are sweeter and more intoxicating than the wine of this world, when He asks her to catch the troubling foxes, she says no. She was not ready... and enters a time of great anguish and travail without His apparent presence, though He is never far away – but hidden. I have been there as you have already read. She must look for Him, and when we seek Him, we will find Him, when we search for Him with all our heart. We realise that there is nothing good in us but Jesus. Left to our own devices, nothing good can grow only weeds in His garden of love within my heart... weeds that choke the vine... so she goes out to look for Him when she has come to her senses, and refuses never to leave Him again. Now her heart is ready to obey, and whatever the pressures, trials, testing, persecution that comes her way, she sees it as the Refiner's fire, she is not afraid because her Beloved is with her in the fire, just like He was with the three Hebrews, friends of Daniel, in the furnace in the Book of Daniel 3. She is now being transformed from glory to glory with unveiled face – with nothing between. Her heart becomes 'One with Jesus'. His will becomes her will. His desires become her desires. His sufferings become her suffering. Where He goes she goes... her love is relentless toward Him as His love has been relentless toward her... Oh what a journey, of great love and passion unfolding between her and her Bridegroom King... Lover of her soul... Jesus.

Malachi 3 talks of being refined as silver. Silver is a symbol of redemption... A woman once went to visit the local silversmith to ask if she could learn about the way silver is refined, so she could better understand Malachi 3. He told her that the silver had to be held in the hottest part of the fire. She asked if there was a stand where he would leave the silver and do other things, but he said no. The silversmith never leaves the silver in its process, holding it all the while. Just thinking of that, the silversmith must endure extreme heat for a long time as he holds it in the flames. The woman then asked how he knows it is finished and ready. His remark was; "That is the easy part, because it is refined and finished when I can see my own reflection in the silver!" Indeed, we are all being refined as silver, He holds us in the fire of trials and testings, but never leaves us... and when He sees the image of Himself in us – we are ready! It's a process in His great love and commitment to us.

This is your journey and it is my journey. This is the path upon which I am walking... it is the path of His Church being prepared for marriage, the Fathers gift of love to His Perfect Son – The King of Kings. He is transforming us to be His Equal, His Bride... not all will be willing, because it comes with a cost... are you willing?

The words our Bridegroom speaks to us in **Song of Songs Chapter 7:1-6**

Oh such transformation has taken place, and in these words we see the love and mercy of the Father's heart, the compassion for the lost as is equal to His heart. It is the fruit of His handiwork within her, as she has surrendered herself totally to His will, and given birth to spiritual sons and daughters to nurture in purity, sharing Godly wisdom to help them grow as Brides to be.

> **Even a King is held captive by your beauty!**
> **How delicious your fair beauty**
> **It cannot be described**
> **As I count the delights you bring to Me—**
> **Love has become the greatest!** (TPT: 4)

Jesus – The King, is held captive by yours and my beauty, others may call us ugly, cod-fish eyes or call us by other physical weaknesses and flaws in our flesh, but this is how we are seen by our Lover. This is the way My Perfect Valentine speaks to me... speaks to you... and I marvel and rejoice because I bring delight to Him! It is what I have searched for my whole life.

Oh, to hear these words of my Beloved, is worth all that I have encountered so far of this journey and yet to encounter. Now you know why I call Him my Perfect Valentine. He does not take for granted what sometimes are feeble attempts by me, for He meets me in my weakness, and there His strength is made perfect. I offer him my loaves and fishes, and He turns them into food for thousands to feast upon. That my love for Him has conquered The Conqueror... that makes me 'more than a conqueror'! I long for Him to take hold of me by His power, and to be possessed as His fruitful bride. There is nothing more I long for. I long to be His and His alone fully! I am lost and undone in His love. I rejoice that my kisses of love for Him awaken those still sleeping... it is my heart's desire... His desire which is being fulfilled in me...

This is my hearts cry: **Song of Songs 7:10 -13**

Although I know I am still catching **foxes**, I see that I am also here... living and sharing the Word of the Lord, sharing my testimony of His amazing all-consuming passionate love and grace, mercy and power to redeem me, the worst of sinners. **Song of Songs 8: 2-3**

This is my desire, my heart cry, this is my prayer to my Beloved to say continue Your work within me, that I might carry You completely within me... **Song of Songs 8:5**

I say Yes Lord Yes!

What will your response be? As I read the amazing words of a Love Song written 3,000 years ago, of the relentless passionate love of Jesus, the Bridegroom-King and the Shulamite (the Church – you and me individually and corporately, male and female) I never cease to be moved by such love. It is such love that will cause cold hearts to burn hot, it is such love that will cause the Church to 'Arise and Shine' for the glory is upon her, shining in the present darkness of this world. It is not the hard heart of an old man with a beating stick... No! This love is pure, unconditional passionate love, that calls us, draws us ever closer into His Chamber within a Chamber – to the mountain top of His Presence. This is where we have overcome the works of the enemy, this is the ultimate place of deliverance and healing, seated at the Kings table to feast upon His Love, where He drinks and drinks and drinks of the precious wine of the fruits He has grown within our hearts.

This is where we will run like the flock of goats down the mountain side of mount Gilead – skipping and jumping rejoicing to lay down our lives for the sake of our Beloved Jesus, and it will not seem like a sacrifice anymore!

[The Bridegroom and Bride in Divine Duet]
¹⁴Arise, My darling!
Come quickly my Beloved.
Come and be the graceful gazelle with Me
Come be like a dancing deer with me.
We will dance in the high place of the sky
Yes, on the mountains of fragrant spice!
Forever we shall be
United as One!

Perhaps you have been kept busy nurturing other's vineyards, and neglected your own. Perhaps you are busy serving in others ministries, supporting their call, their vision, so busy at every church meeting and service, yet in the business of tending others vineyards, you are too tired and busy to tend to your own. It is not wrong to serve in a ministry that the Lord has called us to, but if it takes the place of our own personal relationship with Jesus, then it is wrong. Remember it is not good works even in the Kingdom of God, but by our own heart relationship with The King.

I have come to see that in some cultures, men show there love by the things they do for the loved ones, which can show a busy life, that they unfortunately spend little time actually in the presence of the ones they love and have little conversation with their wife and children. It is actually a picture for most of The Church. We think by doing good works for The Kingdom, it is Love acceptable to God. It is not... it is intimacy with the God – Father, Son and Holy Spirit that is the acceptable offer of love... out of this intimacy will flow naturally good works ordained by God Himself, but not at the cost of neglecting our personal relationship with Him...

My prayer is that we all become willing prisoners of His love.

As for me:

I have thrown away the key, that I be locked forever in His love!

HAPPY FOX HUNTING!

245

Suggested reading

Books by Fenella Stevensen

Rejoice... I Will Fear No Evil (Psalm 23)

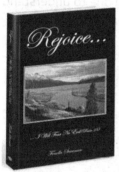

The first autobiography by Fenella Stevensen: Life looks positive as a young woman still in my late teens, when I fall madly in love with my Prince Charming, a wonderful man of good looks, money and power... until he attempts to kill me with the carving knife.

Meeting my Perfect Valentine, becomes a major turning point in my life, directing me through important choices to be made and amazing experiences where I travel and begin to fulfil my childhood dreams. It is a story of growth, pushing boundaries, dealing with pain, re-learning basic truths, and actually beginning to love myself. Having always been told I was ugly – well that I have eyes like a cod fish – would you like to kiss a cod?

Rejoice... The Bricks Have Fallen; I Will Rebuild (Isaiah 9:10)

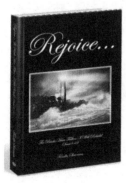

The second part of the Rejoice books by Fenella, telling of the hard and heart breaking times that almost broke her, but finding her way back.......
Happiness is short lived in marriage – eleven days to be exact, followed by a seven year nightmare before finally bailing ship. The first book begins with physical abuse, but my marriage was a relationship of emotional abuse, that led me to attempt suicide as the only way out. Having counselled and helped others, I couldn't help myself!

Returning to my Perfect Valentine, He empowers and encourages me to break free from the chains of self-pity, low self-worth, and the constant cloud over me as a failure.

Books by Brian Simmons

The Sacred Journey – a compelling read to those who long to understand the 'most beautiful love song ever written' – Song of Songs by King Solomon. This book will change your life as you understand the relentless pursuit of Jesus for each one of us willing to be His bride. It is not a book for females but male and female combined that make up the Church of God. It will open wide the hearts and minds of each one to understand the Prophetic meaning which was written 3,000 years ago.

And to visit His website for the books of the Bible currently translated – The Passion Translation at http://stairwayministries.org/store/

About the Author

Fenella Stevensen... by the time this book is published will have just celebrated 60 yrs. A British citizen, resident in Malta and Missionary to Africa and beyond, teaching in YWAM, Church leaders, congregations and one to one. I have, since the age of five years old, known I would be a missionary in a mud hut in Africa. Thankfully the homes are mostly brick now, at least where I stay – but I have stayed in a Mud House.

I became a Born-Again Christian when I was 26 years old in Torquay, and served for some years as a missionary with YWAM. All of this is in my first Book: 'Rejoice... I Will Fear No Evil' after which I made a life changing decision that took me into a spiritual wilderness, a distant land of bitterness, anger and rebellion. I thought the wilderness often as the wasted years, but found them to be preparation for the things to come, a learning ground of invaluable lessons. My second Book: 'Rejoice... The Bricks Have Fallen; I Will Rebuild' covers the pains and heartaches of this part of my journey, but it also covers the return to 'My Perfect Valentine'. I have never professed to be a writer, my school grades for English language and literature were below the marks of a Pass... so I could hardly imagine one day I would write one book let alone three.

My life is as a single – divorced woman, whose heart and soul desire is to walk in surrendered obedience to the voice and will of the Lord Jesus, and to share the Gospel in all its fullness, which is the Incomparable, Unconditional Love of God, and His Amazing Grace, Who, despite our flaws and weakness, loves us and sets us free from the restraints of this world, and to empower us to soar on Eagles Wings in His Spirit as He transforms us from glory to glory into the image of Christ.

I am passionate for Him and for the people He sends me to. The Lord has given me spiritual sons and daughters (Christian and Muslim) and grandchildren in Uganda, Kenya, Tanzania, Rwanda, Ethiopa and India. I who have never born a child, is now receiving restoration of all that the locust had eaten... and the prophetic words of Isaiah 54 I am now living them.

I am a Bride-to-Be of Christ, whose heart has been completely chased and wooed by the Lover of my Soul, Jesus... and it is my privilege and joy to spend my days sharing of this great and wonderful truth with hearts the Lord has prepared to listen.

If any of you would like to know more of this ministry and the things I am involved in, or would like to support that which the Lord has called me to do, then please find me at

Facebook: Fenella Stevensen

Email: fenellastevensen@gmail.com